S0-BRA-204

SILVER BURDETT English

Nancy N. Ragno
Marian Davies Toth
Betty G. Gray

SILVER BURDETT COMPANY MORRISTOWN, NJ

Atlanta, GA · Cincinnati, OH · Dallas, TX · Northfield, IL · San Carlos, CA · Agincourt, Ontario

Centennial Edition

Acknowledgments

Cover: Victoria Beller-Smith for Silver Burdett

Contributing Artists: Michael Adams; Ray Burns; Rick Cooley; René Daly; Marie DeJohn; Bert Dodson; Roberta Eagan; Pamela Ford-Johnson; Hal Frenck; Kathleen Garry-McCord; Nancy Hannons; Chris Holzer; Robert Jackson; John Jones; Jane Kendall; Norma Rahn; Sally Schaedler; Rosalyn Schanzer; Den Schofield; Jim Spence; Sally Springer; Suzan Swan; Irene Trivas; George Ulrich; Herman Vestal; James Watling

Photographs: Unit 1 3: © Harald Sund, 26: Victoria Beller-Smith for Silver Burdett. 30–31: Silver Burdett. 34–37: Victoria Beller-Smith for Silver Burdett. 38: © L. West/National Audubon Society Collection, Photo Researchers, Inc. 41: Silver Burdett. 43: *t.* N.O. Tomalin/Bruce Coleman; *t.m.* William Amos/Bruce Coleman; *m.* N.O. Tomalin/Bruce Coleman; *b.m.* Jeff Foote/Bruce Coleman; *b.* Jen & Des Bartlett/Bruce Coleman. **Unit 2** 47: Elliott Erwitt/Magnum. 81: *t.* Larry May/Shostal Associates; *b.* Joseph Baiocchi Family, circa 1916, courtesy Marie C. Byrne. **Unit 3** 87: Mark Newman/Tom Stack & Associates. 120: Pam Hasegawa for Silver Burdett. 123–124: Silver Burdett. **Unit 4** 129, 159: Silver Burdett. **Unit 5** 169: Silver Burdett. 186: Jacques Jangoux/Peter Arnold, Inc. 187: Clyde Smith/The Stock Shop. 190: Tom Pix/Peter Arnold, Inc. 192: Joe Barnell/Shostal Associates. 195: Silver Burdett. 197: Plimouth Plantation. **Unit 6** 201: E.R. Degginger. 235: Silver Burdett. 237: Detail from "Lewis and Clark at Three Forks." Courtesy, Montana Historical Society, Helena, Montana. **Unit 7** 245: E.R. Degginger. 260: Peter Arnold/Peter Arnold, Inc. 261: J. Gerard Smith. 270: Silver Burdett. **Unit 8** 275: Victoria Beller-Smith for Silver Burdett. 298: *t.* NASA: *b.* E.R. Degginger.

Contributing Writers: Nancy Anderton; Judy Brim; Caribou; Michael Quinn

Acknowledgments continued on page 312

CONTENTS

UNIT ONE

Grammar

Sentences

Composition

Classifying

Late summer evening.

Wind falls still. Cicadas drone.

Swallows fly in sun.

—*Shiki*

1 What Is a Sentence?

> ● A **sentence** is a group of words that expresses a complete thought.

Jana read an article on the history of writing. Then she made some notes for a report. Some of her notes were sentences, and some were not.

Read each group of words below to yourself. Notice which groups of words make sense by themselves. Those groups of words express complete thoughts and are sentences.

1. **Writing began with pictures.**
2. **On rocks and on the walls of caves.**
3. **Ancient people recorded many things.**
4. **Drew pictures of people and animals.**

Notes 1 and 3 are sentences. They name someone or something and tell what that person or thing did.

Notes 2 and 4 are not sentences. Note 2 just names things. Note 4 just tells what happened. Jana will have to change these notes when she writes her report. She will have to make each group of words express a complete thought.

Skills Tryout

Some of the groups of words below are sentences, and some are not. Name the sentences.

1. Three thousand years ago in the Middle East.
2. Scratched lines on wet clay.
3. This writing is called cuneiform.
4. During that time in Egypt, only certain people were allowed to write.
5. Drawn on papyrus or carved on stone.

Practice

A. Write *sentence* or *not a sentence* for each group of words below.

1. Chinese writing began as a kind of picture writing.
2. Scratched on bone, bronze, or stone.
3. Changed very little in the last 3,000 years.
4. Today the Chinese write on paper with a brush and ink.
5. More than 40,000 separate signs are used in Chinese.
6. A difficult task for Chinese students.
7. These signs are sometimes called pictographs.
8. Different pictographs for new words.
9. The sign for *sun* behind the sign for *tree*.
10. This combination means "east."

B. Write the group of words in each pair that is a sentence.

11. **a.** Sitting in the library.
    b. Jana worked on her report every day.
12. **a.** She needed more pictures for her report.
    b. The librarian at the main desk.
13. **a.** After reading Jana's first draft.
    b. Over the weekend she made some changes.
14. **a.** Saw an A+ at the top of her paper.
    b. Jana got an A+ on her report.
15. **a.** Jana's teacher put the report on the bulletin board.
    b. With slight changes and using more pictures.

Application WRITING SENTENCES

Write three sentences of your own. Write about something that you like, such as a hobby or a sport. Be sure your sentences are complete thoughts.

2 Declarative and Interrogative Sentences

- The first word of a sentence begins with a **capital letter**.
- A **declarative sentence** makes a statement and ends with a period (.).
- An **interrogative sentence** asks a question and ends with a question mark (?).

The sentences below make statements.

> **Many foods of today were first found in the New World.**
> **Potatoes come from Peru.**
> **Chocolate was a favorite food of the Aztecs in Mexico.**

Sentences like these are declarative sentences. Each begins with a capital letter and ends with a period.

The sentences below ask questions.

> **Was Thomas Jefferson the first president to eat a tomato?**
> **Where was spaghetti first made?**
> **How many kinds of squash did Native Americans grow?**

Sentences like these are interrogative sentences. Each begins with a capital letter and ends with a question mark.

Skills Tryout

Tell whether each sentence is declarative or interrogative.

1. Wild rice is a special kind of plant.
2. Does anyone know the origin of the hot dog?
3. Yams were brought to America from Africa.
4. What kind of corn is used to make hominy?
5. Alligator pear is another name for avocado.

Practice

A. Write each sentence. Then write *declarative* or *interrogative* to show what kind of sentence it is.

1. Where were peanuts first grown?
2. Spanish explorers brought peanuts to Africa and Spain in the sixteenth century.
3. Did you know that the peanut is a member of the pea family?
4. Tomatoes were once thought to be poisonous.
5. Are the tomato and the potato related?
6. French gardeners grew potatoes for their blossoms.
7. When did people begin to eat vegetables that were found in the New World?
8. Corn and beans were eaten by the Pilgrims.
9. Peppers are called chilies by the people of Mexico.
10. What would pizza taste like without tomatoes?

B. Write each declarative or interrogative sentence. Begin each sentence correctly. Use correct punctuation at the end.

11. how many Native American foods can you name
12. green peppers, corn, and tomatoes were first grown in America
13. bananas are native to South America
14. are pineapples originally from Hawaii
15. what did Europeans eat for Christmas dinner before 1492
16. the turkey should be our national bird
17. is anything more American than pumpkin pie
18. when were jack-o'-lanterns first made
19. the colonists brought apples to America
20. did they bring blueberries, too

Application WRITING SENTENCES

Write three declarative sentences about some of your favorite foods. Then write three interrogative sentences about them.

3 Imperative and Exclamatory Sentences

- An **imperative sentence** gives a command or makes a request. It ends with a period (.).
- An **exclamatory sentence** expresses strong feeling. It ends with an exclamation mark (!).

Remember that sentences make statements or ask questions. Sentences also give commands or make requests. Read the following sentences.

> Look at that strange mask.
> Please tie my shoes for me.

Sentences like these are imperative sentences. Each begins with a capital letter and ends with a period.

Other sentences express strong feelings.

> What a great disguise that is!
> You really fooled me!

Sentences like these are exclamatory sentences. Each begins with a capital letter and ends with an exclamation mark.

Skills Tryout

Tell which sentences below are imperative and which are exclamatory.

1. Put your costume on quickly.
2. How dark it is outside!
3. Please help me fix this crown.
4. You look great in that helmet!
5. Try some of this yellow paint on your mask.

Practice

A. Write each sentence. Then write *imperative* or *exclamatory* to show what kind of sentence it is.

1. I can hardly wait for Alan's party to begin!
2. Meet me there at five o'clock.
3. Watch out for the tub of apples in the basement.
4. What a weird noise that is!
5. Don't be afraid to go down those stairs.
6. That is the most terrifying sound I have ever heard!
7. Let Paula go ahead of you then.
8. Absolutely nothing frightens her!
9. How strange everything looks down here!
10. Please wait for me to catch up with you.

B. Write each imperative or exclamatory sentence. Begin each sentence correctly. Use a period or an exclamation mark at the end.

11. that sounded just like an owl screeching
12. please be careful over there
13. sit down next to me on the bench
14. there's a cat peering in that window
15. reach into this bowl
16. something cold and slimy is in there
17. how awful it feels
18. turn the lights on
19. please look in the bowl
20. what a relief it is to see cold spaghetti

Application WRITING SENTENCES

Write three imperative sentences and three exclamatory sentences about Halloween. Be sure to use capital letters, periods, and exclamation marks correctly.

GRAMMAR and MECHANICS: Imperative and Exclamatory Sentences **9**

4 Complete Subjects and Complete Predicates

- The **complete subject** is all the words in the subject part of a sentence. The subject part names someone or something.
- The **complete predicate** is all the words in the predicate part of a sentence. The predicate part tells what the subject is or does.

You have learned that every sentence expresses a complete thought. To do that, every sentence has two main parts. The subject part names someone or something. The predicate part tells what the subject is or does.

Read the sentences below. The part in blue is the complete subject. The part in green is the complete predicate.

1. Caves may have been the first human dwellings.
2. Simple mud houses were a later development.
3. Castles of stone and iron kept off attackers.
4. Sand castles disappear.

The complete subject may have one word, as in 1 above. The complete subjects in 2, 3, and 4 have more than one word. The complete predicate may also have one word or many words.

Skills Tryout

Name each complete subject and complete predicate.

1. A houseboat provides shelter and transportation.
2. The White House is a home as well as a national monument.
3. Cave dwellers painted animal pictures on the walls of caves.
4. Snow houses can be quite warm.
5. The Pueblos of New Mexico built homes of clay.

Practice

A. Write each sentence. Underline the complete subject once. Underline the complete predicate twice.

1. Settlers in Nebraska built sod houses.
2. People in ancient Egypt lived in mud and brick houses.
3. Tribes of wandering shepherds made tents of skin.
4. Tepees sheltered Native Americans on the Great Plains.
5. Glass houses make good use of solar energy.
6. The dwelling place of the future may be a space station.
7. Stone cottages with tile roofs are common in Ireland.
8. Woven grass kept the rain out of Hawaiian homes long ago.
9. A tree house is a temporary dwelling.
10. Some people like to live in log houses.

B. Add a complete subject or a complete predicate to each group of words below. Write the complete sentence.

EXAMPLE: _____ were made of wood.
ANSWER: The stairs were made of wood.

11. The carpenter _____.
12. _____ is on the top floor.
13. _____ has just been painted.
14. The old brick house _____.
15. _____ lives in a twelve-story building.
16. Two new apartment houses _____.
17. _____ lived in a cottage in the woods.
18. _____ stood on a rocky island.
19. We _____.
20. A log cabin _____.

Application WRITING SENTENCES

Write five sentences about the kind of house you would like to live in some day. Be sure each sentence has a complete subject and a complete predicate.

5 — Simple Subjects

- The **simple subject** is the main word in the complete subject.

Remember that the complete subject is all the words in the subject part of a sentence. The most important word in the complete subject is called the simple subject.

Read the sentences below. The complete subject of each sentence is shown in blue. The simple subject is underlined.

1. School is very exciting this year.
2. Every school in town has a computer.
3. My English class goes to the computer lab twice a week.
4. Luís Ramos used the computer today.
5. He made this design.

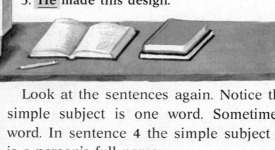

Look at the sentences again. Notice that most of the time the simple subject is one word. Sometimes it is more than one word. In sentence 4 the simple subject is two words because it is a person's full name.

Skills Tryout

A line has been drawn between the complete subject and the complete predicate of each sentence below. Name the simple subject in each sentence.

1. Our whole class | was surprised.
2. A strange machine | sat on the desk.
3. The first lesson on the computer | was easy.
4. Leroy Johnson | showed us what to do.
5. Computers | can solve problems quickly.

Practice

A. Read each sentence below. A line has been drawn between the complete subject and the complete predicate. Write each complete subject. Draw a line under the simple subject.

1. Scientists | use special computers for difficult problems.
2. Ordinary people | can use computers easily.
3. Every computer | has a memory.
4. Information | is stored in the memory.
5. The computer's memory | contains instructions.
6. The instructions | are in a special language.
7. The words in this language | look like English.
8. Some meanings | are different, though.
9. Special commands | tell the computer when to count.
10. A touch of the finger | stops the machine.

B. Write the simple subject of each sentence.

11. This button turns on the machine.
12. An arrow on the screen lights up.
13. The keys on the right make the arrow move.
14. Words appear on the screen.
15. Emma's friends in the class want to work with the computer.
16. The class uses the computer for writing.
17. Some programs will correct misspelled words.
18. Two students draw pictures with the computer.
19. The computer in Mrs. Walker's class can talk.
20. Sarah Easton hopes to have a computer of her own.

Application WRITING SENTENCES

Write five sentences. Use each word below as the simple subject of a sentence. Remember that the complete subject can contain one word or many words.

machine   button   arrow   picture   key

6 — Simple Predicates

- The **simple predicate** is the main word or words in the complete predicate.

You have learned that the complete predicate is all the words in the predicate part of a sentence. The simple predicate is the most important word or words in this part. The simple predicate is the word or words that show action.

Julia's class was writing about sports. Here are some of the sentences the students wrote. The complete predicate of each sentence is shown in green. The simple predicate is underlined.

1. Balls bounce.
2. The Aztecs played ringball.
3. The pitcher, a left-hander, was throwing mostly fastballs.
4. The soccer ball in the garage had lost most of its air.

In sentences 1 and 2 the simple predicate is one word. In sentences 3 and 4 the simple predicate is more than one word.

Skills Tryout

Here are some more of the sentences Julia's class wrote. A line has been drawn between the complete subject and the complete predicate of each sentence. Name the simple predicate.

1. The game of golf | was invented in Scotland.
2. The surprised umpire | lost his glasses.
3. Sally Jo, a champion rodeo rider, | practices every day for six hours.
4. The player in the red shirt | has made three fouls in just the first half of the game.
5. The winner of last year's prize | is playing again this year.

Practice

A. Read each sentence below. A line has been drawn between the complete subject and the complete predicate. Write each complete predicate. Draw a line under the simple predicate.

1. Many different sports | are played today.
2. Some sports | develop skills for daily use.
3. Soccer | is growing more popular than ever.
4. Baseball | requires speed and practice.
5. Water sports | teach confidence to sailors and swimmers.
6. A swim on a hot day | cools the body.
7. The ability to float | has saved many lives.
8. Practice with jacks | makes fingers nimble.
9. Exercise in the open air | helps your heart and lungs.
10. Sports | have proved useful in many ways.

B. Write the simple predicate of each sentence.

11. Our team has made another touchdown.
12. The quarterback had called a new play.
13. The new shortstop threw the ball to second.
14. She was trying for a double play.
15. Ellen, our best hitter, has broken her wrist.
16. Julio scored several goals a game.
17. The great goalie prevented the other team from scoring.
18. The large chestnut horse cleared the first fence easily.
19. Marcy Jackson, a new young rider, won the blue ribbon.
20. Lee likes water sports.

Application WRITING SENTENCES

Write five sentences about sports you like. Use the words below as simple predicates.

a. have played   **c.** was practicing   **e.** scored
b. ran   **d.** had won

GRAMMAR: Simple Predicates **15**

7 Subjects in Imperative Sentences

- *You* (understood) is the subject of an imperative sentence.

Maria's class was reviewing declarative and imperative sentences. She looked at the examples on the chalkboard.

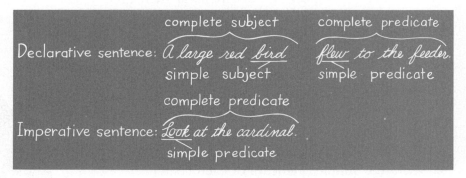

"Mr. O'Connor," she said, "something is missing. The imperative sentence does not have a complete subject. How can we find the simple subject?"

He explained, "The simple subject of any imperative sentence is *you*. However, the word *you* is not usually written or spoken. We say that it is 'understood.'"

In the sentence below, the simple subject is *you* (understood).

(You) Watch the birds from the window.

Skills Tryout

Name the simple subject in each sentence below. Some of the sentences are imperative.

1. Fill the bird feeder every day.
2. The nuthatch walks down the side of the tree.
3. Mix peanut butter and oatmeal together.
4. Birds with short, stubby beaks crack seeds.
5. Throw stale bread covered with bacon grease on the ground.

Practice

A. Write each sentence. Underline the simple subject. Write *(You)* if the subject is understood.

EXAMPLE: Start feeding in September.
ANSWER: (You) Start feeding in September.

1. One interesting hobby is bird-watching.
2. Birds of all kinds can be seen in the park.
3. Borrow a pair of field glasses.
4. Look for finches in the pine trees.
5. Your own backyard is a good place for bird-watching.
6. Robins look for worms in the ground.
7. A thrush in a nearby park brightens the day with song.
8. Get some books about birds from the library.
9. Ask the librarian for more information about birds.
10. Set up a bird-feeding station near the kitchen window.

B. Write each sentence. Then write *declarative* or *imperative* to show what kind of sentence it is. Underline the simple subject in each declarative sentence. Write *(You)* for each imperative sentence.

11. Different birds eat different kinds of food.
12. Supply a variety of foods.
13. The bright red cardinal likes sunflower seeds.
14. Mix fats with peanut butter.
15. Keep the squirrels away.
16. Hummingbirds will sip nectar and sugar water.
17. Put the food on the ground.
18. Some birds eat only from the ground.
19. A hungry jay will drive away other birds.
20. Enjoy your new hobby.

Application LISTENING

Write five imperative sentences you have heard in advertisements on television or radio.

8 — Synonyms and Antonyms

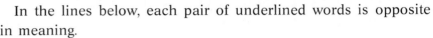

- **Synonyms** are words that have almost the same meaning.
- **Antonyms** are words that have opposite meanings.

In the lines below, each pair of underlined words is opposite in meaning.

Sing a song of people
   Walking <u>fast</u> or <u>slow</u>;
People in the city,
   <u>Up</u> and <u>down</u> they go.

Words with opposite meanings, like *fast* and *slow*, are antonyms.

Words can also have similar meanings, like the underlined pair below.

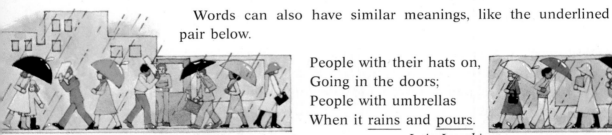

People with their hats on,
Going in the doors;
People with umbrellas
When it <u>rains</u> and <u>pours</u>.
    —*Lois Lenski*

Words with similar meanings, like *rains* and *pours*, are synonyms.

Skills Tryout

Tell whether the underlined words in each sentence below are synonyms or antonyms.

1. Felix looked <u>left</u> and <u>right</u> at all the buildings.
2. He had expected a <u>tiny</u>, <u>little</u> house.
3. This building was <u>tall</u> and <u>towering</u>.
4. People hurried <u>in</u> and <u>out</u> of the doors.
5. City life was certainly not <u>calm</u> and <u>quiet</u>.

Practice

A. Write each pair of words below. Then write *S* after each pair of synonyms. Write *A* after each pair of antonyms.

1. boring, dull
2. bright, dim
3. smooth, level
4. narrow, wide
5. rush, hurry
6. loud, noisy
7. early, late
8. near, far
9. rough, jagged
10. like, dislike

B. Write the underlined word. Beside it write the word in parentheses ( ) that is a synonym for the underlined word.

11. Felix came from a <u>small</u> town.   (big, little)
12. He thought it would be <u>easy</u> to find his way around in the city.   (simple, hard)
13. The city was <u>bigger</u> than he thought.   (newer, larger)
14. The buildings were <u>huge</u>.   (old, gigantic)
15. Poor Felix felt very <u>confused</u>.   (happy, puzzled)

C. Write the word in parentheses ( ) that is an antonym for the underlined word.

16. Polly <u>arrived</u> here at the same time as Felix.   (left, came)
17. The streets were <u>empty</u> all day.   (crowded, vacant)
18. Polly <u>talked</u> to all the people she met.   (spoke, listened)
19. It took her a <u>long</u> time to make friends.   (lengthy, short)
20. She never noticed how <u>clean</u> the streets were.   (dirty, neat)

Application USING LANGUAGE

Write five sentences describing a place you have visited. Use a synonym or antonym for each of the words below.

big   beautiful   empty   exciting   busy

Four Kinds of Sentences *pages 4–9*

A. Write each sentence. Then write *declarative, interrogative, imperative,* or *exclamatory* to show what kind of sentence it is.

1. Do you know how to train animals?
2. Toby is taking her dog to obedience school.
3. She rewards Tuffy for behaving well.
4. What a good dog he is!
5. Please call your dogs to you.
6. Is Tuffy paying attention to Toby?
7. Come here right now, Tuffy.
8. Tuffy runs immediately to Toby's side.
9. How cute he looks!
10. Will he be able to do that trick again?

Complete Subjects and Complete Predicates *pages 10–11*

B. Write each sentence. Underline the complete subject once. Underline the complete predicate twice.

11. A gull sits on its nest.
12. An egg starts to hatch.
13. The chick pecks inside the shell.
14. Its neck muscles are very strong.
15. The newborn chick rests in the nest.
16. The mother and father gull keep it warm.
17. The chick's feathers dry after a while.
18. The parents feed it.
19. The chick stands up soon.
20. The baby gull can walk on the first day.
21. It learns to fly in a few weeks.
22. The gull grows very fast.
23. It catches fish in the sea.
24. The young bird joins the other gulls.
25. The grown bird belongs with the adults now.

Simple Subjects *pages 12–13*

C. Write the simple subject of each sentence.

26. The new teacher gives the class an assignment.
27. Each student must write a report.
28. The librarian helps them.
29. Nancy is writing about the solar system.
30. The books on this shelf are for her.

Simple Predicates *pages 14–15*

D. Write the simple predicate of each sentence.

31. Eric was waiting for the mail.
32. He heard the letter carrier at the door.
33. Four envelopes were lying in the mailbox.
34. Eric saw a letter for him.
35. He opened the envelope eagerly.

Synonyms and Antonyms *pages 18–19*

E. Decide whether the word in parentheses ( ) is a synonym or an antonym for the underlined word. Then write *synonym* or *antonym*.

36. Max tried to grow a tree. (attempted)
37. Leroy saves seeds. (keeps)
38. Janet threw the ball. (caught)
39. The pot was filled with moist soil. (damp)
40. Miki accepted our advice. (took)
41. Let's sell this car. (buy)
42. The cat was contented after it ate. (happy)
43. The last page of this book is missing. (first)
44. Mark was early. (late)
45. Some guests left before dessert. (several)

See also Handbook pages 314–321.

Sentence Combining

Grammar and Writing Workshop

- Sentences with repeated ideas can be combined.

Read the sentences below.

A. Karl read the article about operas.
B. Karen read the article about operas. (and)
A + B. Karl and Karen read the article about operas.

Sentence A tells what Karl read. Sentence B tells that Karen read the same thing. The second sentence repeats an idea. Sentence A + B tells as much as both sentences A and B. The longer sentence does not repeat a fact.

Sentence A + B was made by combining, or joining, the subjects of sentence A and sentence B. The repeated idea in B was removed. The word *and* was used to add the new idea (Karen) in B to the fact in sentence A. As a result, one strong sentence took the place of two sentences.

Other sentences can be combined in this way.

C. Karen bought two opera tickets.
D. Karen gave one to me. (and)
C + D. Karen bought two opera tickets and gave one to me.

Sentence C and sentence D each tell one thing that Karen did. The word *and* was used to combine the predicates of these sentences, creating sentence C + D. This new sentence does not repeat an idea.

Now it's your turn to combine sentences. As you read each pair of sentences on page 23, find the idea in each second sentence that already appears in each first sentence. Find the new idea in each second sentence. Then you will be able to combine each pair of sentences into one good sentence.

Combine-a-Pair   Combine each pair of sentences below. Use the clues in parentheses ( ) the way they were used on page 22. Write each new sentence.

1. Richard sat next to me in Mr. Cohen's music class.
   Karen sat next to me in Mr. Cohen's music class. (**and**)

2. Karen enjoys the music of Mozart.
   Karen sings with the school choir. (**and**)

3. Richard takes trumpet lessons.
   Richard practices for a half hour every day. (**and**)

4. Kathy attends a special music school during the summer.
   Kathy hopes to become a professional singer. (**and**)

5. The choir appeared in the spring concert.
   The band appeared in the spring concert. (**and**)

6. Parents look forward to this event each year.
   Relatives look forward to this event each year. (**and**)

No-Clue Time   Combine each pair of sentences without clues. Write each new sentence.

7. We went to the theater last night.
   We saw an opera.

8. We found our seats.
   We sat down as the curtain went up.

9. The singers performed with great beauty and skill.
   The musicians performed with great beauty and skill.

10. The star of the opera stepped forward.
    The star of the opera bowed gracefully.

11. I borrowed a record of the opera from the library.
    I listened to it for days.

12. My sister really enjoyed that record!
    I really enjoyed that record!

9 — Finding Words in a Dictionary

- **Guide words** in a dictionary show the first and the last entry word on a page.

A dictionary contains thousands of words in alphabetical order. Each word that is defined is called an **entry word**. How can you find the word you want? Luckily, there are some shortcuts to help you.

The first shortcut is to think of the dictionary in three parts: the front, *a–g;* the middle, *h–p;* and the back, *q–z.* Decide in which part your word appears. Then open to that part. As a challenge, try to open to the first letter of the word you want.

Front   a b c d e f g

Middle   h i j k l m n o p

Back   q r s t u v w x y z

The second shortcut is to use the guide words. The first guide word is the first entry word on the page. The second guide word is the last entry word. All the other entry words on the page fall between the guide words in alphabetical order.

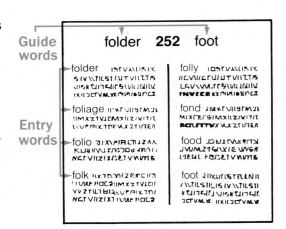

Skills Tryout

Tell in which part of the dictionary each word appears.

1. tradition
2. ballot
3. hive
4. mole
5. primitive
6. culture

Practice

A. Write each word. Then write *front, middle,* or *back* to show in which part of the dictionary it appears.

1. fantasy
2. rhyme
3. suburb
4. customs
5. longitude
6. ancient
7. nature
8. hero
9. elastic

B. Guide words for dictionary pages 218–221 are shown at the right. Write words **10–25**. Then write the page number for each entry word.

| bunt **218** burro | burrow **219** butterfly |
| buttermilk **220** cabbage | cabin **221** calabash |

10. bushel
11. bygone
12. cactus
13. burglar
14. burlap
15. buttercup
16. cafeteria
17. cable
18. cadet
19. buzzard
20. burnt
21. bureau
22. cabbage
23. caboose
24. burr
25. business

C. Write each set of guide words. After each set write three words that could be entry words on that page. You may use a dictionary if you wish.

26. guide words: changeless—chasm
27. guide words: monopoly—more
28. guide words: plum—point
29. guide words: royal—sack
30. guide words: something—sour

Application USING STUDY SKILLS

How long does it take you to find a word in the dictionary? Find out. Have a friend write a word and then time you as you look it up. Record your time. Repeat this activity with other words and try to improve your time.

10 Using a Dictionary

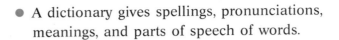

- A dictionary gives spellings, pronunciations, meanings, and parts of speech of words.

*Did I spell asthma right?...What does leonine mean?...
Do you write on stationary or stationery?...
How is rendezvous pronounced?...*

The answers to all these questions can be found in one book, the dictionary. Of all reference books the dictionary is probably the one you will turn to most often. Why is the dictionary so useful? To find out, study the dictionary entries and pronunciation key below. Notice what kind of information they give.

Pronunciation   Part of Speech

Entry word— **leg end** (lej'ənd), *n.* 1. A story coming down from earlier times, which many people have believed.

Meanings— 2. Such stories as a group. 3. What is written on a coin or medal or below a picture.
leg en dar y (lej'ən der'ē), *adj.* Of or

relating to a legend or legends; not historical.
leg er de main (lej'ər də mān'), *n.* 1. Sleight of hand; conjuring tricks. *A common demonstration of legerdemain is to pull a rabbit from an empty hat.* 2. Trickery.

Example sentence

Pronunciation Key— hat, āge, cãre, fär; let, ēqual, tėrm; it, īce; hot, ōpen, ôrder; oil, out; cup, pút, rüle; **ch**, child; **ng**, long; **sh**, she; **th**, thin; **ᴛʜ**, then; **zh**, measure; ə represents *a* in about, *e* in taken, *i* in pencil, *o* in lemon, *u* in circus.

Skills Tryout

Use the dictionary entries above to answer these questions.

1. Which entry word has three numbered meanings?
2. The last vowel sound in *legendary* is $\bar{e}$. Which word in the pronunciation key shows how to pronounce $\bar{e}$?
3. Which entry includes an example sentence?
4. Which two entry words are nouns (marked *n.*)?
5. What is the number of the meaning that *legend* has in this sentence? *The legend on a dime is "IN GOD WE TRUST."*

Practice

A. Use the following dictionary entries for questions **1-5**.

bunk er (bung'kər), *n.* 1. An area or bin for storing fuel on a ship. 2. A sand trap or mound of earth used as an obstacle on a golf course.

buoy (boi), *n.* 1. A floating object kept in a certain place on the water to show safe areas or dangerous areas. 2. A life buoy; something used to keep a person afloat in the water.

buoy an cy (boi'ən sē), *n.* 1. Power to float. 2. Lightheartedness; cheerfulness; hopefulness.

1. Which entry word rhymes with *annoy*?
2. What is the number of the meaning that *buoyancy* has in the following sentence? *The waterlogged wood had lost much of its buoyancy.*
3. Which entry word names a place?
4. What part of speech is each entry word?
5. What kind of buoy is thrown to swimmers in trouble?

B. Use a dictionary to answer the following questions.

6. What is the portcullis of a castle?
7. Which word is spelled incorrectly and how should it be spelled: *perceive, porcupine, porcelaine, portrait*?
8. Which of these words names something to eat: *sepia, filigree, chambray, victuals*?
9. Does *lien* rhyme with *mean, mine,* or *men*?
10. What does *leghorn* mean in the following sentence? *She wore a leghorn.*

Application   USING STUDY SKILLS

Use a dictionary to write a word quiz for your classmates. Write five questions like those in **Practice B**. Choose unfamiliar words to make your quiz more challenging. You might exchange papers with a classmate and see who can answer the questions in the shortest time.

11 — Using a Thesaurus

- A **thesaurus** contains lists of synonyms and antonyms.

There are two books a writer cannot do without. The first is a dictionary. The second is a thesaurus.

Thesaurus means "treasury," and a thesaurus is truly a treasury of words. A thesaurus is somewhat like a dictionary. It has entry words in alphabetical order. However, a thesaurus lists many synonyms and antonyms for each entry word. This makes it the writer's book of word choices.

There is a thesaurus on pages 395–414 of this book. Browse through it, and look at pages 396–400. Every entry word, synonym, and antonym included in the Thesaurus is listed there.

Study the thesaurus entry below for the word *courage*.

	Part of speech	Definition

Entry word ——— **courage** (n)—the strength of mind or will to face danger.
Example sentence—— Fire fighters showed <u>courage</u> in battling the blaze.

boldness—show of scorn for danger; daring. The <u>boldness</u> of the plan surprised us.
bravery—fearlessness in the face of danger or difficulty; courage. The <u>bravery</u> of the hostages was astounding.
Synonyms ——— *heart*—enthusiastic courage. It takes <u>heart</u> to persist.
heroism—willingness to take risks to help others; valor. Davy Crockett's <u>heroism</u> is admired.
valor—willingness to take risks to help others; heroism. Knights of old showed <u>valor</u> in battle.

Cross-reference ——— See also *spirit* (n).
Antonyms ——— ANTONYMS: cowardice, fear (n), timidity

Skills Tryout

Use the thesaurus entry above to answer these questions.

1. What part of speech are *courage* and its synonyms?
2. Which two synonyms have a definition that is the same?
3. Which words are antonyms of *courage*?

Practice

A. Write each sentence. Complete it with a synonym for *courage*. Use a different synonym in each sentence.

1. With _____, Columbus sailed the unknown seas.
2. Gilda showed _____ by spending a night in the haunted house.
3. The _____ of his plan surprised everyone.
4. After Mary saved the child from the fire, she was awarded a medal for _____.
5. The cheering crowd gave the team _____.

B. In each sentence below, replace the word *large* with a synonym that makes sense. (Turn to *large* in the Thesaurus for a list of synonyms.) Write the new sentences.

6. The movie *King Kong* starred a large gorilla.
7. Kong perched on top of a large New York skyscraper.
8. He swatted passing airplanes with his large paw.
9. Through the years a large number of people have seen *King Kong* and its sequels.
10. In one movie, Kong fought a large dinosaur.

C. Find the five antonyms for *large* listed in the Thesaurus. Write a sentence for each one. If you wish, write the five sentences about some small fairy-tale creatures.

Application USING STUDY SKILLS

Here are two riddle clues for the word *vigor*:

> You need _____ to play tennis.
> I am an antonym of weakness.

Choose three words from the Thesaurus on pages 395–414. They can be entry words, synonyms, or antonyms. Write two riddle clues for each word. You might put them in a class riddle box and pick each other's riddles to solve.

12 — What Is a Paragraph?

- A **paragraph** is a group of sentences that tells about one main idea.

Clear writing is a matter of grouping things together in a meaningful way. A word is a group of letters that has meaning. A sentence is a group of words that expresses a complete thought. A paragraph is a group of sentences that tells about one main idea.

The paragraph below shows how sentences work together to tell about one idea. The first sentence states the main idea. The other sentences tell more about it.

Computers come in all shapes and sizes. Some are larger than refrigerators. Others are as small as books. A few are even tiny enough to fit in a pocket.

Notice that the first sentence starts a little bit to the right. It is **indented.** An indented line signals the beginning of a new paragraph.

Skills Tryout

Some of the sentences below belong together in a paragraph. Others do not. Tell which sentences belong in the paragraph.

1. Computers are getting smaller all the time.
2. One of the first computers, named UNIVAC, filled a room.
3. Today's personal computers fit on desk tops.
4. A desk is an important piece of furniture in an office.
5. Desk-top computers may someday be replaced by even smaller computers.
6. Cars are getting smaller, too.

Practice

A. Decide which sentences below belong in a paragraph about robots. For each sentence write *yes* or *no*.

1. Robots are machines run by computers.
2. Some robots have become movie stars.
3. C-3PO became famous in *Star Wars*.
4. Space movies draw large crowds to theaters.
5. A robot may look very human.

B. Which main idea does each sentence tell about? Write *X* or *Y*.

MAIN IDEA X: Some computers can talk.
MAIN IDEA Y: Some spaceships are giant robots.

6. Computer voices, however, don't sound human.
7. Computers can't produce human tones and rhythms.
8. The spaceship that went to Mars had no crew.
9. Computers guided the ship to its landing.
10. Think about the sound of a sigh or a groan.
11. You can't get computers to make those sounds.
12. Robot arms gathered samples from the soil.
13. Future computers will have better speech.
14. Robot eyes sent pictures back to earth.
15. Someday, computers may sound just like people.

C. Make a paragraph about main idea X or Y above. Start with the main idea. Add all the sentences that tell about that main idea. Write the sentences in paragraph form, leaving out the numbers. Be sure to indent the first line.

Application WRITING A PARAGRAPH

Imagine yourself in the future with a robot of your own. Describe your robot in a paragraph. Begin by completing this sentence for the main idea: *My robot looks like a* _____. Then add sentences that give more details about how it looks.

13 — Topic Sentence and Supporting Sentences

- The **topic sentence** states the main idea of a paragraph.
- **Supporting sentences** develop the main idea.

All the sentences in a paragraph tell about the main idea. Most paragraphs have one sentence that states the main idea. That is the topic sentence. The other sentences develop or explain the main idea by giving details. Those are the supporting sentences.

Notice the role of each sentence below.

Topic Sentence: Some creatures move about in unusual ways.
Supporting Sentence: Kangaroos hop.
Supporting Sentence: Sidewinders travel sideways.
Supporting Sentence: Oysters propel themselves backward.

The sentences can be grouped together to form a paragraph. Simply indent the first line.

Some creatures move about in unusual ways. Kangaroos hop. Sidewinders travel sideways. Oysters propel themselves backward.

Although the topic sentence usually comes first in a paragraph, it can come in other positions. Sometimes it comes last. The topic sentence in the paragraph below is underlined. Notice how the supporting sentences lead to the main idea.

Toadfish make a croaking noise. Dolphins chatter at a high pitch. Some whales sing haunting melodies. <u>The ocean is alive with sound</u>.

Skills Tryout

Tell which sentence is the topic sentence and which are the supporting sentences.

1. The bat sends out a high-pitched sound.
2. The sound bounces off objects.
3. A bat has a built-in radar system.
4. These bouncing sounds tell the bat where things are.

Practice

A. Use the sentences below to write a paragraph. Identify the topic sentence and write it first. Then complete the paragraph by writing the supporting sentences.

1. Grasshoppers are the color of grass.
2. Some animals' colors help them hide from enemies.
3. Certain butterflies match the bark of trees.
4. Leopards' spots blend with the shadows of leaves.
5. Polar bears are the color of snow.

B. The sentences below are topic sentences. Write two supporting sentences for each.

6. Some animals have homes underground.
7. Dogs are wonderful pets.
8. Circus animals have to be well trained.

C. Write a topic sentence and two or more supporting sentences for each subject.

9. Why people like zoos   10. The silliest animal of all

Application WRITING A PARAGRAPH

Animals in books and movies often act like people. Choose an animal character you have read about or seen. Write a paragraph about its human actions. Underline the topic sentence.

14 — The Writing Process

What happens when you write? What really goes on when you write a story or a letter? Have you ever thought about it? Take a moment to think about it now. Discuss it with your classmates. Try to describe what happens when you write.

Everyone writes differently. In general, however, all writers follow four steps:
1. **prewriting**
2. **writing**
3. **revising**
4. **publishing**

This is "the writing process."

A description of the writing process begins on the next page. Read it and think about it. Does it sound like what happens when *you* write?

1. Prewriting

Prewriting is getting and exploring ideas. Getting ideas is not always easy, though. Do you ever feel like saying, "I don't know what to write about"? If so, don't worry. All writers sometimes feel that way.

There are many ways to get ideas. Here are a few:

- Notice how a thing looks, smells, sounds, tastes, or feels.
- Read a poem or story and jot down your thoughts about it.
- Talk with someone to get information about a topic.

In no time you will have at least one good idea. This is the surprising part: One idea is all you need to start writing.

2. Writing

Is it true that you must know everything you will write before you start writing? No. You can start writing with just one small idea. You will get more ideas as soon as you start to write. Remember: Thinking helps you write, but also writing helps you think!

WRITER'S HINT: As you write, it helps to know two things:

1. **Purpose** Why are you writing? To tell a story? To persuade someone to share an opinion you have?

2. **Audience** Who will read what you write? Will your reader be someone your own age? Someone younger? An adult?

Knowing your purpose and audience helps you write more effectively.

This is the time to get all your ideas on paper. Don't worry about neatness or spelling. Don't worry about putting your ideas in the best order. Just keep on writing as long as ideas are coming. When you have written everything you want to say, stop. You have written your first draft.

3. Revising

Vision means "seeing." *Revision* means "seeing again." Revising is taking another look at what you have written. It is trying to see through the eyes of the person who will read it. It is adding or changing to make it clearer or better. It is rewriting to improve.

4. Publishing

Publishing is sharing what you have written. You can mail a letter or place a story in the class library. You can put a poem on the bulletin board or read a report aloud.

Be courteous to your reader. Before you publish, proofread what you have written. Fix any errors, and make a correct copy.

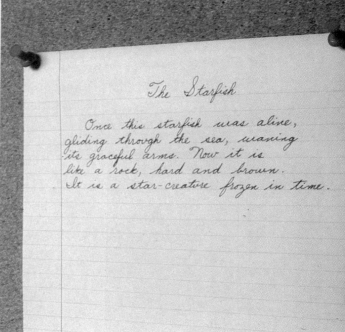

The Starfish

Once this starfish was alive, gliding through the sea, waving its graceful arms. Now it is like a rock, hard and brown. It is a star-creature frozen in time.

15 — Writing a Comparison Paragraph

Writing Project

- A **comparison paragraph** tells about the likenesses between two objects, persons, places, or ideas.

Scientists often compare things and describe how they are alike. That is how they classify plants and animals. Writers also like to describe how things are alike. Have you ever thought that an anthill is like a small city or that clouds sometimes look like castles? Writers often make such comparisons.

In this lesson you will look at two things and think about how they are alike. Then you will write a comparison paragraph to describe the likenesses. Later you will share your paragraph with your classmates. As you work, you will practice the four steps of the writing process.

1. Prewriting

Look at the flower and the butterfly. In what ways are they alike? Discuss your ideas with your classmates. Then read the list of likenesses below. Did you think of the same likenesses? What others did you think of?

Likenesses

Both flowers and butterflies

are delicate	live a short time
are small	appear in spring
are alive	move in the breeze
are colorful	are seen in gardens

One reminds us of the other.
Butterflies remind us of flying flowers.
A field of flowers looks like a butterfly party.

▶ Now select your own topic. Here are some suggestions:

- Compare something in space to something on earth.
- Compare something very large to something very small.
- Compare your pet to a wild animal.
- Compare *any* two things you choose.

Write down three pairs of things you could compare. Decide which pair is the most interesting or the most fun. You have chosen your topic.

▶ Form a mental picture of the two things you have chosen to compare. (Get real pictures of them if you can.) Make a list of likenesses. Write some ideas about how one reminds you of the other.

2. Writing

Sometimes it is hard to start writing a paragraph. You have your list of likenesses, but what should you say first? How can you form a topic sentence for your paragraph?

You could begin with a question like this: "Have you ever noticed that flowers are like butterflies?" Or you could begin with a statement: "My dog is like a wolf in three ways." Notice that each topic sentence names the two things being compared: flowers and butterflies, a dog and a wolf.

▶ Now write your own topic sentence. Be sure to name the two things you are comparing. Then write as many ideas as you can about how they are alike. As you write, you might use some of the connecting words in the box. They can help connect the details in your paragraph.

Don't worry about spelling or handwriting. Just try to capture all your ideas. This will be your first draft.

Connecting words
both   also
besides
in addition
similarly
moreover
in each case
in fact
furthermore
to me
it seems that
in my view
I notice that

3. Revising

▶ Read your first draft to yourself or to someone else. How does it sound? Can you improve your writing? Use this checklist to help you think about your paragraph.

Revision Checklist
- Did I write a topic sentence that tells the main idea?
- Did I write supporting sentences to develop the main idea?
- Did I tell how two things are alike?
- Did I use connecting words?
- Does each sentence express a complete thought?

Writers use editing marks when they revise their writing. The sample shows how editing marks can be used to make changes. As you read the sample, notice how it was changed to make each sentence express a complete thought.

Sample draft with editing marks:

> Have you ever ~~notissed~~ *noticed* that flowers are like butterflies? Both are soft and *delicate*. ~~Are like butterflies on stems.~~ *To me, flowers* The both *wave like* tiny flags in the breeze.

Revised paragraph:

> Have you ever noticed that flowers are like butterflies? Both are delicate and bright. Both wave like tiny flags in the breeze. To me, flowers are like butterflies on stems.

▶ Now make any changes you want to improve your paragraph, using the editing marks on the next page.

4. Publishing

▶If you plan to let others read what you have written, proofread for errors. Use the checklist below as a guide. Use the editing marks to make corrections.

Proofreading Checklist

- Is the first word of the paragraph indented?
- Does each sentence begin with a capital letter and end with the right punctuation mark?
- Is each word spelled correctly?
- Have I used my best handwriting?

EDITING MARKS

——— cross out
∧ add
↻ move
= capital letter
/ small letter
¶ indent
◯ check spelling

▶A bulletin board is a good place to publish your writing. Draw or find pictures of the two things you compared. Post the pictures beside your paragraph on a bulletin board.

You and your classmates might like to try this variation: Scramble the pictures and the paragraphs. Title the bulletin board "Guess the Comparisons." Read each other's paragraphs and identify the pictures that belong with each one.

Writing Project

A Class Thesaurus

Make an illustrated class thesaurus that you can add to during the year. With your classmates make a list of overused words. Then choose one of the words for your thesaurus entry. (Each person should choose a different word.)

Set up your thesaurus entry like the one on this page. First, write the word and its part of speech. Next, write a short definition and a sentence that shows the meaning of the word. Finally, list several synonyms and antonyms for the word. Illustrate your thesaurus page yourself or use a magazine picture as an illustration.

Collect the entries and put them in alphabetical order. Use divider pages with alphabet tabs if you wish. If you write the thesaurus entries on loose-leaf paper and put them in a three-ring binder, you can easily add more pages later.

pretty (adjective) — pleasing to the senses; nice-looking. These pretty flowers bloom in the fall.

Synonyms: attractive, handsome, lovely, striking

Antonyms: homely, plain, ugly, unattractive, unsightly

Science

Classify means "to put things together that belong together." Classifying is especially important in science. Scientists classify animals, plants, and planets. They classify stars, storms, and stones. They classify the many items in the world of nature so that they can study them more easily.

▶ Now you try it. Classify the animals in the photographs. Think about how they are alike and how they are different. On a sheet of paper, copy the four characteristics below. After each one, list the animals that have that characteristic. You may use an encyclopedia if you need help.

1. Has a backbone
2. Eats meat or fish
3. Feeds young on milk
4. Lives in water

Writers at Work Imagine trying to keep track of all the foods a zoo needs to buy! That is the responsibility of the people who work in a zoo's commissary, or supply store.

▶ Pretend that you work in a zoo commissary. Below is a list of foods zoo animals eat. Rewrite the list so that it will be easier to use as a grocery checklist. Put foods that belong together in groups. Write a heading such as Fruits or Seafood for each group.

ants, oranges, raw horsemeat, cereal, sunflower seeds, crickets, bamboo leaves, trout, mice, acorns, eggs, carrots, hay, bananas, oats, lettuce, raisins, bread crumbs, rice, milk, potatoes, cabbage, apples, cracked corn, peanuts, thistle seeds, mixed birdseed, wax worms, eucalyptus leaves, codfish, ground meat, shrimp

Timber wolf

Jellyfish

Crocodile

Eagle

Whale

Checkpoint: Unit 1

Sentences *pages 4–17*

A. Write each sentence. Then write *declarative, interrogative, imperative,* or *exclamatory* to show what kind of sentence it is.

1. What a windy day it is!
2. I just found a dollar.
3. How deep is this lake?
4. Is that book enjoyable?
5. Please answer the phone.
6. We won the track meet!

B. Write each sentence. Underline the complete subject once. Underline the complete predicate twice.

7. Our science class took a trip to the weather station.
8. Brightly colored flags hung all around the football field.
9. A small group of students started the hiking club.
10. The tallest building in town is four stories high.
11. Mrs. Starzyck needs a hammer and some nails.
12. That gray cat with stripes lives in the back alley.

C. Write the simple subject of each sentence. Write (*You*) if the subject is understood.

13. Bring a bag lunch for the school picnic.
14. One loud cricket has been chirping all night.
15. Follow the trail for at least two miles.
16. Take these fresh flowers to Mr. Watson.
17. The bus from New York usually arrives on time.

D. Write the simple predicate of each sentence.

18. Seven circus clowns rode in the tiny bus.
19. Pam's older brother is driving her home from the movie.
20. The baby robin had fallen from its nest.
21. A small stream flows past our house.
22. Michael was using a new kind of baseball glove.

Checkpoint: Unit 1

44

Synonyms and Antonyms *pages 18–19*

E. Write each pair of words. Write *S* after each pair that are synonyms. Write *A* after each pair that are antonyms.

23. timid, shy   **25.** misty, clear
24. swiftly, slowly   **26.** comical, funny

Dictionary *pages 24–27*

F. Read each set of guide words. Write the word in parentheses ( ) that would appear on the same page.

27. close—club (clue, cloud)   **29.** mist—mixer (mitt, milk)
28. rake—range (rate, rally)   **30.** head—heard (hero, heal)

G. Read the dictionary entries. Answer each question.

wield (wēld), *v.* 1. To use a tool or weapon. 2. To exercise power.
wisp (wisp), *n.* 1. A thin, slight piece or strand. 2. Something delicate.

31. What part of speech is *wisp*?
32. Does *wield* rhyme with *child, kneeled,* or *filled*?

Thesaurus *pages 28–29*

H. Read the thesaurus entry. Answer each question.

rare (adj)—uncommon; often valuable. The <u>rare</u> gem was priceless.
scarce—hard to find.
unusual—out of the ordinary.
ANTONYM: **common**

33. What are the two synonyms for *rare*?
34. What is the antonym for *rare*?

Paragraphs *pages 30–33*

I. Write a topic sentence and two supporting sentences about this main idea: *Why people have pets.*

See also Handbook pages 314-321, 368.

Grammar
Nouns

Composition
Narrating

Old Log House

On a little green knoll
At the edge of the wood
My great great grandmother's
First house stood.

The house was of logs
My grandmother said
With one big room
And a lean-to shed.

The logs were cut
And the house was raised
By pioneer men
In the olden days.

I like to hear
My grandmother tell
How they built the fireplace
And dug the well.

They split the shingles;
They filled each chink;
It's a house of which
I like to think.

Forever and ever
I wish I could
Live in a house
At the edge of a wood.

—*James S. Tippett*

1 Nouns

- A **noun** names a person, place, thing, or idea.

Mr. Shaw's class learned that nouns are naming words. The class made a chart to show that nouns can name persons, places, things, and ideas.

Examples of Nouns			
Persons	student	teachers	Nicholas
Places	country	Greece	islands
Things	houses	ships	food
Ideas	democracy	bravery	humor

Mr. Shaw asked, "How are the nouns that name people, places, and things alike?"

Mark said, "They all name someone or something that we can see or touch."

"What about the nouns that name ideas?" asked Mr. Shaw.

"They name things we can't see or touch," said Isabel.

Skills Tryout

Each of the sentences below has three nouns. Read the sentences and name the nouns.

1. The class studied life in ancient Greece.
2. Tim read a book about the country.
3. The students saw statues in a museum.
4. Ancient Greeks studied mathematics and music.
5. This report is about their houses and their cities.

Practice

A. Write the following sentences. Underline all the nouns in each sentence.

1. The Greeks liked sunshine.
2. Ancient Greeks lived in plain and simple houses.
3. The warm weather made the garden a popular place.
4. Families worked and played under the trees.
5. Many people lived in cities.
6. Towns were planned with great thoughtfulness.
7. The adults met their friends at the open markets.
8. Temples and theaters were also important buildings.
9. Wide streets led into town.
10. Walls surrounded the city for safety.

B. Write the following sentences. Complete each sentence with one of the nouns below. Use the noun that best fits the sentence.

chairs	clothes	beds	writers	windows
nails	house	comforts	tables	heat

11. Many _____ have left descriptions of ancient Greece.
12. The Greeks enjoyed many of the _____ of life.
13. Each room in a Greek _____ had a different use.
14. Some rooms contained _____ for sleeping.
15. Some clothing was hung on _____ in the walls.
16. Other _____ were stored in chests.
17. Greeks did not sit on _____ to eat their meals.
18. Instead, their _____ were placed beside couches.
19. Their _____ was supplied by charcoal stoves.
20. The _____ were left open for fresh air.

Application WRITING SENTENCES

Write five sentences. Use one of the nouns below in each.

people   friendliness   building   chairs   warmth

2 Singular and Plural Nouns

- A **singular noun** names one person, place, thing, or idea.
- A **plural noun** names more than one person, place, thing, or idea.

Nouns can name one thing or more than one thing. In other words, nouns can be singular or plural. Most nouns add an ending in the plural. Some nouns change their spelling. A few nouns are the same in the singular and the plural.

Here are the singular and plural forms of some nouns.

Singular	Plural
cat horse book	cats horses books
church wish glass box	churches wishes glasses boxes
baby berry city	babies berries cities
monkey tray boy	monkeys trays boys
life knife calf	lives knives calves
foot goose woman	feet geese women
moose sheep deer	moose sheep deer

Rules for spelling plural nouns are on page 326 in the Grammar Handbook. Use them to help you do these exercises.

Skills Tryout

Tell whether each of these nouns is singular or plural.

1. wish	**3.** monkeys	**5.** dash	**7.** knives	**9.** women
2. toy	**4.** box	**6.** feet	**8.** rake	**10.** kite

Practice

A. Write the underlined noun in each sentence. Then write *singular* if the noun is singular. Write *plural* if it is plural.

1. The smallest <u>muscle</u> is in the ear.
2. The tallest <u>women</u> are over seven feet tall.
3. One cat had a litter of thirteen <u>kittens</u>.
4. What is the largest <u>ruby</u> in the world?
5. Are the most expensive <u>dresses</u> from Paris?
6. What <u>holidays</u> are celebrated by the most people?
7. These <u>sheep</u> have the longest horns in the world.
8. What country has the greatest number of <u>wolves</u>?
9. The largest <u>flag</u> in the world is in the United States.
10. This <u>mouse</u> weighs less than an ounce.

B. Write the plural of each of these nouns.

11. ax
12. army
13. glass
14. moose
15. turkey
16. goose
17. village
18. ostrich
19. shelf
20. bat

C. Write each sentence. Use the plural form of the noun in parentheses ( ).

21. Saturn and Jupiter each have sixteen (satellite).
22. Where are the tallest (chimney) in the world?
23. The two largest (radish) weighed twenty-five pounds each.
24. One pie was made from 4,950 pounds of (cherry).
25. Seven (woman) stood together at the South Pole in 1969.

Application WRITING SENTENCES

Write two sentences using each of these nouns. In one sentence use the singular form. Use the plural form in the other sentence. You will write six sentences in all.

arch   bridge   balcony

3 Common and Proper Nouns

- A **common noun** is the general name of a person, place, or thing.
- A **proper noun** names a particular person, place, or thing.

Ms. Easton wrote these words on the chalkboard.

state   scientist   bridge
California   Luther Burbank   Golden Gate Bridge

"Thomas, tell us about these words," she said.

"They are all nouns," Thomas said.

Julia added, "California is the name of a particular state. Luther Burbank is the name of a particular scientist."

Billy Joe raised his hand. "The Golden Gate Bridge is a particular bridge."

"You're all correct," Ms. Easton said. "The general name of a person, place, or thing is a common noun. The particular name of a person, place, or thing is a proper noun. Notice that a proper noun can be more than one word."

Skills Tryout

Julia's class read about California. Here are some sentences from their book. Tell whether the underlined nouns are common or proper.

1. San Diego has an almost perfect climate.
2. This city has delightfully warm days and cool nights.
3. The part of the coast called Big Sur attracts many tourists.
4. The automobile made Los Angeles a place of freeways.
5. Open fields, not buildings, once lined Wilshire Boulevard.

Practice

A. In each sentence below, the nouns are underlined. Write each noun. Then write *common* or *proper* to show what kind of noun it is.

1. Death Valley is the lowest, hottest desert in America.
2. Settlers lived in towns with names like Furnace Creek.
3. Sequoia National Park is not far from this desert.
4. The General Sherman Tree is the largest tree in the state.
5. Many beautiful churches and missions are found between Carmel and San Luis Obispo.
6. Father Junipero Serra built chapels at the missions.
7. Grapes for raisins are grown in the valleys.
8. People seeking gold hurried to Sutter's Creek.
9. Now tourists visit Sutter's Mill on the creek.
10. Another favorite attraction is Yosemite National Park.

B. Write each sentence. Draw one line under the common nouns. Draw two lines under the proper nouns.

11. Many movies are made in Hollywood.
12. Giant redwood trees grow in Muir Woods National Monument.
13. The highest peak in the Sierra Nevada is Mount Whitney.
14. Lake Tahoe is a beautiful place for a vacation.
15. Disneyland charms adults as well as children.
16. The Sacramento is the longest river in California.
17. The Golden Gate Bridge is a famous landmark.
18. Fisherman's Wharf is a popular restaurant in San Francisco.
19. Many seals live on the rocks along the coast.
20. San Diego is a large city near Mexico.

Application WRITING SENTENCES

Write five sentences about a place you would like to visit. Use at least five common nouns and five proper nouns.

4 Capitalizing Proper Nouns

> ● A proper noun begins with a capital letter.

A proper noun always begins with a capital letter. If a proper noun has more than one word, each important word is capitalized.

The chart below gives some rules and examples for capitalizing proper nouns.

Capitalizing Proper Nouns	
Rule	Examples
1. Capitalize the names of people and pets.	Stacy Mrs. Green Lassie the Johnsons Bostonians
2. Capitalize every important word in the names of particular places and things.	United States Pacific Avenue Rocky Mountains Sears Tower George Washington Bridge Philadelphia New Jersey Statue of Liberty
3. Capitalize the names of months, days, and holidays.	April October Friday Fourth of July Memorial Day

Skills Tryout

Name the proper nouns in each sentence below. Tell which letters should be capitalized.

1. The harrisons flew to florida last week.
2. The park hotel is in everglades national park.
3. On friday we'll drive to key west on the gulf of mexico.
4. The audubon house is on whitehead street.
5. The whole family will fly back to logan airport in boston.

Practice

A. Write each sentence. Capitalize the proper nouns.

1. The town of plymouth is in massachusetts.
2. People from all over the united states visit the town each november.
3. They remember the first thanksgiving.
4. Actors dress up as pilgrims for the dinner.
5. Some visitors cross main street to look at plymouth rock.
6. It is on the shore at the edge of cape cod bay.
7. At a little store sharon and louise bought postcards.
8. They bought pictures of nantucket and the town of sandwich.
9. On the way home they visited the thornton burgess museum.
10. They saw some glass plates with pictures of peter rabbit and joe otter.

B. Write a proper noun for each common noun below.

11. state
12. lake
13. president
14. school
15. holiday

16. city
17. bridge
18. river
19. street
20. pet

Application FILLING OUT FORMS

Copy the form below and fill it out. Make up the information you need.

ALPHA TRAVEL AGENCY

Trip for:
Name _____
Street _____
City _____ State _____ Zip _____
Going to _____
Leaving on _____

5 Abbreviations

- An **abbreviation** is a shortened form of a word. Many abbreviations begin with a capital letter and end with a period.
- An **initial** is the first letter of a name. It is written with a capital letter and followed by a period.

In these messages the letters in red are abbreviations. The letters in blue are initials.

B. J. called. Don't forget soccer practice on Sat., 9 A.M. Your appointment is for Mon., Nov. 3, at 4 P.M., with Dr. S. A. Wheeler, 1482 Prospect Rd.

The chart below lists some common abbreviations.

Abbreviation	Explanation	Abbreviation	Explanation
Mr.	Mister (a man)	St.	Street
Ms.	a woman	Ave.	Avenue
Mrs.	a married woman	Blvd.	Boulevard
Sr.	Senior (older)	Dr.	Drive
Jr.	Junior (younger)	Rd.	Road
Dr.	Doctor	Rte.	Route
A.M.	before noon	P.M.	after noon
Mon. Tues. Wed. Thurs. Fri. Sat. Sun.			
Jan. Feb. Mar. Apr. Aug. Sept. Oct. Nov. Dec.			

Skills Tryout

Explain the initials and abbreviations in the messages below.

1. Meet T. J. at 126 Brewer St.
2. Club meeting Fri., 3 P.M.
3. R. L. to dentist Thurs.
4. Nov. 19: Adam's birthday
5. Call Mr. Warshawsky
6. B. K.'s home: 11 Elm Dr.

Practice

A. Each message below contains initials or an abbreviation written incorrectly. Write each message. Make the abbreviation or initials correct.

1. The students in mrs Gelardi's class have a bulletin board.
2. They collect their messages at 9 am every day.
3. Oliver Mayo, jr, sent Louise a note.
4. Meet me at the Garden st door after school.
5. One message says, "Hear dr Giddings speak today."
6. Public debate will start at 4 pm in the auditorium.
7. Writer m a Banks will speak to the science fiction book club.
8. Winter vacation begins on dec 21.
9. We have invited ms Taft's class to our play.
10. They will take a field trip on apr 3.

B. Each sentence or message below contains a word that can be abbreviated. Write the sentence or message using the correct abbreviation.

11. The following messages have been left for Doctor Romero.
12. Martha Potts cannot be here Monday night.
13. She would like an appointment for January 11 instead.
14. The patient at 15 Valley Road called.
15. Please telephone Mister Reese immediately.
16. George Young, Senior, called yesterday.
17. The hospital on Central Boulevard has room for him.
18. You have a conference this Saturday at the medical school.
19. You can get there quickly on Route 3.
20. Please fill out this form before February 1.

Application USING LANGUAGE

Look for abbreviations and initials in newspapers and magazines. Find at least five examples of each. List them in columns like these:

Abbreviations	Initials	Meaning	Where Found

6 — Possessive Nouns

- A **possessive noun** shows ownership.

Remember that a noun names a person, place, thing, or idea. The underlined word in each sentence below is a possessive noun. The possessive form of a noun shows that the person or thing named owns something.

1. Do not seek to escape the flood by clinging to a <u>tiger's</u> tail.
2. To get the <u>hens'</u> eggs, you must put up with the cackling.
3. <u>Children's</u> laughter outlives their tears.

In sentence 1 the underlined possessive noun is singular. In sentences 2 and 3 the underlined possessive nouns are plural.

The chart below lists the rules for forming possessive nouns. You add an apostrophe and *s* or only an apostrophe.

To form the possessive of	Add	Examples
a singular noun	's	tiger's tail, Charles's face
a plural noun ending in -s	'	hens' eggs, racers' engines
a plural noun not ending in -s	's	children's laughter, deer's hoofs women's offices

Skills Tryout

Name the possessive noun in each sentence below. Tell whether it is singular or plural.

1. Martina's grandmother came to visit.
2. All the cousins' voices blended together.
3. Her stories always kept the children's interest.
4. The stories' last words were always proverbs.
5. "All in a day's work," she would say.

Practice

A. Write the sentences. Draw one line under each possessive noun that is singular. Draw two lines under each possessive noun that is plural.

1. The fox's tail will show no matter how hard he tries to hide it.
2. Fools' names, like their faces, are often seen in public places.
3. You cannot hold two cows' tails at once.
4. The chicken hawk's prayer does not catch the chicken.
5. People's purses will never be bare
   If they know when to buy, to spend, and to spare.
6. Beware of a wolf in sheep's clothing.
7. A friend's frown is better than a fool's smile.
8. Poor folks' wisdom goes for little.
9. In a fiddler's house all are dancers.
10. Merchants' goods are bought and sold.

B. Write the possessive form of each noun given.

11. flower
12. officers
13. tribe
14. men
15. hotel
16. neighbors
17. niece
18. coaches
19. chimpanzee
20. actors

21. leader
22. navy
23. carpenters
24. canary
25. wife
26. nephew
27. man
28. worker
29. lions
30. mouse

Application WRITING SENTENCES

Make up a funny saying or proverb. Use a possessive noun in your saying.

7 Borrowed Words

- Many English words have been borrowed from other languages.

A great many of the words you use every day have come into English from other languages.

Some Borrowed Words	
chocolate	This word comes from the Aztecs of Mexico. When Spanish explorers in Mexico first tasted chocolate, they had no Spanish word for it. They used the Aztec word *chocólatl.*
alligator	When Spanish explorers first saw this animal, they had no name for it. It looked like a big lizard, so they named it *el lagarto,* the Spanish word for "lizard."
dandelion	This word comes from French. The yellow flower looks a little like a lion's head and mane. The petals are tooth-shaped. The French name is *dent-de-lion,* or "tooth of the lion."
raccoon	This is a Native American word. It comes from the Algonquin word *äräkhun.*

Skills Tryout

Name the word for each meaning.

chipmunk   catsup   almanac   kindergarten   wagon

1. _____ comes from the Arabic word *al-manākh* (calendar).
2. _____ comes from the German words *kinder* (children) and *garten* (garden).
3. _____ comes from the Algonquin word *atchitamō* (a squirrel).
4. _____ comes from the Dutch word *wagen* (a four-wheeled cart).
5. _____ comes from the Malayan word *kĕchap* (a spicy sauce).

Practice

A. Write the word for each meaning. You may use a dictionary.

plaid	canyon	muumuu	piano	corridor
bouquet	knapsack	kimono	parka	succotash

1. a robe (from Japanese)
2. a deep, narrow valley (from Spanish)
3. a backpack (from German)
4. a patterned cloth (from Scottish Gaelic)
5. a long, loose dress (from Hawaiian)
6. a musical instrument (from Italian)
7. a warm jacket with a hood (from Aleut)
8. a bunch of flowers (from French)
9. lima beans and corn cooked together (from Algonquin)
10. a hallway (from Italian)

B. Write the sentences using the words below.

mosquito	caftan	opossum	patio	yogurt
algebra	boulevard	sesame	ballet	barrette

11. A word from French for a hair clip is _____.
12. A word from Spanish for a biting insect is _____.
13. A word from Algonquin for a small animal that lives in trees is _____.
14. A word from Turkish for a soft dairy food is _____.
15. A word from French for a flavorful seed is _____.
16. A word from French for a wide street is _____.
17. A word from Arabic for a branch of mathematics is _____.
18. A word from French for a kind of dance is _____.
19. A word from Persian for a loosely fitting cloak is _____.
20. A word from Spanish for an open courtyard is _____.

Application USING LANGUAGE

Write six sentences of your own. In each sentence use one of the borrowed words listed in **Practice B.**

Singular and Plural Nouns   *pages 48–51*

A. Write the underlined noun in each of the sentences below. Then write *singular* if the noun is singular. Write *plural* if it is plural.

1. All the <u>children</u> brought their sleeping bags.
2. They soon left the <u>cities</u> behind.
3. Which <u>man</u> bought a ticket to Boston?
4. Molly bought <u>necklaces</u> for gifts.
5. Ana planned to go to some <u>parties</u>.
6. Everyone else went for a ride on the <u>donkeys</u>.
7. The <u>goose</u> chased Jean.
8. They saw an animal in the <u>bushes</u>.
9. Andy spotted a baby <u>deer</u> under a tree.
10. It was as cute as the <u>calf</u> on the farm.

Common Nouns and Proper Nouns   *pages 52–53*

B. Write each underlined noun. Then write *common* or *proper* to show what kind of noun it is.

11. That girl is my <u>cousin</u>.
12. She lives on <u>Pine Avenue</u>.
13. It's near the <u>street</u> where we live.
14. <u>Gerry Doe</u> is my mother's brother.
15. He and my mother grew up in <u>Idaho</u>.
16. They moved to this <u>state</u> fifteen years ago.
17. First they lived on <u>Kerr Lake</u>.
18. Now we all live near the <u>river</u>.
19. <u>Brookside Park</u> is not far from here.
20. We take our <u>dog</u> there to run.

Capitalizing Proper Nouns *pages 54–55*

C. Write each sentence. Capitalize all the proper nouns.

21. Our neighbor, mary franklin, works at the supermarket.
22. Her work week begins on monday and ends on saturday.
23. She says that may and june are the busiest months.
24. The market is in ohio, but it sells food from europe.
25. The oranges come from california and from florida.

Abbreviations *pages 56–57*

D. Write the abbreviation for each underlined word.

26. Norman Lincoln, <u>Junior,</u> is our dentist.
27. He was recommended by <u>Doctor</u> Eleanor Amatucci.
28. You have an appointment with him on <u>Wednesday</u> morning.
29. Western <u>Avenue</u> is his street.
30. You have to go back in <u>September</u> for a checkup.

Possessive Nouns *pages 58–59*

E. Write the possessive form of each noun.

31. Tess   32. women   33. babies   34. toy   35. girls

Borrowed Words *pages 60–61*

F. Write the word on the right that fits each meaning.

36. a furry animal   (Algonquin)   soprano
37. a musical instrument   (Hawaiian)   bureau
38. a high voice   (Italian)   raccoon
39. a salad of raw cabbage   (Dutch)   ukulele
40. a chest of drawers   (French)   coleslaw

See also Handbook pages 322–329, 378–381, 383.

Writing with Nouns

Grammar and Writing Workshop

● Use exact nouns to give details in your writing.

1. A book is a useful tool for a writer.
2. A thesaurus is a useful tool for a writer.

These sentences are very much alike. In sentence 1, however, the noun *book* is not exact. After all, a book called *Favorite Elephant Jokes* would not be a very useful tool for a writer! The noun *thesaurus* is much more exact than the vague noun *book*. It makes sentence 2 clearer and more interesting than sentence 1. Some other exact nouns for *book* are *dictionary, atlas, encyclopedia,* and *storybook*.

Here is another pair of example sentences.

We usually eat out on a weekday.
We usually eat out on Wednesday.

The Noun Game Here is a list of vague nouns. What exact nouns could replace each one?

Choose a noun from the list and write it. See how many exact nouns you can write in two minutes. Be sure that they could replace the vague noun in a sentence.

hobby	insect	vegetable
sport	relative	house

How many exact nouns did you write? Find a classmate who chose the same vague noun. Did he or she think of any exact nouns that are not on your list? Do you have any that are not on your classmate's list?

Choose another vague noun from the list and start again. You might form teams with one or more of your classmates.

The Noun Switch Write each sentence. Replace the underlined word or words with a more exact noun.

EXAMPLE: <u>Clothes</u> are sold in department stores.

ANSWER: Jackets are sold in department stores.

1. Our day at the fair was ruined by the <u>weather</u>.
2. Bobby almost forgot to bring the <u>food</u> to the picnic.
3. Allison used <u>a color</u> in her painting.
4. The <u>worker</u> answered the telephone.
5. Put your suitcase in the <u>room</u>.
6. Is it time for <u>the meal</u> yet?

No-Clue Time Now replace nouns without using clues. Find the vague word or words in each sentence below. Think of a more exact noun that could replace it. Write the new sentence.

7. Nathan borrowed my tool, but he never returned it.
8. A person entertained us at the charity bazaar.
9. Lou Belle is always the winner when we play a game.
10. The invention is a great time-saver.
11. We went swimming in the body of water.
12. These shoes are worn-out.

Using the Thesaurus

Find the entry for *story* in the Thesaurus that begins on page 395. Then write each sentence below. Replace the noun *story* with a different synonym in each sentence.

a. We studied the story of the science of aviation.
b. That story tells why giraffes have long necks.
c. Find facts about that president's childhood in a story.
d. The story of the cross-country ski trip was fascinating.
e. "The Three Little Pigs" is a story loved by children.

8 Reading a Tall Tale

- A **tall tale** is a story in which things are exaggerated, or bigger than life.

There are many tales about Paul Bunyan. The stories say that he invented logging. Most of the tales are set in the old logging camps of North America.

The Paul Bunyan stories were started by the loggers themselves. Often they would gather around the camp stove in the evening to talk. They would tell stories about things real people had done. They would also tell tales that exaggerated, or stretched, the truth. Some of the stories were fanciful ones about a giant logger named Paul Bunyan. They told about his enormous size and his great strength. As the stories were told and retold, they became even more exaggerated.

As you read the logger's story that follows, see if you can tell why it is called a tall tale.

Paul Bunyan and

Some folks don't believe the tales I tell. They call them tall tales. Let me tell you a story about a man named Paul Bunyan. You can judge the tale for yourself.

Some people say Paul was the world's largest baby. That may be true. He weighed fifty pounds an hour after he was born. Paul was like most babies in many ways. But his appetite wasn't like most! He could eat as much as a grown man. Also, his baby voice could be heard over forty miles away.

Paul was a husky fellow right from the start. They say he grew strong and tall quickly. Soon his mother had to sew wagon wheels on his shirts. She used them in place of buttons. Finding a place for Paul to sleep was a real problem. His father solved

Babe the Blue Ox

it by making a boat in the shape of a cradle. Once Paul rocked his cradle very hard. The rocking created giant waves that flooded towns along the coasts of Maine and Canada.

Exactly how big was Paul Bunyan? No one knows for sure. Some say he was two hundred and forty-two ax handles high. Others say he was so tall that he could have plucked the moon from the sky.

Everything about Paul was powerful, even his words. One year it was unusually cold. That year Paul's words froze as soon as they hit the air. His loggers put the frozen words in a stewing pot. They put the pot on the bunkhouse stove and let the words thaw. An hour later Paul's words came roaring out of the pot. They almost knocked the walls down. That happened the year before the Winter of the Blue Snow.

I was with Paul during the Winter of the Blue Snow. From then until now no one has seen a sight so beautiful. At first, little snowflakes like mirrors of blue sky danced in the wind. Then the wind blew harder, and the flakes grew bigger. With the rising wind the blue flakes grew thicker and thicker. Soon it was hard to tell where the sky ended and the earth began. For six days and seven nights the blue snow floated and fell on Paul's forests.

One day, Paul was out shoveling the blue snow. Suddenly he tripped over a thing as big as a mountain. The thing groaned a bit. Then it shivered and sent blue snowflakes fluttering over the entire state. Paul saw a blue tail flip its way out of the snowdrift. Then he saw two satiny blue ears.

"What is this!" exclaimed Paul. The thing made a faint mooing sound.

Paul grabbed the tail and ears at the same time and pulled with all his might. From the snowdrift came a wobbly, shivering

blue baby ox. The calf's shiny nose was black. All other parts—its horns, eyes, fur, tail, and even its hooves—were blue. The blue ox was the largest baby ox that anyone had ever seen. Paul named his new pet Babe.

Paul had trouble picking up the baby ox. But he managed to cradle it in his huge arms and carry it home. He wrapped the shivering animal in some warm blankets. All night long he sat patting the blue head and stroking the blue back. By morning, Babe was feeling better. He ate one hundred gallons of moose moss soup. Later he took a walk with Paul in the slushy blue snow.

Well, Babe grew up to be a great help to Paul. He was so strong that he could carry a whole pine forest on his back. The ox was also as big as he was strong. Loggers had to use field glasses to see from one end of Babe to the other. Once they measured the distance between Babe's eyes. It was exactly one hundred and forty-two ax handles plus one plug of tobacco. How big was Babe? This fact will give you some idea. Once a pioneer family fell into one of Babe's footprints. They had to walk for weeks before they were able to get out.

When I left Paul Bunyan's camp after the Winter of the Blue Snow, he gave me a present. It was a certificate written in blue ink made from the melted blue snow. Using a tree for a pen, Paul wrote, "Your tales are taller than I am." Now what do you think of that?

About the Tall Tale

1. *Exaggerated* means "bigger than life" or "more than in real life." Explain how the details about Paul and Babe are exaggerated.
2. What makes this story a *tall* tale?

Activities

A. A tall tale exaggerates. Imagine you are as big as Paul Bunyan. Write what you might use for each item below.

   1. a bathtub   2. a coat hook   3. a dinner plate

B. Make up a tall tale in which *you* are the hero.

   For example, tell about a game you played. Did you win? (Say you did, even if you didn't.) How did you do it? What fantastic plays did you make? Did you use unbelievable speed? Incredible intelligence?

   Or tell about some housework you did. Did you clean the whole house or apartment? (Say you did, even if you didn't.) How fast did you do it? What amazing tools or methods did you use?

   Make up your tall tale by starting with something you really did. Then stretch the truth. Exaggerate as much as you can. You may tell or write your tall tale.

9 — Understanding Character, Setting, and Plot

> ● Three things make up a story: **character**, **setting**, and **plot**.

No two stories are exactly alike. Yet most stories contain the same three ingredients. Read this "story recipe" to find out what they are.

A Story

1. Take one or more <u>characters</u>.

2. Put them in a <u>setting</u>.

3. Add a <u>plot</u>.

Combine ingredients. Serve with an interesting title.

The characters are the people or animals in a story. In some stories the characters are fantastic beings, such as creatures from outer space. The author of a story describes the characters by telling how they look, how they act, what they say, and what they think.

The setting is where and when a story takes place. For example, an old, abandoned house on a stormy autumn night might be the setting for a chilling ghost story.

The plot tells what happened. It gives a story its beginning, middle, and end. Usually a problem is introduced at the beginning of the story. Action and excitement build. The most exciting or important event comes near the middle of the story. The end of the story explains how the problem was solved.

Skills Tryout

Tell whether each of these is an example of character, setting, or plot.

1. Paul Bunyan and Babe
2. a lonely log cabin
3. a robbery occurs
4. early spring

Practice

A. Write *character, setting,* or *plot* to show what each sentence illustrates.

1. One winter, Paul set up camp in eastern Montana.
2. Paul threw a tree to the drowning woman.
3. Carrie was strong, but she was not a good swimmer.
4. Paul made a dam to stop the river.
5. The river flowed through a tree-lined canyon.

B. Think of a short story you have enjoyed. Choose a story from a book or a television program. Write answers to these questions about the story.

6. Who is the main character in the story?
7. What is the story's setting?
8. What problem does the main character face?
9. What is the most important event in the story?
10. How does the story end?

Application WRITING A PARAGRAPH

Supply one ingredient for a story. You may choose character, setting, or plot. Write a paragraph describing the character, setting, or plot you invent.

You and your classmates may want to write your paragraphs on index cards and place the cards in three piles. Make one pile for character, one for setting, and one for plot. You could then draw cards from the piles and use them to write a story.

10 — Writing a Book Report

- A **book report** tells what a book is about and gives an opinion of the book.

Read this book report. What does it tell about the book?

Nightbirds on Nantucket
by Joan Aiken

This adventure story takes place in the 1700s. It begins off the coast of England, where Dido Twite, an orphan, is drowning. She is saved by the absent-minded Captain Casket. The Captain sends Dido and his daughter, Pen, to Nantucket to visit Pen's Aunt Tribulation. Dido is a courageous girl, but Pen is afraid of everything, including the cruel Aunt Trib. The girls do not know that she is not really Pen's aunt, but a spy.

The story is filled with danger and suspense. However, the events and characters are exaggerated in a hilarious way. I enjoyed reading this exciting, fun-filled book.

Notice these things about the book report.

1. The title and author are named. The title of the book is underlined. In a book title the first word, the last word, and all important words are capitalized.
2. The report describes the book's characters, setting, and plot, but it does not tell the whole story.
3. The report gives an opinion about the book.

Skills Tryout

Tell which of these should be included in a book report and which should not.

1. a few sentences about the author's life
2. the title and author of the book
3. the titles of other books the author has written
4. a brief description of the characters, plot, and setting
5. praise of the book, even if you did not like it

Practice

A. Write answers to these questions about the book report on page 74.

1. What words are underlined? Why?
2. Which word in the book title is not capitalized? Why?
3. What information is given about the setting of the book?
4. What words are used to describe Dido Twite?
5. How is Pen's personality different from Dido's?
6. What is Captain Casket like?
7. What is the person posing as Aunt Trib like?
8. In what way is *Nightbirds on Nantucket* like a tall tale?
9. Does the report make you want to read the book? Why or why not?
10. What is the book reporter's opinion of the book?

B. Write a book report, using the information on page 74 as a guide. Illustrate your report if you wish.

Application ORAL REPORTING

Sometimes you want to tell others about a book you have read. Tell the class about the book you reported on for **Practice B**. If you like, read a passage from the book. Do not give away the ending, though! Know your report well enough that you can look at your audience while you speak.

11 — Writing a Tall Tale

Writing Project

- A **tall tale** is a story that stretches the truth about the character, plot, or setting.

You have probably heard many tall tales. The tales about Paul Bunyan and Pecos Bill are well-known ones. Tall tales stretch the truth by exaggerating things. Paul Bunyan didn't really flood the coastal towns of Maine by rocking a boat. Each time the story was repeated, however, it became "taller." People enjoy reading about events that are exaggerated, or made bigger than life. Which would you rather read about—a girl riding a skateboard or a skateboard that can fly?

Tall tales are passed on when people retell stories they have heard. In this lesson you will write a tall tale for your friends to pass on. You will try to build a real experience into a story no one will ever forget.

1. Prewriting

A story ladder will help you get ready for writing. In this example, the ladder is divided into three parts. The order in which things happened is important when you write a tall tale. On this story ladder the ideas are in the right order, from bottom to top.

Read this writer's story ladder. Try to identify these story parts: character, setting, and plot. Can you find the exaggerations that will make this story a tall tale?

becomes a movie star
collie is writing a book

picture in newspaper
collie was made fire chief

barn was on fire
collie carried out 12 cows

▶ Before you make your story ladder, select a topic for a tall tale. Think of a few personal experiences and write down your ideas. Here are some suggestions that may help you think of your own topics:

- the first time I rode a roller coaster
- the best project I ever made
- what happened on my last birthday
- the day I hit a home run
- the most famous person I've met

Discuss your topics with a classmate. Choose the one that will make the tallest tale.

▶ Make a story ladder by writing down what happened to you. Start at the bottom of your ladder and write your ideas in the order in which things happened. You do not need to use complete sentences. As you add ideas, stretch the facts. If you rode in a one-mile bike race, make it a cross-country race. If you went camping, make it a camping trip in the jungle. Include as many exaggerations as you can.

2. Writing

Now you are ready to turn your story ladder into a tall tale. How would you begin if you were telling your story to a friend? You can write your tall tale as if you were saying it out loud. If you can't get started, practice it out loud first. You might begin by saying, "Once when I was eight years old ... ." Or say, "I'll never forget the day ... ."

The topic sentence will tell your reader what your story is about. "I'll never forget the day my collie became a hero." From this topic sentence the reader knows what to expect. The reader will want to find out why the collie was a hero.

▶ Write your topic sentence. Briefly tell what your tall tale is about. Then add ideas from your story ladder. Explain what happened, one step at a time. The words in the box may help you explain the events in the right order. Don't worry about handwriting or spelling now. You will make changes in this first draft later.

first	next	last	then	after
finally	before	later	now	meanwhile

3. Revising

▶ Think of someone who knows the real story behind your tall tale. Read that person your exaggerated version. Ask the following questions:

Did I leave anything out?
Is there anything you want to know more about?
What part do you like best?

Listen to the comments and make notes. How can you change your story to make it better? Use this checklist to help you think about your writing.

Revision Checklist
- Did I write a topic sentence that tells the main idea?
- Did I include these three story parts: character, setting, and plot?
- Did I exaggerate the facts?
- Did I use words that show the order in which things happened?
- Did I take out unnecessary words?

Read the sample on the next page and notice how the story is improved by taking out unnecessary words.

> ¶ I'll never forget the one day my collie dog became a very important ~~heroe~~ (hero). Buddy ~~lifted~~ (carried) twelve cows

I'll never forget the day my collie became a hero. Buddy carried twelve cows out of a burning barn. The next day his picture was in the newspaper. The town decided to make Buddy a fire chief, and a few years later he was starring in movies. Now my collie is writing a book about his life.

▶ Now use the editing marks to make changes that will improve your tall tale.

4. Publishing

▶ Before you share your writing, proofread for errors. Use the Proofreading Checklist in the Young Writer's Handbook on page 377. Make corrections, using the editing marks.

▶ Many tall tales were told in the American Old West. People would sit around a campfire and share stories for hours. Try this with your classmates. Sit in a circle. Take turns reading your tall tales. When you have finished, ask the group which parts were true and which parts were exaggerated. Decide whose tale was the tallest.

Writing Project

A Folk Hero Map

Key:
A. Appleseed, Johnny - Midwest
B. Bunyan, Paul - Northwest
C. Clementine - California
D. Frietchie, Barbara - Maryland
E. Pecos Bill - Texas
F. Betsy Ross - Pennsylvania
G. Slue Foot Sue - Texas
H. Stormalong - New England

Draw big pictures of folk heroes on heavy paper. Use bright colors and bold outlines. Cut out the figures. Paste them on a map of the United States to show where their stories are set. Add a key. List the heroes in alphabetical order.

Social Studies

Storytellers were the world's first historians. Much of what we know about early people and countries comes from the stories storytellers told. Even before people kept written records, storytellers kept events of the past alive.

▶ Now you try it. Tell a story about a character from history. Choose a hero or heroine who is interesting to you. Davy Crockett, Sacagawea, Clara Barton, and Martin Luther King, Jr., are examples of people you might want to tell about. Tell about one important event in the person's life. Use the library to obtain a factual account of what happened.

Writers at Work Historians are writers who help us understand the present by explaining the past. They examine the events of history and the people who shaped them. Then they tell the story in a logical order.

▶ Choose an object like one of those shown on this page. You might choose an old photograph from a family album, a famous painting, or a stamp showing a historical event or person. Then do some detective work. Learn about the history behind the object. Find out about the time period, the person, or the event. You can get information by asking questions of family members or by using a reference book. Write a paragraph that tells what you learned.

Nouns   *pages 48–53*

A. Write the plural form of each noun.

1. box
2. cup
3. woman
4. dress
5. donkey
6. knife
7. penny
8. moose
9. beach

B. Read each noun. If it is a common noun, write *common*. If it is a proper noun, write *proper*.

10. Chicago
11. singer
12. playground
13. Main Street
14. post office
15. Atlantic Ocean

Capital Letters and Periods   *pages 54–57*

C. Write each sentence. Capitalize the proper nouns.

16. The stepfords spent a week in new york city.
17. Their hotel was near the empire state building.
18. They took a ferry ride to the statue of liberty.
19. They brought me a poster from the whitney museum.

D. Write each sentence. Abbreviate the underlined words.

20. Our class will hold a bake sale on September 29.
21. The public library is on Marlboro Boulevard.
22. Mary wrote a letter to Mister James Doyle.
23. I have a piano lesson every Saturday.
24. Take Route 39 to the apple orchard.

Apostrophes   *pages 58–59*

E. Write the possessive form of each noun.

25. men
26. aunt
27. teachers
28. Frances
29. river
30. sheep

Book Report   *pages 74–75*

F. Choose what should be included in a book report and what should not. Write *yes* or *no*.

31. where the author lives
32. the names of the main characters
33. a description of the book's setting
34. a description of how each chapter begins
35. the title of the book

Stories   *pages 66–73*

G. Read the paragraph. Then write answers to the questions.

Mark Twain wrote a tall tale about a man named Bemis who was chased by a buffalo. Bemis was riding his horse across the plain when the buffalo charged him. In running from the buffalo, Bemis and his horse overtook a rabbit and a coyote and nearly passed an antelope. The charging buffalo mowed down weeds and stirred up a whirlwind of sand. Then Bemis's saddle broke, and he was thrown 400 feet into the air. He landed in a tree with his saddle. Bemis still was not safe. The buffalo began to climb the tree. So Bemis took his lasso and waited until the buffalo was only ten feet away. Then he roped the buffalo, tied it to the tree and escaped.

36. Where does the story take place?
37. Who are the characters in the story?
38. How does the story end?
39. Write one sentence from the story that contains an exaggeration.

H. Imagine that you are going to write a tall tale by building on a real experience that you have had. Write a topic sentence for your tall tale.

See also Handbook pages 322–329, 373, 378–381, 383, 385.

Cumulative Review

Sentences   *pages 4–17*

A. Write each declarative, interrogative, imperative, or exclamatory sentence. Begin each sentence correctly. Use correct punctuation at the end.

1. did you bake these muffins
2. what a pretty song that is
3. wear your hat and mittens
4. this is a robin's nest
5. how tame this squirrel is
6. turn off the lights
7. here is the newspaper
8. when does the movie start

B. Write the complete subject of each sentence. Underline the simple subject. Write (*You*) if the subject is understood.

9. An alligator crawled out of the swamp.
10. Listen to the sound of the crickets.
11. A group of hikers climbed the mountain.
12. Show our guests to their rooms.
13. My coat is hanging in the hall.

C. Write the complete predicate of each sentence. Underline the simple predicate.

14. Amy is wearing her new glasses today.
15. Mr. Spencer weeded his vegetable garden.
16. Some cows escaped from the barnyard.
17. The band was practicing for the concert.

Nouns   *pages 48–53*

D. Write each sentence. Underline the nouns in each sentence.

18. Ms. Ross brought her class to the museum.
19. A statue of a soldier was near the entrance.
20. One room contained ancient coins and tools.
21. The students saw several famous paintings.

Cumulative Review

E. Write the plural form of each noun.

22. pencil 24. goose 26. life
23. sheep 25. patch 27. butterfly

F. Write *common* or *proper* for each noun.

28. Maine 30. Red Sea 32. bookstore
29. college 31. doctor 33. Tom Sawyer

Capital Letters and Periods *pages 52–57*

G. Write each sentence. Capitalize the proper nouns.

34. Our family took a trip to north carolina.
35. A beach along the atlantic ocean was our first stop.
36. We drove through the blue ridge mountains.
37. At fort raleigh everyone bought postcards.
38. I visited the wright memorial in kitty hawk.
39. We arrived home on the fourth of july.

H. Write each sentence. Abbreviate the underlined words.

40. Eileen has a guitar lesson this <u>Thursday</u>.
41. Watch out for the traffic jam on <u>Route</u> 5.
42. <u>Doctor</u> Ludwig gave my hamster some medicine.
43. In <u>January</u> we held a snow sculpture contest.
44. The Rays are building a house on Morningside <u>Drive</u>.

Apostrophes *pages 58–59*

I. Write the possessive form of each noun.

45. James 48. mice 51. city
46. customer 49. bridge 52. women
47. students 50. athletes 53. pigeons

Grammar
Verbs

Composition
Informing

The Three Horses

Three horses came
to the meadow's edge—
they poled their noses
over the hedge.

One was grey,
one was white,
and one was black
as a winter's night.

I patted the white horse,
I stroked the grey,
and I rode the black horse
far away.

—*Ivy O. Eastwick*

1 Action Verbs

- An **action verb** shows action.

You have learned to identify the predicate part of a sentence. You also know that the main word or words in the predicate is the simple predicate. The simple predicate is often an action verb. An action verb tells what the subject of the sentence does.

In the poem below, the underlined words are action verbs. Each one shows an action.

> The black cat yawns,
> Opens her jaws,
> Stretches her legs,
> And shows her claws.
> —*Mary Britton Miller*

What actions do the verbs *yawn*, *open*, *stretch*, and *show* describe? Here are some more verbs that show actions of a cat. What other action verbs could be added to the list?

scratch   purr   run   leap

Skills Tryout

Name the action verb in each sentence.

1. Two scientists traveled to Nepal.
2. They studied the habits of tigers in the wild.
3. They watched the tigers for months.
4. They learned many interesting facts.
5. Their article describes the life of a tiger.

Practice

A. Each sentence below contains an action verb. Write each sentence and underline the verb.

1. The tigers make their home in a large valley.
2. Tall, thick grass covers much of the ground.
3. Rivers run through the valley.
4. In hot weather the tigers cool themselves in the water.
5. The tigers hunt various kinds of deer.
6. They hide in the tall grasses.
7. Tigers live alone, not in groups.
8. Young tigers stay with their mothers for two years.
9. Each tiger controls its own territory.
10. It roams long distances inside this area.

B. Write the sentences. Use an action verb to complete each sentence.

EXAMPLE: Angelo _____ a tiny kitten.
ANSWER: Angelo found a tiny kitten.

11. It _____ outside the front door in the rain.
12. Angelo _____ it with a towel.
13. He _____ the kitten to his mother.
14. Then they _____ it something to eat and drink.
15. The kitten _____ its paws carefully.
16. It _____ straight into Angelo's room.
17. With a loud "meow," it _____ onto the bed.
18. It _____ down right in the middle of the pillow.
19. Angelo _____ its sleek, soft head.
20. The kitten _____ happily before it fell asleep.

Application WRITING SENTENCES

Suppose you were an animal. Would you be a wild animal or a pet? Write five sentences. Explain how you move and what you do. Use a different action verb in each sentence.

2 — Linking Verbs

> - A **linking verb** shows being. It links the subject with a word or words in the predicate.

You have learned that a verb can show action. It can tell what the subject does.

Tim <u>skates</u> in the winter.   **Lana <u>swims</u> in December.**

A verb can also show being. Read the examples below.

1. Hawaii <u>is</u> warm all year.   **2. Kim <u>was</u> a fine surfer.**

In sentence 1 the verb *is* links, or connects, the subject *Hawaii* with the word *warm*. In sentence 2 the verb *was* connects the subject *Kim* with the word *surfer*. Both *is* and *was* are forms of *be*, the most common linking verb.

Other linking verbs are *seem, look, feel, taste,* and *smell.*

The breeze <u>feels</u> delightful.   **Orchids <u>look</u> fragile.**

Using the Forms of *Be*		
Use *am/was*	with *I*	I am/I was
Use *is/was*	with *she, he, it,* and singular nouns	She is The water was
Use *are/were*	with *we, you, they,* and plural nouns	They are The boats were

Skills Tryout

Name the linking verb in each sentence. Name the words in the subject and the predicate that the linking verb connects.

1. Hawaiian winters are mild.
2. Sunny days seem endless.
3. My aunt is a hula teacher.
4. Surfing looks dangerous.
5. Pineapples taste wonderful.
6. A coconut smells sweet.

Practice

A. Write each sentence. Underline the linking verb. Use an arrow to connect the two words that the verb links.

EXAMPLE: Some waves are very large.

ANSWER: Some waves <u>are</u> very large.

1. December was too cold.
2. Every year the winter seems longer.
3. Hawaii was our destination.
4. The sun feels warm on our faces.
5. Fresh coconuts taste creamy.
6. Even the cabdrivers look happy.
7. Tanaka is a fire-walker.
8. Honolulu is the capital of Hawaii.
9. Liliuokalani was the last queen of Hawaii.
10. The volcanoes were quiet during our stay.

B. Write the sentences. Choose the correct form of *be* to complete each sentence. Refer to the chart on page 90.

11. Palm trees _____ heavy with fruit. (was, were)
12. I _____ glad we spent our vacation there. (is, am)
13. Fresh pineapple _____ new to me. (was, were)
14. You _____ right about the beaches. (was, were)
15. Coral reefs _____ homes for many fish. (is, are)
16. Feather cloaks _____ the badges of royalty. (was, were)
17. They _____ still bright today. (is, are)
18. We _____ eager to try the outrigger canoes. (was, were)
19. Haleakala _____ a very large volcano. (is, are)
20. It _____ inactive today. (is, are)

Application WRITING SENTENCES

Imagine that you are making a travel brochure. Write five sentences about a dream vacation. Use each of the following words as a linking verb: *is, are, seem, look, feel.*

3 — Main Verbs and Helping Verbs

- A **helping verb** works with the main verb.

Remember that the simple predicate can contain more than one word.

1. Kay and Nick <u>are</u> <u>practicing</u> for a contest.
2. They <u>have</u> <u>danced</u> together for two years.
3. Someday they <u>will</u> <u>become</u> professional dancers.

In the sentences above, *are*, *have*, and *will* are helping verbs. They work with the main verbs *practicing*, *danced*, and *become*. The **main verb** is the most important verb in the predicate.

Using Helping Verbs

When the helping verb is *am*, *is*, *are*, *was*, or *were*, the main verb often ends in *-ing*.	I <u>am</u> <u>practicing</u>. You <u>are</u> <u>practicing</u>. They <u>were</u> <u>practicing</u>.
When the helping verb is *has*, *have*, or *had*, the main verb often ends in *-ed*.	He <u>has</u> <u>danced</u>. We <u>have</u> <u>danced</u>. They <u>had</u> <u>danced</u>.
When the helping verb is *will*, the main verb is unchanged.	She <u>will</u> <u>become</u> a dancer. You <u>will</u> <u>become</u> a dancer. I <u>will</u> <u>become</u> a dancer.

Skills Tryout

Tell whether the underlined word in each sentence is a main verb or a helping verb.

1. They <u>will</u> present the fourth annual ballet competition.
2. Dancers <u>have</u> arrived from all over the world.
3. The town was <u>preparing</u> to house and feed everyone.
4. The judges <u>are</u> arriving today.
5. This contest has <u>provided</u> much excitement.

Practice

A. Write each sentence. Draw one line under the main verb. Draw two lines under the helping verb.

1. This contest has attracted many talented people.
2. It is growing more important every year.
3. The winners will appear with a professional company.
4. Each dancer is performing twice.
5. They all have worked very hard for this chance.
6. They will exercise for two hours every morning.
7. Kay has stretched her leg muscles.
8. Nick was bending forward and backward.
9. The musicians had practiced, too.
10. Soon everyone will compete.

B. Write the sentences. Use the helping verb *are*, *have*, or *will* to complete each sentence.

11. Kay and Nick _____ performing today.
12. They _____ prepared two dances.
13. In one, Kay _____ wear special shoes.
14. In them she _____ stand on the tips of her toes.
15. The two young dancers _____ feeling very nervous.
16. The judges _____ watching carefully.
17. Both dancers _____ turned in circles across the stage.
18. They each _____ balanced on one foot with their arms gracefully and proudly raised.
19. Now they _____ bowing to the audience.
20. The judges _____ make their decision soon.

Application WRITING SENTENCES

Write five sentences about a contest. Your sentences may be about entering, preparing for, competing in, or winning a contest. Use one of these helping verbs in each sentence.

am   is   are   was   were   has   have   had   will

4 Verbs with Direct Objects

- The **direct object** receives the action of the verb.

The direct object is another part of the complete predicate. It comes after an action verb and is often a noun. The direct object answers the question *whom* or *what*. In the sentences below, the underlined nouns are direct objects.

Clouds hold <u>moisture</u>.   (hold what?)

Clouds produce <u>rain</u>.   (produce what?)

The rain soaked <u>Jesse</u>.   (soaked whom?)

You can find the direct object in a sentence by asking "whom?" or "what?" after the verb.

In the sentences below, the underlined nouns are direct objects. They receive the action of the verbs *absorb* and *cause*.

Clouds absorb much <u>energy</u> from the earth.

Large air masses cause <u>changes</u> in the weather.

Skills Tryout

Read these sentences. Name the action verb and the direct object in each one.

1. Weather information helps gardeners.
2. Weather satellites photograph clouds.
3. Air holds more moisture on a hot day.
4. A weather vane shows the direction of the wind.
5. An anemometer measures its speed.

Practice

A. Write each sentence. Draw one line under the action verb. Draw two lines under the direct object.

1. Weather satellites take pictures of the clouds.
2. Wind draws moisture from the skin.
3. During tornadoes, people seek shelter.
4. A meteorologist studies weather.
5. The hurricane damaged the coastline.
6. Tornadoes cause the most damage of any storm.
7. Sometimes a powerful thunderstorm scares my dog.
8. Huge cumulonimbus clouds bring thunderstorms.
9. Bodies of water affect the weather of the nearby land.
10. Weather follows regular patterns in most cases.

B. Write the direct object of each sentence. Then write *what* or *whom* to show what question the direct object answers.

11. The meteorologist predicted a huge snowstorm.
12. The first flakes hit the ground at six o'clock.
13. The snow almost covered my window by midnight.
14. The mayor warned the motorists about the blizzard.
15. High winds caused drifts four feet high.
16. I called my sister over to my window.
17. My sister Ellen brought an extra blanket for warmth.
18. Three feet of snow covered our driveway.
19. The superintendent closed the schools.
20. We invited our friends for lunch.

Application WRITING SENTENCES

Pretend that a storm is brewing. You can feel that it is about to begin. Write five sentences about a storm—before, during, or after. Use an action verb and a direct object in each sentence.

5 Tenses of Verbs

- The **tense** of a verb shows the time of the action.

The form of a verb shows when the action takes place.

1. Fire fighters <u>protect</u> people's lives.
2. The class <u>learned</u> about fire prevention.
3. Carefulness and safety <u>will</u> <u>prevent</u> fires.

In sentence 1 the verb is in the present tense: *protect*. In sentence 2 it is in the past tense: *learned*. In sentence 3 it is in the future tense: *will prevent*.

A verb in the **present tense** shows action that happens now.

They <u>protect</u>.　　He <u>learns</u>.　　It <u>prevents</u>.

A verb in the **past tense** shows action that already happened. The past tense of a verb is usually formed by adding *-ed*.

They <u>protected</u>.　　They <u>learned</u>.　　They <u>prevented</u>.

A verb in the **future tense** shows action that will happen. The future tense is usually formed with the helping verb *will* or *shall*.

They <u>will</u> <u>protect</u>.　　They <u>will</u> <u>learn</u>.　　They <u>will</u> <u>prevent</u>.

Skills Tryout

The verbs in the sentences below are underlined. Tell whether each verb is in the present, past, or future tense.

1. Noreen <u>wanted</u> a job as a fire fighter.
2. Next month the fire department <u>will</u> <u>offer</u> the test.
3. Noreen <u>asks</u> for an application at the station.
4. She <u>worked</u> hard before the test.
5. She <u>will</u> <u>study</u> at the fire academy for six weeks.

Practice

A. Write the verb in each sentence. Then write *present, past,* or *future* to show what tense it is in.

1. The men and women prepare for the test.
2. They jogged eight miles every day.
3. They carried sandbag dummies up and down the stairs.
4. Some of them also lift weights.
5. For strength, Noreen eats only healthful foods.
6. They will drag eighty pounds of hose.
7. They will climb a ladder to a second-story window.
8. They will run up five flights of stairs.
9. The test lasts just over four minutes.
10. Noreen finished it in less than three minutes.

B. Each underlined verb below is in the present tense. Write each sentence. Change the verb to the tense shown in parentheses ( ).

EXAMPLE: The fire fighters <u>wear</u> leather hats. (future)
ANSWER: The fire fighters will wear leather hats.

11. Day shifts <u>last</u> nine hours. (future)
12. Noreen <u>stays</u> at the firehouse all day. (past)
13. The fire alarm <u>interrupts</u> dinner. (past)
14. The engines <u>race</u> to the fire. (future)
15. The fire fighters <u>need</u> air masks. (future)
16. They <u>enter</u> the burning building. (past)
17. Noreen <u>pulls</u> the hose up the stairs. (past)
18. Gallons of water <u>pour</u> out of the hose. (past)
19. Noreen <u>struggles</u> with the heavy hose. (past)
20. After work the fire fighters <u>rest</u> at home. (future)

Application WRITING SENTENCES

Write five sentences that tell about fire fighters at work. Use action verbs in the present, past, and future tenses.

6 — Using the Present Tense

- A verb in the present tense must agree with the subject of the sentence.

When you studied linking verbs, you learned that certain forms of *be* are used with certain subjects.

I <u>am</u> fond of whales. Whales <u>are</u> sea mammals.
The narwhal <u>is</u> a whale with a tusk like a unicorn's horn.

When the correct verb form is used, a subject and verb are said to agree.

Action verbs must also agree with their subjects. This means knowing when to use *-s* or *-es* in the present tense.

Using the Present Tense

With a singular noun, use *-s* or *-es*.
A seal eat<u>s</u> fish.   A seal catch<u>es</u> fish.

With a plural noun, do not use *-s* or *-es*.
Seals eat fish.   Seals catch fish.

With *he, she,* or *it*, use *-s* or *-es*.
She like<u>s</u> science.   She stud<u>ies</u> sea life.

With *I, you, we,* or *they*, do not use *-s* or *-es*.
We like science.   We study sea life.

Skills Tryout

Name the form of the verb in parentheses ( ) that correctly completes each sentence.

1. Maureen (work, works) as a marine biologist.
2. She (supply, supplies) facts about sea turtles.
3. Sea turtles (lay, lays) their eggs in the sand.
4. Shorebirds (eat, eats) the turtle eggs.
5. Humans also (hunt, hunts) turtles for food.

Practice

A. Write each sentence. Use the correct form of the verb in parentheses ( ).

1. The elephant seal (get, gets) its name from its large nose.
2. During mating season its nose (fill, fills) with air.
3. The male seals (roar, roars) their readiness to fight.
4. They (like, likes) a diet of penguins and fish.
5. After eating, a leopard seal (sleep, sleeps) on land.
6. Only its nostrils (show, shows) above the water.
7. The walrus (live, lives) in a small family group.
8. Its tusk (serve, serves) as a powerful weapon.
9. A walrus mother (swim, swims) with her infant on her back.
10. It (use, uses) its bristly mustache for hunting fish.

B. Write each sentence. Use the correct present-tense form of the verb in parentheses ( ).

11. Our boat _____ in an hour. (leave)
12. I _____ an otter family over there. (see)
13. Sea urchins _____ a tasty meal for otters. (provide)
14. Like their land relatives, sea otters _____ a lot. (play)
15. While napping they _____ their eyes with their paws. (cover)
16. A sea otter _____ a rock to open shellfish. (use)
17. It _____ on squid and fish, too. (feed)
18. A thick coat _____ the otter warm. (keep)
19. Their webbed feet _____ them swim easily. (help)
20. The animal _____ to the ocean floor. (dive)

Application WRITING SENTENCES

If you were a body of water, would you be a stream, a lake, a river, or an ocean? Write five sentences telling about the water life around you. Use these verbs in the present tense: *float, dive, breathe, sleep, search.*

USAGE: Subject-Verb Agreement **99**

7 Spelling Verbs Correctly

- The spelling of some verbs changes when *-es* or *-ed* is added.

You have learned that the past tense of a verb is usually formed by adding *-ed*. Remember, too, that the present tense of a verb may end in *-es*.

Note the spelling of the underlined verb in each sentence.

Verb: I try on my costume.
Verb + -es: She tries on her costume.
Verb + -ed: They tried on their costumes.

If a verb ends in a consonant and *y*, change the *y* to *i* before adding *-es* or *-ed*.

Note the spelling of the underlined verbs below.

Verb: You hop across the stage.
Verb + -ed: You hopped across the stage.

If a one-syllable verb ends in one vowel and one consonant, double the final consonant before adding *-ed*.

Skills Tryout

Read the sentences. For sentences 1, 2, and 4 spell the present-tense form of the verb in parentheses ( ). For sentences 3 and 5 spell the past-tense form.

1. Our director (worry) too much.
2. An actor (study) the script.
3. One of the dancers (stub) his big toe.
4. The reporter (hurry) to write her review.
5. We (plan) to have a party after the show.

Practice

A. Write each verb. Then write its past-tense form.

1. rip
2. worry
3. carry
4. defy
5. mat
6. sip
7. hurry
8. supply
9. tan
10. rub
11. marry
12. tug
13. pry
14. trip
15. plot
16. slam
17. plug
18. pad
19. dry
20. fan

B. Write each verb. Then write its -es present-tense form.

21. envy
22. fly
23. apply
24. bury
25. fry
26. rely
27. cry
28. try
29. satisfy
30. reply

C. Write each sentence. Use the past tense of the verb in parentheses ( ).

31. In the first act Basil (spy) on the Duke.
32. In the morning the Duke (deny) the theft.
33. In the second act Alice (pin) the message to Basil's door.
34. The Duchess (copy) the message.
35. Fortunately the author of the play (plan) a happy ending.

Application WRITING SENTENCES

Write five sentences. Use the past tense of:

imply   grip   stop   notify   mop

Write five sentences. Use the -es present-tense forms of:

occupy   pry   deny   study   multiply

8 — Using Irregular Verbs

- **Irregular verbs** do not form the past and past participle by adding -*ed.*

You have learned that the past tense of most verbs is formed by adding -*ed.* Irregular verbs are verbs that do not follow this rule.

The forms of some common irregular verbs are shown below. The **past participle** is the form used with the helping verb *has, have,* or *had.*

Present	Past	Past Participle
come	came	(has, have, had) come
do	did	(has, have, had) done
eat	ate	(has, have, had) eaten
fall	fell	(has, have, had) fallen
fly	flew	(has, have, had) flown
give	gave	(has, have, had) given
go	went	(has, have, had) gone
grow	grew	(has, have, had) grown
ride	rode	(has, have, had) ridden
run	ran	(has, have, had) run
see	saw	(has, have, had) seen
take	took	(has, have, had) taken
wear	wore	(has, have, had) worn
write	wrote	(has, have, had) written

See pages 330–333 of the Grammar Handbook for the forms of *be* and *have.* These two irregular verbs deserve extra study.

Skills Tryout

Name the past and past participle of each verb. Use the helping verb *has* with each past participle.

1. see **2.** give **3.** write **4.** do **5.** eat

Practice

A. Write each sentence. Use the past tense of the verb in parentheses ( ).

1. Hooray! Our tickets finally (come).
2. Our family (fly) to Cairo with a tour group.
3. Our group (see) the three pyramids at Giza.
4. We (do) a great deal of walking that day.
5. Ken (wear) out two pairs of sneakers on the trip.
6. We (take) a trip up the Nile on our way to Alexandria.
7. Cotton (grow) on the Nile banks in ancient times, too.
8. Rain (fall) unexpectedly when we were in Alexandria.
9. Marta (write) postcards from her high-rise hotel.
10. My parents (give) a farewell gift to our tour guide.

B. Write each sentence. Use the past participle of the verb in parentheses ( ).

11. Our passports had already (came).
12. Cecily had (eat) Egyptian food many times.
13. I had (do) all the packing for the trip.
14. Jim had never (fall) off a camel before.
15. Ellie has (run) a mile at dawn every day.
16. She had (go) to the train with us.
17. Mom and Dad have (take) the last camels to the hotel.
18. I have (see) twenty souvenir stands in three days.
19. Dust, wind, and rain have (wear) away the temple steps.
20. The pilot has (fly) this route many times before.

Application WRITING SENTENCES

Have you ever visited a special place that you clearly remember? Use vivid details to tell about your visit. Write eight sentences. Use these forms of irregular verbs.

ate	went	rode	ran
given	grown	ridden	written

9 — Using Irregular Verbs

- Some irregular verbs follow a pattern in the way they are formed.

Some irregular verbs follow a pattern in forming the past and past participle. The irregular verbs below are grouped by patterns to help you memorize them.

Some have the same past and past participle.

Present	Past	Past Participle
bring	brought	(has, have, had) brought
catch	caught	(has, have, had) caught
find	found	(has, have, had) found
say	said	(has, have, had) said
think	thought	(has, have, had) thought

Some form the past participle by adding -n to the past.

Present	Past	Past Participle
break	broke	(has, have, had) broken
choose	chose	(has, have, had) chosen
freeze	froze	(has, have, had) frozen
speak	spoke	(has, have, had) spoken

Some change one vowel in the past and in the past participle.

Present	Past	Past Participle
drink	drank	(has, have, had) drunk
ring	rang	(has, have, had) rung
sing	sang	(has, have, had) sung
swim	swam	(has, have, had) swum

Skills Tryout

Name the past and past participle of each verb.

1. find   2. think   3. break   4. choose   5. sing

Practice

Write each sentence. Use the past or the past participle of the verb in parentheses (   ).

1. Ronnie (say) that he could hardly wait for summer.
2. The lake (freeze), but he dreamed of warm weather.
3. He had (speak) to Gary about the vacation program.
4. Everyone (think) it would be fun to do again.
5. They had (swim) every day at the community center.
6. Cheryl complained that she had (freeze) in the cold water.
7. No one had (catch) a cold, though.
8. A bell always (ring) to call the campers.
9. All the campers (bring) bag lunches with them.
10. They (drink) juice with their sandwiches.
11. After lunch they had (break) into different groups.
12. Some of the campers (sing) in a chorus.
13. Some (choose) colored glass for their crafts projects.
14. One day Gary had (bring) fishing poles for everyone.
15. He had (say) that they were going on a trip.
16. Darryl had (choose) the seat next to Leona.
17. Everyone had (sing) loudly during the bus ride.
18. At the park they (swim) in the lake.
19. Then they (find) a place to go fishing.
20. No one (speak) while they baited their hooks.
21. Suzanne had (think) she would be bored.
22. She was surprised when she (catch) so many fish.
23. She (break) the camp record.
24. At sundown Ronnie had (ring) the bell for taps.
25. After they had (drink) some cocoa, everyone went home.

Application LISTENING

Listen for irregular verbs in the conversations of people around you. Write six sentences using verbs that you hear. Use the past tense or the past participle of an irregular verb in each sentence.

10 — Troublesome Verb Pairs

- Use the verb *can* to mean "to be able to do something." Use the verb *may* when you ask or give permission.
- Use the verb *sit* to mean "to rest." Use the verb *set* to mean "to put or place something."

The verbs *can* and *may* are often confused.

Use *can* when you mean "to be able." Use *may* when you ask or give permission.

The verbs *sit* and *set* are often confused.

Use *sit* when you mean "to rest." Use *set* when you mean "to put or place something."

Skills Tryout

Name the verb in parentheses ( ) that correctly completes each sentence.

1. Did you (sit, set) the paper plates on the table?
2. Is there anyone who (can, may) blow up these balloons?
3. Where will everyone (sit, set) during the show?
4. (Can, May) I taste the popcorn now?
5. In which room (can, may) Eva practice her juggling act?

Practice

A. Write each sentence. Use the correct verb in parentheses ( ).

1. Yes, you (can, may) bring a friend to the party.
2. The extra guests will (sit, set) on the floor.
3. (Can, May) we eat before the magic show begins?
4. Magic Marla (sit, set) a covered basket on the table.
5. A good magician (can, may) fool the audience every time.
6. Magic Marla asked Leroy to (sit, set) in the Chair of Invisibility.
7. How did she (sit, set) it down again?
8. (Can, May) you figure out how it's done?
9. A good juggler (can, may) juggle five objects at a time.
10. The juggler's dog likes to (sit, set) and beg.

B. Write the sentences. Use *can, may, sit,* or *set* to complete each sentence.

11. You _____ begin eating right after the show.
12. Where should we _____ for the refreshments?
13. Nicky, _____ you reach the jar of pickles?
14. Please don't _____ a place for me at that table.
15. Who _____ reach the pitcher of juice?
16. If you _____ it on the edge, it will fall off.
17. You _____ leave the table when you're finished.
18. Let's _____ in the living room and tell jokes.
19. _____ I borrow that deck of cards for a card trick?
20. If you _____ here, you'll be able to see her better.

Application LISTENING

Listen to how people use *can, may, sit,* and *set* in conversation or on television. Write five sentences that you hear.

11 — Prefixes

- A **prefix** is a letter or letters added to the beginning of a word. The prefix changes the meaning of the word.

Many words have two parts—a base word and a prefix. A **base word** is the simplest form of a word. It has no letters added to its beginning or end. In the word *reheat*, *heat* is the base word.

The letters *re-* in *reheat* are a prefix. They add the meaning "again" to the word *heat*.

Here are some more examples of prefixes.

Prefix	Meaning	Example
dis-	opposite of, away from	disagree
mis-	wrong, wrongly	misjudge
pre-	before	prejudge
re-	again, back	rebuilt
un-	not, opposite of	uncover

Skills Tryout

In each sentence find the word that starts with a prefix. Name the prefix.

1. Kathleen reread her family's history.
2. Brian Molloy had been unhappy in Ireland.
3. Brian disagreed about Ireland with his cousin in Boston.
4. His cousin gave him a preview of life in America.
5. Brian thought he would be misguided to stay in Cork.

Practice

A. Write the sentences. In place of the words in parentheses ( ), use words that have the prefixes below. Use the underlined words as the base words.

dis-   mis-   pre-   re-   un-

1. Adam's grandmother (<u>called</u> back to mind) the old days.
2. Her parents had nothing but (wrong <u>fortune</u>) in Poland.
3. Many people were (not <u>able</u>) to make a living there.
4. They wanted to (<u>build</u> again) their lives in the New World.
5. In New York they met with official (opposite of <u>approval</u>).
6. There was a (wrong <u>understanding</u>) about their papers.
7. As a health (<u>caution</u> before) they were put in quarantine.
8. This was not an (opposite of <u>usual</u>) experience.
9. However, their (opposite of <u>content</u>) didn't last long.
10. They were soon busy with (<u>arranged</u> before) jobs.

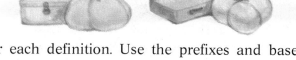

B. Write a word for each definition. Use the prefixes and base words below to form the words.

<u>Prefixes</u>: dis-   mis-   pre-   re-   un-
<u>Base Words</u>: appear   divided   fit   pay   place

11. divided again
12. not divided; united
13. to give money before
14. to give back money
15. to go away

16. to come back
17. to put in the wrong place
18. to put back into place
19. a wrong or bad fit
20. not in fit condition

Application USING LANGUAGE

Write a list of words that have prefixes. Include at least five words that begin with each prefix below. Try to list words that were not used in this lesson.

dis-   mis-   pre-   re-   un-

Action Verbs and Linking Verbs   *pages 88–91*

A. Write the verb in each sentence. Write *linking* if it is a linking verb. Write *action* if it is an action verb.

1. Your skin is part of your body.
2. It weighs twice as much as your brain.
3. Skin covers your body.
4. Skin is necessary for another reason.
5. It controls the temperature of your body.
6. Sometimes your body feels too hot.
7. Then you perspire.
8. The extra heat leaves through the skin.
9. It cools your body.
10. You feel cooler as a result.

Main Verbs and Helping Verbs   *pages 92–93*

B. Write each sentence. Draw one line under the main verb. Draw two lines under the helping verb.

11. Perry was looking for clues.
12. He has found a button on the ground.
13. A button had fallen off the suspect's coat.
14. We will check this button against the others.
15. They are waiting for an answer.

Direct Objects   *pages 94–95*

C. Write each sentence. Underline the direct object.

16. Jessica and Joshua made dinner.
17. First they boiled water.
18. Then they added some rice.
19. Jessica sliced two large tomatoes.
20. Joshua mixed the dressing.

Grammar Review

Tenses of Verbs *pages 96–97*

D. Write the verb in each sentence. Then write *present* or *past* to show the tense of the verb.

21. Jonathan dried his hair thoroughly.
22. We decided on the 4:30 train.
23. A crab scurries out from under a rock.
24. The old clock on the tower stopped.
25. She babies her little brother.

Irregular Verbs *pages 102–105*

E. Write the present, past, and past participle forms of each underlined verb.

26. They <u>choose</u> the players for our team.
27. The telephones <u>ring</u> all day long.
28. I <u>wear</u> a sweater over my shirt.
29. They <u>eat</u> lunch before noon.
30. I <u>find</u> books on my desk every morning.
31. <u>Think</u> of an answer.
32. They <u>give</u> me good ideas.
33. Campers <u>swim</u> across the lake.
34. Snowflakes <u>fall</u> quietly.
35. They <u>go</u> downstairs.

Troublesome Verb Pairs *pages 106–107*

F. Write each sentence. Use the correct verb in parentheses ( ).

36. We have enough chairs for everyone to (sit, set) down.
37. (Can, May) I borrow your table?
38. We usually (can, may) move the folding chairs.
39. Please (sit, set) them against the wall.
40. Let's (sit, set) awhile before we start working.

See also Handbook pages 330–343.

Grammar Review

Writing with Verbs

- Use exact verbs to make your writing more interesting.

Grammar and Writing Workshop

Read the sentences below.

1. Jim drank a glass of water.
2. Jim gulped a glass of water.

The only difference between these two sentences is the verb. Both sentences tell that Jim drank water. Sentence 2, however, shows that Jim was very thirsty. Using an exact verb like *gulped* makes sentence 2 clearer and more interesting than sentence 1.

The sentence below gives a different picture of drinking.

Jim sipped the water.

Look for chances to use exact verbs in your writing. One word can make the difference between a dull sentence and an interesting one.

The Verb Game   Here is a list of verbs. What exact verbs could replace each one?

Choose a verb from the list and write it. Think of exact verbs that could replace it in a sentence. Write as many exact verbs as you can in two minutes.

run	think	look
eat	smile	walk

How many exact verbs did you write? Think about how the meanings of your verbs are different from each other.

Find a classmate who chose the same verb. What exact verbs appear on his or her list?

Choose another verb from the list and start again.

The Verb Switch Write each sentence. Replace the underlined word with a more exact verb.

EXAMPLE: Nancy laughed at Caitlin's joke.
ANSWER: Nancy chuckled at Caitlin's joke.

1. Ricardo hurt his ankle in a soccer game.
2. The unhappy shopper asked to see the manager.
3. Samantha cut her hair last weekend.
4. We walk home after school every day.
5. The speaker talked about meeting famous people.
6. Cars moved along the highway.

No-Clue Time Now replace verbs without using clues. Find the verb in each sentence. Think of a more exact verb that could replace it. Write the new sentence.

7. Did you damage the car?
8. Aunt Marsha went to the market.
9. Danny filled a suitcase with enough clothing for a week.
10. Denise made a bookcase for her mystery novels.
11. Nick cooked a chicken for his parents.
12. Please put these flowers in a vase.

Using the Thesaurus

Suppose that someone delivers a speech about an American hero, then answers questions from the audience. Then suppose that you are writing an article for your school newspaper about what the speaker said. You would not want to repeat the words *said* and *asked* too often.

Find the entries for *say* and *ask* in the Thesaurus. Choose four words that are synonyms for *say* and four words that are synonyms for *ask*. Now write eight sentences about the speech, using these eight verbs.

12 Analyzing a News Story

- A **newspaper story** gives the most important facts first.

Newspaper stories give information. They are set up to inform the reader quickly and efficiently. Study the parts of the newspaper story below to see how this is done.

Headline

ZOO SEEKS HOME FOR ABANDONED SKUNK

Lead Paragraph

HOMETOWN, Ohio—Last night zoo keeper Tina Lopez discovered an abandoned skunk in a cardboard box left outside the zoo's Small Mammal House. Her attention had been attracted by a scratching noise coming from the box.

Body

A note in the box read: "I am Sweetums. Please give me a home. My owner cannot keep me. I am descented and cannot live in the wild."

Ms. Lopez stated that the zoo cannot keep Sweetums. In recent years the zoo has been flooded with requests to accept wild animals that people have purchased as pets. The zoo cannot accommodate them.

Ms. Lopez said, "People sometimes buy an animal meant to live in the wild because as a baby it is cute. When the animal grows up, they don't know what to do with it. This has become a real problem for the zoo."

Meanwhile, Hometown Zoo is searching for a zoo that will adopt Sweetums and give her a comfortable home.

Notice that the headline attracts attention and tells what the story is about. The lead paragraph tells the most important facts. It answers such questions as *Who? What? When? Where? Why?* and *How?* The body of the story gives other facts in order of decreasing importance.

Skills Tryout

Answer these questions about the news story on page 114.

1. Where did the story happen?
2. When did it happen?
3. What happened?
4. Why did it happen?
5. Who made the discovery?
6. How did that person happen to make the discovery?

Practice

A. Write a headline for each of these news events.

1. A student from your school wins $100 in a poetry contest.
2. A family you know discovers oil on their property.
3. A TV celebrity will speak to your class.
4. You are chosen to star in a spy movie.
5. A dog in your town saves a child from drowning.

B. Read the ideas for news stories below. Choose one and write a lead paragraph for it. Your paragraph should answer these questions: What happened? When did it happen? Where did it happen? Why did it happen? How did it happen? Who did it happen to?

6. The circus is coming to your community.
7. Scientists have uncovered dinosaur bones in your town.
8. A rare bird (make up its name) is seen in your state.
9. A pirates' treasure chest is found in North Carolina.
10. Students from your school have set a record for making the world's longest banana split.

Application USING STUDY SKILLS

Cut out several news stories from your local newspaper. In each story underline the sentences that tell *who, what, when, where, why,* and *how.*

13 A TV Interview

- Before you interview someone, decide on several main topics you want to find out about.
- Prepare questions that focus on your main topics.

Conducting an interview is one way of obtaining information. When you interview someone, you tap that person's experience and knowledge. In some ways, being an interviewer is like being a photographer. You choose the subject, and you focus on it.

You have probably seen many TV interviews. A TV interviewer is responsible for getting information to the viewers. The interviewer is the one who keeps the conversation focused. That is why it is important to prepare for an interview.

Here are some hints for preparing for a TV interview. First choose some main topics. Then develop questions that relate to the topics. Try to avoid questions that can be answered by *yes* or *no*. Those are conversation stoppers. Instead, use these six question words: *who, what, when, where, why,* and *how.* Write your questions on cards. Cards are easy to handle.

When you are well prepared with questions, you can concentrate on listening. That is your most important job during the interview itself. Notice what happened during this interview with Julie Cline when the interviewer didn't listen.

Interviewer: How many hours a day do you and your brother practice skating together?

Julie Cline: Six hours a day, but he's in the hospital now.

Interviewer: Do you plan to become a professional skater?

Obviously, the interviewer concentrated too much on preplanned questions and failed to follow up on an important point brought out in the interview.

Skills Tryout

Pretend that you are going to interview these people. Name two main topics you might want to find out about from each.

1. the fire chief
2. a mountain climber
3. the new director of parks and recreation

Practice

A. Write two main topics you might ask about when interviewing each person below.

1. a forest ranger
2. the owner of a new movie theater
3. a horse trainer
4. the gymnastics coach
5. the student who won a national science award

B. Write three specific questions you might ask when interviewing each person below. Use *who, what, when, where, how,* or *why.*

6. a newspaper reporter
7. the director of a computer camp
8. the captain of a cruise ship
9. a dolphin trainer
10. the director of a movie being filmed in your town

C. Write the name of one person you would like to interview. Then write three specific questions you would like to ask that person.

Application CONDUCTING AN INTERVIEW

Choose a member of your class to interview. Decide what the main topics will be. Prepare several questions on each topic. Then interview your classmate.

14 Writing Quotations

- Use **quotation marks** (" ") to show the exact words of a speaker.

When you repeat exactly what someone has said, you are quoting that person. The repeated words are a **quotation**. When you quote someone in writing, you set off the quotation with quotation marks. Here are two ways to write a quotation.

Rita said, "Thanks for lending me your bike."
"Thanks for lending me your bike," said Rita.

Notice that each quotation begins with a capital letter. A comma separates the speaker from the quotation. The comma comes before the quotation marks.

Sometimes what you are quoting is a question or an exclamation. Then a question mark or an exclamation mark is used at the end of the quotation instead of a comma.

"Will you let me use your skates?" her sister asked.

Sometimes a quotation is divided. If the quotation is one sentence, use commas to separate the quotation from the speaker.

"Of course," replied Rita, "you may use them."

If a divided quotation is two sentences, use a period after the speaker. Capitalize the second sentence.

"I can't wear them," she added. "They're too small for me."

When you write quotations, try not to use *said* all the time. Use a variety of verbs, such as *whispered, shouted, suggested, remarked,* and *replied.*

Skills Tryout

Tell where quotation marks should be placed.

1. I can't find my boa, wailed Tim.
2. You're always losing that snake, said his sister.
3. His father asked, When did you last see it?
4. It was on my bed, Tim answered, a minute ago.
5. Don't sit down! warned his father. Your blankets are moving.

Practice

A. Write the sentences. Place quotation marks where they belong.

1. Paula brought a frog to school, said Bonnie.
2. I know, Janet replied. I found it in my desk.
3. Kevin asked, Where is it now?
4. You'll find out soon enough, warned Scott.
5. Just wait, giggled Patty, until you open your lunch box!

B. Write the sentences correctly. Add correct punctuation. Use capital letters where needed.

6. Where are all these ants coming from asked Laura
7. Look at Amy's desk said Megan it's covered with ants
8. Greg shouted they're crawling up my legs
9. Did somebody spill something sticky asked Mark
10. I think said Kim that someone broke open the ant farm

Application WRITING QUOTATIONS

Check your quotation skills. Listen to a conversation between two or more people. Write at least three quotations from the conversation. Be sure to write each speaker's exact words. Try not to use *said* more than once. Choose livelier verbs.

15 — Writing a News Story

Writing Project

- A **news story** gives brief, exact information about a current event.

Everywhere, every day, exciting things are happening. Each day is filled with news. A building catches fire. The school board elects new members. A snowstorm hits your area. How do people keep informed? News reporters research and write the stories. In this lesson you will be a reporter and write a school news story. Later you will share your story in a class newspaper.

1. Prewriting

Reporters collect and write the news. This is called *covering* a story. Reporters obtain information in three ways. They observe carefully, ask questions, and collect details.

Look at the photograph. If you were a reporter, how would you cover this story?

First, observe. Notice the girl. She is holding a grocery sack full of money. The police officer is counting the money. The two people are in front of a store. Observe everything, but record only the facts.

Second, ask questions. *Who* is the girl? *What* is the total amount of money she found? *When* did she find the money? *Where* did she find the money? *Why* did she return the money? These are the five *W* questions.

Third, collect details. After readers get the most important facts, they may want to know more details. *Does the money belong to someone? Where does the girl live? What is the police officer's name?*

▶ Think about a news story you could write. Talk to other students and teachers about news being made in your school. With your classmates prepare a list of topics for a class newspaper. Here are some possible topics for school news stories:

- new books in the library
- a spelling bee
- a student moving away
- safety week posters
- new band members

Take turns choosing a topic from the class list. Help each other choose topics related to your personal interests.

▶ Make preparations to cover your news story. List the questions *Who? What? When? Where?* and *Why?* in your notebook. How will you find the answers to these questions? You might interview a person who can give you the information you need. If you are writing about a school activity, you might plan to attend.

Now you are ready to cover your news story. As a reporter, remember to observe, ask questions, and collect details.

2. Writing

A news story begins with a *lead paragraph*. The lead paragraph tells the most important facts of the story by answering the five *W* questions. For example, a lead paragraph may begin like this: "Yesterday afternoon Michelle Zolton discovered $500 in front of a store on Elm Street."

▶ Write the lead paragraph for your news story. Then use your observations, answers, and details to write the body of your news story. After the most important facts, add detail sentences in the order of their importance. Use specific action verbs to make your story interesting.

Complete the first draft of your news story by writing a headline and a by-line. Write a headline that attracts attention and tells what the story is about. Write your by-line (your name) below the headline.

3. Revising

▶ Read your first draft to yourself or to someone else. Does it sound like other news stories you have read? Use this checklist to help you think of improvements you can make.

Revision Checklist
- Did I begin with the most important facts of my story?
- Are the details given in the order of their importance?
- Are the facts correct?
- Did I answer the five W questions?
- Did I use specific words?

Read the sample and notice how the news story is made better by using specific words.

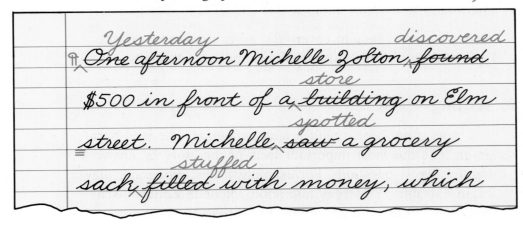

> *Student Recovers Money*
> *By Ellen Hilker*
>
> Yesterday afternoon Michelle Zolton discovered $500 in front of a store on Elm Street. Michelle spotted a grocery sack stuffed with money, which she immediately turned over to Officer Richard Heller. The owner of the money has not been identified.
> Michelle Zolton attends Kennedy Elementary School. She was on her paper route when the incident occurred.

EDITING MARKS

—	cross out
∧	add
⟲	move
≡	capital letter
/	small letter
¶	indent
◯	check spelling

▶ Use the editing marks to make changes that will sharpen your news story. Is your final story brief, exact, and clear?

4. Publishing

▶ Check your news story for errors. Use the Proofreading Checklist in the Young Writer's Handbook on page 377. Use the editing marks to make corrections.

▶ Work as a class to turn a bulletin board into a giant newspaper. Cover the board with old newspapers. Use large sheets of clean paper to make separate news pages. Draw columns and print your stories neatly. Add pictures and other features that will make your newspaper realistic. When you are finished, invite other classes to read your newspaper.

Writing Project

123

A TV News Program

Have a class TV news show. Include interviews, sports, and the weather along with interesting news events.

First make the frame of a television set. Cut a large rectangle out of a side of a very large cardboard carton. Place the carton on a table so that the "screen" will face the viewers.

Choose several news events. Find a large photograph or make a large drawing to illustrate each story. Glue each illustration on cardboard.

Prepare for your telecast by jotting down notes about your news stories. Display your illustrations from inside the carton as you narrate your stories.

Science

In this unit you learned that newspaper stories inform readers quickly and efficiently. They present information in a brief, direct way. Another way to present information concisely is by using graphs, tables, and charts. You will find many of these when you study science.

▶ Try your skill at reading this scientific chart. Choose a planet other than Earth. Use the chart to tell how the planet compares with Earth.

Planet	Greatest Distance from Sun (in millions of mi.)	Greatest Distance from Earth (in millions of mi.)	Length of Year (in Earth time)	Length of Day (in Earth time)
Mercury	43	136	88 days	176 days
Venus	67.7	160	225 days	116.7 days
Earth	94.5	—	365 days	24 hours
Mars	154	248	687 days	24.6 hours
Jupiter	507	600	11.9 years	9.9 hours
Saturn	932	1030	29.5 years	10.4 hours
Uranus	1860	1960	84 years	16 hours
Neptune	2821	2750	164.1 years	18.5 hours
Pluto	4571.2	4670	247 years	6.4 days

Speakers at Work Weather forecasters study weather maps and photographs taken by satellites. After they have studied these resources, they tell people what weather to expect.

▶ Try it. Observe the sky, the winds, and the temperature in your area. Then tell what you think the weather will be like tomorrow. If possible, use a tape recorder to record your prediction. Tonight, compare your forecast with the one given on television or radio. Tomorrow, see who was right—you, the weather forecaster, or both of you.

Checkpoint: Unit 3

Verbs *pages 88–107*

A. Write the verb from each sentence. Then write whether it is an *action verb* or a *linking verb*.

1. A large flock of birds flew across the sky.
2. Robby is the leader of our scout troop.
3. This apple juice tastes quite sweet.
4. Kim rode her pony along the trail.

B. Write whether each underlined word is a *main verb* or a *helping verb*.

5. Nathan and Peggy are planning the class picnic.
6. We will visit the Museum of Science next Friday.
7. Aunt Bev is writing a book of poems.
8. The volleyball team has practiced hard for this game.

C. Write the direct object of each sentence.

9. Waves rocked the small wooden rowboat.
10. Donna lost a quarter in the washing machine.
11. My father repairs bicycles as a hobby.
12. The sparrow closely guarded its eggs.

D. Write the verb in each sentence. Then write *present*, *past*, or *future* to show what tense it is in.

13. Jane will travel to Washington during spring vacation.
14. Mr. Fisher opened a new hardware store.
15. The science club meeting will end shortly.
16. I mow the neighbor's lawn on Saturdays.

E. Write the past and the past participle of each verb. Use the helping verb *has* with each past participle.

17. grow   18. see   19. write   20. give

Checkpoint: Unit 3

F. Write the past and the past participle of each verb. Use the helping verb *has* with each past participle.

21. choose   **22.** bring   **23.** ring   **24.** speak

G. Write the verb in parentheses ( ) that correctly completes each sentence.

25. (May, Can) I borrow your scissors?
26. Please (sit, set) those flowers on the desk.
27. My dog will (sit, set) on command.
28. (May, Can) you walk on your hands?

Prefixes   *pages 108–109*

H. Read each definition. Write a word that has the same meaning by adding the prefix *dis-*, *mis-*, *pre-*, *re-*, or *un-* to the underlined word.

29. opposite of <u>honest</u>   **32.** not <u>true</u>
30. to <u>behave</u> wrongly   **33.** to <u>pay</u> before
31. to <u>tell</u> again   **34.** opposite of <u>usual</u>

Quotations   *pages 118–119*

I. Write each sentence correctly. Add punctuation marks where they belong. Use capital letters where needed.

35. Can you steady the ladder for me Chong asked
36. I know said Ann that my shoes are here somewhere
37. Vinnie whispered it's spooky in the attic
38. Please hurry begged Liz. the movie has already started

News Stories   *pages 114–115*

J. Write a headline for the news event below.

A gorilla escapes from its cage in the local zoo.

See also Handbook pages 330–343, 382–383, 385.

Grammar
Pronouns

Composition
Persuading

The Twins

In form and feature, face and limb,
  I grew so like my brother,
That folks got taking me for him,
  And each for one another.
It puzzled all our kith and kin,
  It reached a fearful pitch;
For one of us was born a twin,
  Yet not a soul knew which.

One day, to make the matter worse,
  Before our names were fixed,
As we were being washed by nurse,
  We got completely mixed;
And thus, you see, by fate's decree,
  Or rather nurse's whim,
My brother John got christened me,
  And I got christened him.

—Henry S. Leigh

1 — Pronouns

- A **pronoun** takes the place of a noun or nouns.

In the sentences below, the words in blue are pronouns. The words in red are the words the pronouns replace.

1. a. The students saw a Laurel and Hardy movie.
   b. They saw an old Laurel and Hardy movie.
2. a. Laurel dropped a piano.
   b. Laurel dropped it.
3. a. The piano fell on Hardy's foot.
   b. The piano fell on his foot.

Sometimes pronouns can be used in place of nouns. In sentence 1b the plural pronoun *they* replaces *students*. In sentence 2b the singular pronoun *it* replaces *piano*. In sentence 3b the singular pronoun *his* replaces *Hardy's*.

The following chart shows the singular and plural pronouns.

Singular Pronouns	Plural Pronouns
I, me, my, mine you, your, yours she, he, it, her, him hers, his, its	we, us, our, ours you, your, yours they, them, their, theirs

Skills Tryout

Name the pronoun in each sentence below.

1. We watched a silent movie.
2. Michael had borrowed it from the library.
3. Lily offered her seat to Diane.
4. Mr. Oppenheim asked me to turn out the lights.
5. Could you see the screen easily?

Practice

A. Write each sentence. Underline the pronoun.

EXAMPLE: Vote for your favorite movie star.
ANSWER: Vote for your favorite movie star.

1. Was Charlie Chaplin your first choice?
2. In this film a young woman helps him.
3. The Little Fellow becomes her friend.
4. They walk down the road together.
5. The Marx Brothers—Groucho, Harpo, Chico, and Zeppo—always make us laugh.
6. Their act is usually the same.
7. Chico and Harpo often get them into trouble.
8. Chico outsmarts his brother Groucho.
9. We love to hear Harpo play the harp.
10. Our favorite Marx Brothers film is *A Night at the Opera*.

B. Write both sentences in each pair. Underline the pronoun in sentence **b**. Underline the noun or nouns in sentence **a** that the pronoun replaces.

11. **a.** Marla decided to make a movie.
    b. She would be the producer and director.
12. **a.** Dennis and Cory heard about the movie.
    b. Marla wanted them to be the stars.
13. **a.** Marla filmed Dennis's special stunts.
    b. His best stunt is tightrope walking.
14. **a.** Cory's scene also had a special effect.
    b. Her finest scene featured a disappearing act.
15. **a.** Marla showed the movie to her family.
    b. Marla's brother and sister enjoyed it very much.

Application LISTENING

Listen to a radio or TV program. List each pronoun that you hear used. Keep track of how many times each pronoun is used. Which pronoun was used the most?

2 Subject Pronouns

- The **subject pronouns** are *I, you, she, he, it, we,* and *they.*

Some pronouns can take the place of a noun used as the subject of a sentence. In the sentences below, the subjects are underlined. Each subject is a noun or a subject pronoun.

1. a. <u>Mr. Tourneau</u> visited the fifth grade.
   b. <u>He</u> talked about Canada.
2. a. <u>Ottawa</u> is the capital of Canada.
   b. <u>It</u> is a city in the province of Ontario.

Notice that in sentence **1b** the pronoun *he* stands for the noun *Mr. Tourneau.* In sentence **2b** the pronoun *it* stands for the noun *Ottawa.*

The subject pronouns are *I, you, she, he, it, we,* and *they.* The pronoun *I* is always capitalized.

Subject Pronouns		
Singular	Used for	Plural
I you she, he, it	talking about yourself talking to someone talking about someone or something	we you they

Skills Tryout

Name the subject pronoun in each sentence.

1. We live in Buffalo, New York.
2. Yesterday I studied several maps of Canada.
3. It is the second largest country in the world.
4. Did you know that Canada has ten provinces?
5. They are areas that are like states.

Practice

A. Write each sentence. Underline the subject pronoun.

1. We went to the province of Quebec.
2. It was settled by the French in the early 1600s.
3. Today they speak both French and English there.
4. You can see signs written in both languages.
5. I heard German and Italian spoken in Ontario.
6. In Manitoba you may hear people speaking Ukrainian.
7. We traveled across the entire Trans-Canada Highway.
8. It is 4,280 miles long.
9. In Nova Scotia I talked to a Scottish Canadian dancer.
10. She danced a lively Highland fling.

B. Write each sentence. Use a subject pronoun in place of the underlined word or words.

11. Jeannette Clery speaks both French and English.
12. After the dance competition, Maureen and Patrick had tea.
13. Nova Scotia was a new home for many Scottish people.
14. The Scots and the Irish settled in eastern Canada.
15. James MacGregor Anderson played the bagpipes.

C. Write the sentences. Complete each sentence with the singular (S) or plural (P) subject pronoun that you use to talk about yourself.

16. (S) went to Vancouver.
17. (P) waited in Toronto.
18. (P) liked Winnipeg.
19. (S) sailed to Halifax.
20. (P) skied in Montreal.
21. (S) saw a caribou.

Application WRITING SENTENCES

Write five sentences about a country you would like to visit. Use at least one subject pronoun in each sentence.

3 Object Pronouns

- The **object pronouns** are *me, you, him, her, it, us,* and *them.*

You have learned that some pronouns take the place of nouns used as the subject of a sentence. Other pronouns replace nouns used as direct objects. Remember, a direct object comes after an action verb. In the sentences below, the direct objects are underlined.

1. a. Señora Campos told the <u>class</u> about Argentina.
   b. Argentina interested <u>us</u>.
2. a. Many Argentines raise <u>cattle</u> or <u>sheep</u>.
   b. Cowboys bring <u>them</u> to market to sell.

In sentence 1b the pronoun *us* stands for the noun *class*. In sentence 2b the pronoun *them* stands for the nouns *cattle* and *sheep*. Pronouns that replace nouns used as direct objects are called object pronouns. Look at the chart of object pronouns.

Object Pronouns		
Singular	Used for	Plural
me	talking about yourself	us
you	talking to someone	you
him, her, it	talking about someone or something	them

Skills Tryout

Name the object pronoun in each sentence.

1. Ramona told us about South America.
2. Sal asked her to talk about the countries there.
3. Ramona described them well.
4. Peru particularly interested me.
5. Ramona described it as mountainous.

Practice

A. Write the second sentence of each pair. Underline the object pronoun.

1. Copper ore comes from Chile. Mining companies sell it around the world.
2. Many farmers in Ecuador grow bananas. Merchants buy them after the harvest.
3. Señora Torres exports coffee. Brazilian coffee growers supply her with coffee.
4. Manfred visited an oil well in Venezuela. A relative invited him there.
5. Sam worked on a cattle ranch in Argentina last year. Sam may take you along next year.

B. Write each sentence. Use an object pronoun in place of the underlined words.

6. Puerto Rico welcomed <u>Christopher Columbus</u> in 1493.
7. Columbus claimed <u>the island</u> for Spain.
8. Columbus's crew tasted <u>the fruits and vegetables</u>.
9. Later they told <u>Queen Isabella</u> about the strange foods.
10. The Spaniards did not like <u>the corn</u>.

C. Write the sentences. Complete each sentence with the singular (S) or plural (P) object pronoun you use to talk about yourself.

11. A guide told _(P)_.
12. Felipe invited _(S)_.
13. Carlos helped _(S)_.
14. The captain knew _(P)_.
15. A friend asked _(S)_.
16. Sonia saw _(P)_.

Application LISTENING

Listen to a conversation between two people. Write five sentences you hear that use object pronouns.

4 — Possessive Pronouns

- A **possessive pronoun** shows ownership.

You have learned that possessive nouns show ownership. Pronouns can show ownership, too.

1. a. Molly's room is messier than Arthur's room.
   b. Her room is messier than his room.
2. a. However, both rooms are neater than Gloria's.
   b. However, both rooms are neater than hers.

In sentence 1b the pronouns *her* and *his* replace the possessive nouns *Molly's* and *Arthur's*. In sentence 2b the pronoun *hers* replaces *Gloria's*.

Pronouns that show ownership are called possessive pronouns. Some possessive pronouns are used before nouns: *That is her room.* Other possessive pronouns are used alone: *That room is hers.* The possessive pronoun *his* can be used both ways.

Used Before Nouns	Used Alone
my, your, his, her its, our, their	mine, yours, his, hers ours, theirs

Notice that no apostrophe (') is used in a possessive pronoun.

Skills Tryout

Name the possessive pronoun in each sentence.

1. Cleaning up is our job today.
2. My brother is washing the dishes.
3. The easiest chore is mine.
4. I will clean your room.
5. Yours is the neatest room.

Practice

A. Write each sentence. Use the pronoun in parentheses (   ) that correctly completes the sentence.

1. Frank and Pam want to clean (their, theirs) bookcase.
2. Charlotte has offered (her, hers) help.
3. We think that the best plan is (our, ours).
4. Please bring (your, yours) ladder.
5. (My, Mine) is too short to reach the top shelves.
6. (Our, Ours) first step is to take everything out.
7. The books about snakes are (your, yours).
8. Which books are (their, theirs)?
9. Where is (my, mine) car magazine?
10. Pam says the mystery stories are (her, hers).

B. Write each sentence. Use a possessive pronoun in place of the underlined word or words.

11. Eddie helped Eddie's sister bathe the dog.
12. They put Eddie and Doris's dog in the tub.
13. The dog has the dog's own shampoo.
14. Doris decided to use Doris's instead.
15. Doris said that drying the dog was Doris's job.
16. The towel she used was Eddie's.
17. Doris brushed the dog with Grandma's old hairbrush.
18. Eddie trimmed the pet's nails.
19. Then they put one of Bob's scarves on the clean dog.
20. Have you ever had a chore like Eddie and Doris's?

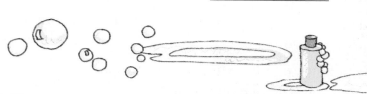

Application WRITING SENTENCES

Write five sentences about a clean-up project you have been involved in at home. Use at least one possessive pronoun in each sentence.

5 Using Pronouns Correctly

- Use a subject pronoun as the subject of a sentence.
- Use an object pronoun after an action verb.

Philip wrote the following letter to his friend Roberto.

Dear Roberto,

My family and I are inviting you to our house. You can help Lois and me. We have a new puppy. She and I are training him.

Your friend,
Philip

The words underlined in red are subject pronouns. Philip used them in the subjects of sentences. The words underlined in blue are object pronouns. Philip used them after action verbs.

Philip used all the pronouns correctly. When Philip named himself and someone else, he always named himself last: *she and I* and *my family and I.*

Skills Tryout

Name the pronoun in parentheses ( ) that correctly completes each sentence.

1. My brother and (I, me) are making kites.
2. Can you help him and (I, me)?
3. Alice and (we, us) will fly the kites on Saturday.
4. You will see her and (we, us) at the park.
5. (She, Her) and the other children will be in a kite-flying contest.

Practice

A. Write each sentence. Use the word or words in parentheses ( ) that correctly complete the sentence.

1. (I and Dora, Dora and I) would like to thank you for the tour of your bakery.
2. You helped (she, her) and me with our project.
3. (She, Her) and I enjoyed meeting your helpers.
4. You and (they, them) explained everything so clearly.
5. We especially liked watching you and (they, them).
6. Dora's brother asked her and (I, me) about our report.
7. I told (he, him) about your bakery.
8. (He, Him) and Rhoda tasted the rolls you made.
9. Our friends and (we, us) would like to visit again.
10. Would you show (we, us) how to make bread?

B. Write each sentence. Use the pronoun in parentheses ( ) that correctly completes the sentence. Then write whether the pronoun you used is a subject or an object pronoun.

11. Alex and (I, me) wrote to the Tiny Toy Company.
12. (He, Him) and I asked for some information.
13. The president of the company answered (he, him) and me.
14. She thanked Alex and (I, me) for our letter.
15. She told (we, us) about the company.
16. (She, Her) and the vice-president invited our parents and us to visit the company.
17. Our parents and (we, us) accepted the invitation.
18. The president showed (they, them) and us the factory.
19. We thanked (she, her) and the vice-president.
20. Then (they, them) and we said good-by.

Application WRITING SENTENCES

Write five sentences about a factory or a business you would like to visit. Use at least one subject pronoun or object pronoun in each sentence.

6 Contractions

- A **contraction** is a shortened form of two words.

You know that the pronouns *I, you, she, he, it, we,* and *they* are used as subjects in sentences. These subject pronouns may be combined with the verbs *am, is, are, has, have, had, will, shall,* and *would.* The combined forms are called contractions.

Each of the underlined words in the following conversation is a contraction.

Peggy: "Hello, Uncle Sy. I'm coming to Tennessee."
Uncle Sy: "We're glad to have you."
Peggy: "I'll be arriving in a few days."
Uncle Sy: "Your Daddy said he'd be coming, too."
Peggy: "He's packing his bags now."

Study the contractions listed below. Notice that an apostrophe (') shows where a letter or letters have been left out.

Pronoun + Verb	=	Contraction
pronoun + <u>am</u>	=	I'm
pronoun + <u>are</u>	=	you're, we're, they're
pronoun + <u>is</u> or <u>has</u>	=	he's, she's, it's
pronoun + <u>have</u>	=	I've, you've, we've, they've
pronoun + <u>had</u> or <u>would</u>	=	I'd, you'd, he'd, she'd, we'd, they'd
pronoun + <u>shall</u> or <u>will</u>	=	I'll, we'll
pronoun + <u>will</u>	=	you'll, he'll, she'll, they'll

Skills Tryout

Say the contraction for each pair of words.

1. they have   **2.** it is   **3.** we will   **4.** I am   **5.** you are

Practice

A. Write the contraction for each pair of words.

1. I will	**6.** you would	**11.** I had
2. we are	**7.** it has	**12.** you will
3. he would	**8.** we shall	**13.** she had
4. she has	**9.** they are	**14.** I would
5. they had	**10.** she is	**15.** you have

B. Write the contraction in each sentence. Then write the words from which the contraction is formed.

16. I'm going camping in a Tennessee mountain range.
17. It's called the Great Smoky Mountains.
18. The mountains look smoky because they're covered with a blue-gray haze.
19. After camping we'll go to Oak Ridge.
20. We've always wanted to visit the American Museum of Science and Energy in Oak Ridge.
21. We're also planning a trip to Memphis.
22. I'd like to visit Nashville, too.
23. They've named it the country-music capital of the world.
24. You've probably heard of the Grand Ole Opry House.
25. Uncle Sy said he'll take us there for a concert.

Application WRITING SENTENCES

Every state has interesting parks, museums, and historical sites to visit. Write five sentences that tell about places of interest in your own state. Use at least five contractions in your sentences.

7 — Homophones

- **Homophones** are words that sound alike but have different meanings and spellings.

Read the poem below. Pay special attention to the underlined words.

> For I, sir, ay yes, I eye a dear deer,
> And a hare with hair that is half of a pair
> While I pare a pear beside a new gnu
> And shoo a bare bear away from my shoe—
> And all this I do at ten to two, too!
> —*Eve Merriam*

Words like *I* and *eye* or *pair, pare,* and *pear* are called homophones. They sound alike but their meanings and spellings are different.

The possessive pronouns *their, its,* and *your* are often confused with the contractions *they're, it's,* and *you're.* These homophones are underlined in the sentences below.

1. They're playing with their dog.
2. It's a shame that the dog dropped its bone in the water.
3. You're afraid of your own reflection, Rover!

Skills Tryout

Name the six pairs of homophones in the lines below.

> For I had four cents for fare for the fair,
> But it didn't make sense to go in 'where
> I'd wear a tie that was not in a knot,
> So instead I watched blue smoke that blew,
> And then flew straightway up the flue.
> —*Eve Merriam*

Practice

A. Write the homophones from each sentence.

1. It's hard to start a story when its ending is not clear.
2. They're trying to keep their words simple.
3. Be sure you're using your best ideas.
4. It's a story about a castle and its hidden treasure.
5. Their search ended down there in the dungeon.

B. Write each sentence. Use the homophones in parentheses ( ) that correctly complete the sentences.

6. The (night, knight) was cold and the wind (blue, blew).
7. We could (here, hear) wolves howling at the (pail, pale) moon.
8. We wanted to (flea, flee) but we didn't (no, know) how.
9. Then we saw the (sale, sail) of the ship out at (sea, see).
10. (Our, Hour) own boat had a (whole, hole) in its bottom.
11. What could we (dew, do) to make them (sea, see) us?
12. (Eye, I) (knew, new) there was only (one, won) way.
13. We had to (meat, meet) them out (there, they're).
14. Janet took a (pale, pail) to (bale, bail) out the boat.
15. Craig brought (eight, ate) life jackets and an (or, oar).
16. "(I'll, Aisle) wave a (peace, piece) of cloth," I said.
17. (Would, Wood) we make it to (their, they're) ship?
18. "(Bee, Be) brave and row (right, write) to the ship!"
19. Suddenly we (herd, heard) the ship's captain call, "Ahoy (there, their)!"
20. He had (seen, scene) us!

Application USING LANGUAGE

Use each pair of homophones below in a sentence.

steal, steel   plain, plane   pain, pane

great, grate   shoot, chute

Grammar Review

Subject Pronouns   *pages 130–133*

A. Write each sentence. Use a subject pronoun in place of the underlined word or words.

1. Christopher wanted to try a science experiment.
2. The experiment is not hard to do.
3. Jane Gorman gathered the supplies.
4. Christopher and Jane needed a nail and a battery.
5. The nail must be made of iron.
6. Ms. Gerber had been explaining electromagnets.
7. The next day the students wanted to make one.
8. The directions were on the chalkboard.
9. My brother asked Ms. Gerber a question.
10. Jane and I listened carefully.

Object Pronouns   *pages 134–135*

B. Write each sentence. Use an object pronoun in place of the underlined word or words.

11. Anna told Henry and me about her great-aunt.
12. Aunt Millie had made that quilt.
13. People admired Aunt Millie.
14. Millie's friends liked her quilt designs.
15. The story of Millie's life impressed Henry.

Possessive Pronouns   *pages 136–137*

C. Write the possessive pronoun in each sentence.

16. Rachel wrote her cousin a long letter.
17. Anthony took his package to the post office.
18. This is their newspaper.
19. The news magazine is hers.
20. I recognized the magazine by its cover.

Grammar Review

144

Using Pronouns Correctly   *pages 138–139*

D. Write each sentence. Use the pronoun in parentheses ( )
that correctly completes each sentence.

21. Jan and (I, me) learned about geysers.
22. (She, Her) and Philip borrowed an interesting book.
23. It told (they, them) about hot springs.
24. They and (we, us) read every word.
25. The book showed them and (we, us) Old Faithful.
26. Jan told (he, him) and Philip about her trip.
27. Our parents took Jan and (I, me) to Yellowstone.
28. You and (he, him) have seen our pictures.
29. Philip asked (she, her) and me to show them again.
30. (They, Them) and we enjoyed our vacation.

Contractions   *pages 140–141*

E. Write the contraction for each pair of words.

31. we would   33. she has   35. I will
32. he is   34. they are   36. we have

Homophones   *pages 142–143*

F. Write the homophones from each sentence.

37. Dear, there's a deer in the road.
38. We ate dinner at eight o'clock.
39. Lee put the pale flowers in a pail.
40. A great amount of water poured through the grate.
41. Stan can't wait to lose some weight.
42. I have never seen a more beautiful scene.
43. That is not a square knot.
44. A spark flew up the flue.
45. They're using their own ideas.

See also Handbook pages 344–349, 382, 385.

Writing with Pronouns

Grammar and Writing Workshop

- Use pronouns instead of repeating the same nouns too often.

Read the sentences below.

1. The president told reporters the president believed the president's plan would work.
2. The president told reporters he believed his plan would work.

Sentences 1 and 2 say the same thing. However, sentence 2 is much less awkward.

The same noun is used three times in sentence 1. In sentence 2 the pronouns *he* and *his* replace the nouns *president* and *president's*. The result is a smoother sentence that is easier to read and understand.

Pronouns can help you to improve your writing.

The Pronoun Game In the groups of words below, the underlined words can be replaced by pronouns. Name at least one pronoun from the Pronoun Bank for each group of words.

the governor's mansion
Sally plays
above the clouds
singing with Billy
Norma and Lucy's discovery
for the cook
the writers' stories
spoke to June

the people complain
the explorer arrives
because of Marjorie
the lightning strikes
belonging to Stu and Joe
about the students
the apples ripen
if Jason runs

Pronoun Bank						
we	their	you	she	he	they	me
it	him	her	us	he	them	his	our

The Pronoun Switch   Use pronouns to replace the underlined words in the sentences below. Write each new sentence.

EXAMPLE: Pablo knows that Pablo needs Pablo's rest.
ANSWER: Pablo knows that he needs his rest.

1. Yolanda didn't know that Harvey was waiting for Yolanda.
2. The volcano sent lava streaming down the volcano's sides.
3. Bob ran as Bob saw the snake slithering toward Bob.
4. Ants are famous for ants' incredible strength.
5. Janet handed a sweater to Janet's friend.

Add-a-Pronoun   Use pronouns to complete the paragraph below. Write the paragraph.

Shirley put on _____ bathing suit. _____ walked along the beach. There were many colorful seashells beneath _____ feet. _____ were of many different shapes and colors. Shirley placed some of _____ in her beachbag. The beachbag was a gift from _____ grandfather. _____ was a lighthouse keeper. _____ favorite hobby was needlepoint, which _____ had learned when _____ was a young sailor.

Using the Thesaurus

Write five sentences about different kinds of accidents, but don't use the word *accident.* Find the entry for *accident* in the Thesaurus. Use five different synonyms for *accident* in your sentences.

Then write your five sentences again. Change at least one of the nouns in each sentence to a pronoun. An example is given below.

The Smiths told us about the mishap. They told us about it.

8 Understanding Facts and Opinions

- A **fact** is true information about something.
- An **opinion** is what a person *thinks* about something.

Every day you hear and read messages that try to persuade you. For example, commercials, ads, speeches, and bumper stickers try to persuade you to do something or to think a certain way. How can you judge the truth of what they say? To do this, you must be able to tell facts from opinions.

Sometimes, on the other hand, *you* want to persuade others to share your opinion. You want to be convincing. To do this, you need to back up your opinion with facts.

It is not always easy to tell facts from opinions. An opinion may be stated very positively. It may sound like a proven fact, even though it is just someone's opinion. Here are some hints for telling facts from opinions.

Fact

You can check a fact to see if it is true.
    Check it against your own knowledge or experience.
    Check it by experimenting.
    Check it in a reference book or with an expert.

Examples of Facts
1. The bicycle was introduced in England in 1818.
2. This Whizzo bike weighs twenty-four pounds.
3. The handlebars are made of steel.

Opinion

An opinion cannot be proved true or false. It tells what someone thinks, feels, or believes.

Examples of Opinions
1. Whizzo is the best bike that money can buy.
2. Whizzo is the bike for the space age.
3. Whizzo's streamlined frame is ahead of the rest.

Skills Tryout

Answer these questions about the examples of facts and opinions on the opposite page.

1. How could you check fact 1?
2. How could you check fact 2?
3. How could you check fact 3?
4. Why is the word *best* a clue that opinion 1 is an opinion?
5. How might people disagree about opinion 3?

Practice

A. Write *fact* or *opinion* for each statement below.

1. Racing bikes weigh less than touring bikes.
2. A dirt bike has knobby tires.
3. The Whizzo bike blends raw power with space-age style.
4. The Tour de France is a famous bicycle road race.
5. Dirt-bike racing is a thrilling sport!
6. A ten-speed bike is the bike to use for long rides.
7. A dirt bike has a low seat and wide handlebars.
8. A three-speed bike is best for riding around town.
9. Some ten-speed bikes have drop-style handlebars.
10. The new Whizzo Light-Bike is fantastic.

B. Write an opinion that goes with each of these facts.

11. The Whizzo Light-Bike's frame weighs five pounds.
12. The bike comes in Fire Red, Brilliant Blue, and Silver.
13. The bike costs $450.
14. The dirt-bike race was held in Nashville.
15. Hang-On handlebar grips are made of foam.

Application WRITING A PARAGRAPH

Write a paragraph about bicycles. Start by giving an opinion. Then give at least three facts to back up the opinion.

9 — Using the Telephone

- When you use the telephone, speak clearly and listen carefully.
- When you write a telephone message, give correct and complete information.

No one's voice is as clear on the telephone as it is in person. Some words, such as *mine* and *nine,* may sound almost alike on the phone. For this reason it is important to speak clearly. Pronounce consonants carefully. You also need to pay close attention to the caller's words. Ask the caller to repeat or spell any word that isn't clear.

Do you ever answer a call for someone else? When you do, it is important to be helpful and polite. What you say can persuade the caller to leave a message. Most people would not want to leave a message with someone who says, "Huh? I don't know." They would prefer to leave a message with someone who says, "She's not here right now. May I take a message?"

Notice the parts of the message below. It is important to include these parts when you write a telephone message.

Date and Time — *January 9, 10:15 A.M.*
Person called — *Dad,*

Caller — *Mr. Barrows called.*
Message — *Call him at work.*
Caller's number — *555-9336.*

Message taker's name — *Tommy*

Whenever you take a message, be sure to get all the necessary information. Your attention to details will show the caller that the message is in good hands.

Skills Tryout

Three parts of a phone message are missing from the list below. Tell what they are.

Date and time
Name of person called
Caller's phone number

Practice

A. List the parts that are missing from this phone message.

Sue,
Ms. Stevens, your piano teacher, called.
She has to change your lesson time. Call
her as soon as you can.
Rick

B. Write this phone message correctly. Fill in the missing information. You may make up any information you need.

January 21

Someone called long distance.
(415) 555-3381

C. Write a phone message for someone in your family. Be sure to include all the necessary parts.

Application LIFE SKILLS

The telephone book is full of information, but it is too large to carry everywhere. Many people carry small books in which they have written the numbers they call often.

Prepare a small personal directory for yourself. Write emergency numbers in the front. Then write the names of friends and relatives in alphabetical order. When you write their numbers, remember to include area codes where necessary.

10 — Writing a Friendly Letter

- A friendly letter has five parts: the heading, greeting, body, closing, and signature.

Read this letter. Notice the positions of the five parts.

Heading

235 Elmwood Avenue
Columbus, OH 43220
January 19, 1986

Greeting

Dear Stacy,

Body

It's been a long time since we were at camp together last summer. I wish we could be sitting by the campfire right now. I have two new ghost stories for you.

I'm wondering if I could persuade you to try a different camp next summer. Camp Willow Brook was fun, but I found a new camp that teaches sailing. I'm sending along a booklet that describes the new camp. Let me know what you think.

Closing

Your camping friend,

Signature

Karen

1. The heading shows the address of the writer and the date. Proper nouns are capitalized. A comma is used between the city and the state and between the date and the year.
2. The first word of the greeting is capitalized as well as the proper noun. The greeting is followed by a comma.
3. The closing is followed by a comma. Only the first word in the closing is capitalized.

Turn to page 371 in the Young Writer's Handbook for help in writing social notes such as thank-you notes.

Skills Tryout

Name these parts of a friendly letter.

1. the writer's address and the date
2. the writer's name
3. the writer's message

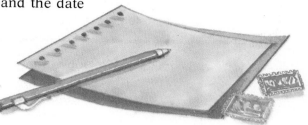

Practice

A. For each item below, write *heading, greeting, body, closing,* or *signature.*

1. Dear Cindy,
2. 203 Green Street
   Cambridge, MA 02139
   January 6, 1986
3. Your cousin,
4. Have you heard the news? We are coming east to visit you during spring vacation. I can't wait!

B. Write these items as if they were parts of friendly letters. Punctuate and capitalize them correctly.

5. dear brian
6. 43 edgewood drive
7. your friend
8. maplewood NJ 07040
9. december 15 1986
10. dear mary ann
11. westport ct 06880
12. your niece
13. 633 winslow road
14. march 12 1986
15. berkeley ca 94702
16. july 31 1986

Application WRITING A FRIENDLY LETTER

Pretend that you belong to a club that you want a friend to join. Write a letter to persuade your friend. Remember to include all five parts. Then address an envelope for the letter. Refer to page 374 in the Young Writer's Handbook for the correct position of addresses on the envelope.

11 Writing a Business Letter

- When you write a business letter, make your message clear and brief.

Read this business letter. Notice that it has six parts.

Heading

44 Seagull Way
Santa Cruz, CA 95065
January 13, 1986

Inside address

Ms. Lynne Evans, Manager
Parkside Art Supplies
215 South Milford Avenue
Santa Cruz, CA 95060

Greeting

Dear Ms. Evans:

Body

Would you consider letting the gymnastics club buy art supplies at a discount? We need to make posters to advertise our annual winter show. We are giving the show to raise money for equipment, and we would appreciate your help.

Closing

Respectfully,

Lee Shen

Signature

Lee Shen

Notice how a business letter differs from a friendly one.

1. An inside address is added. It gives the name and address of the person or company to whom the letter is being sent.
2. The greeting is more formal. If you don't know the exact person's name, use a greeting such as *Dear Sir or Madam, Dear Manager,* or *Dear Parkside Art Supplies.* The greeting is followed by a colon.
3. The body briefly states the facts.
4. The closing is more formal. You could also use *Sincerely* or *Yours truly.*
5. If a business letter is typed, the writer's name is typed four lines below the closing.

Skills Tryout

Name these parts of a business letter.

1. Roadside Lumber Company
   222 Grand Avenue
   Medina, OH 44256
2. Yours truly,
3. Dear Manager:

Practice

A. Write the answers to these questions about a business letter.

1. Which part of a business letter is not part of a friendly letter?
2. What do you do about the greeting if you don't know the name of a specific person?
3. How is the greeting punctuated?
4. How is the closing punctuated?

B. Write these items as if they were parts of business letters. Punctuate and capitalize them correctly.

5. august 25 1986
6. sincerely yours
7. 46 rodeo circle
8. dear mr. wilson
9. cornelius nc 28031
10. 956 north elm street
11. dear shopper's mart
12. coarsegold ca 93614
13. very truly yours
14. forest hills ny 11375
15. may 13 1986
16. 119 seaview lane

Application WRITING A BUSINESS LETTER

Pretend that you are organizing a school newspaper. Write a letter to your local newspaper asking for help. Persuade the editor to send a reporter to talk to your group.

12 — Writing a Persuasive Paragraph

Writing Project

- A **persuasive paragraph** gives the writer's opinion with reasons to support it.

Persuading means getting someone to agree with you or to do what you want. A television commercial may persuade you to buy a product. It gives reasons why you should buy the product. Persuasion can also bring about important changes. Think about these events from history.

Columbus persuaded Queen Isabella to buy him ships.
Henry Ford persuaded people to replace horses with cars.
Women used persuasion to gain the right to vote.

In this lesson, you will write a persuasive paragraph. Your paragraph will make others aware of a problem. You will try to get your classmates to agree with your opinion about what should be done.

1. Prewriting

To persuade someone to agree with you, you have to give reasons for your opinion. One way to think of reasons and organize them is to draw a cluster. Suppose you think the school playground should be fixed. Look at the cluster of reasons on the next page that supports your opinion.

▶ The key word in the cluster shown is *playground*. Write key words for three things you think should be improved. Name something at school, something in your city, and something in the nation.

Decide which key word you know or care the most about. You have selected the topic for your persuasive paragraph.

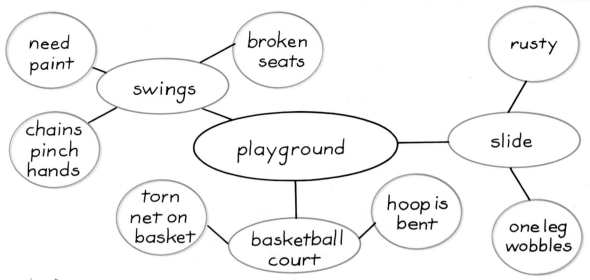

▶ Make a cluster about your topic. Use circles of different colors, as in the example. Put the key word in a black circle in the middle of your paper. Write two or three words that tell more about your key word in red circles. Write more details in the green circles. Be sure to connect your circles to show how the ideas are related.

2. Writing

Begin your persuasive paragraph with a topic sentence that states your opinion. The reader should know from your topic sentence that you are giving an opinion. Begin with words such as *I think*, *I believe*, or *In my opinion*. Read this topic sentence: "I think the school playground needs to be improved."

▶ Write your topic sentence. Then use ideas from your cluster to write reasons that support your opinion, or topic sentence. In writing, some words are more persuasive than others. Use words with strong meanings in your paragraph.

3. Revising

▶Compare your first draft to the cluster you drew. Check your paragraph to see if you have included the important information from your cluster. Now read your paragraph aloud. Are your words strong enough? Do your reasons sound convincing? This checklist will help you improve your first draft.

Revision Checklist
- Did I write a topic sentence that states my opinion?
- Did I include reasons to support my opinion?
- Did I use words with strong meanings?
- Will my reader be persuaded to agree with my opinion?
- Did I combine short, choppy sentences?

Read the sample and notice how combining short, choppy sentences improves the paragraph.

I think the school playground is in ~terrible~ bad condition , and It needs to be ~improved~ improved. Students refuse to play on broken equipment , but Nothing about it has been done. The slide and swings are unsafe. All of the

> I think the school playground is in terrible condition, and it needs to be improved. Students refuse to play on broken equipment, but nothing has been done about it. The slide and swings are unsafe. All of the equipment needs to be repainted. It is impossible to play basketball with a torn net and a bent hoop. Don't you agree the students deserve a better place to play?

EDITING MARKS

— cross out
∧ add
↷ move
≡ capital letter
/ small letter
¶ indent
◯ check spelling

▶ Use the editing marks to make changes in your paragraph.

4. Publishing

▶ Before you share your writing, proofread for errors. Use the Proofreading Checklist in the Young Writer's Handbook on page 377. Make corrections, using the editing marks.

▶ Hang your paragraph on a class bulletin board and ask everyone to read it. Write the name of your topic on an envelope or empty box and place it by the bulletin board. Cut small pieces of paper for ballots. Ask each class member to vote "yes" or "no" on your opinion. Count the votes to see if you were a persuasive writer.

Writing Project

A Company Letterhead

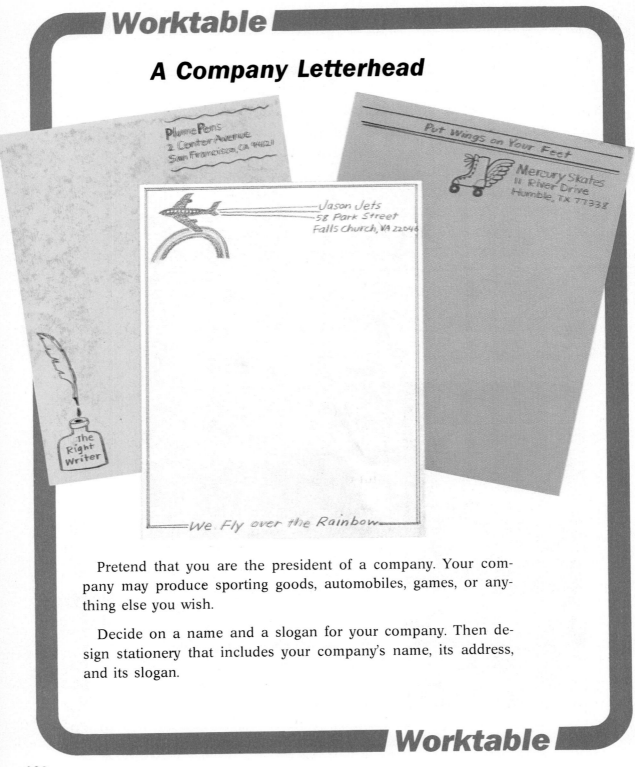

Pretend that you are the president of a company. Your company may produce sporting goods, automobiles, games, or anything else you wish.

Decide on a name and a slogan for your company. Then design stationery that includes your company's name, its address, and its slogan.

Building Bridges

Health

Letter writing can help you learn more about health. You can write to private or government agencies and request up-to-date information about a health topic.

▶ Try it. Write a business letter requesting information about a health topic that interests you. Here are a few suggestions.

● Write to a United States government agency. You might write to the President's Council on Physical Fitness and Sports. Or you might write to the National Clearinghouse on Drug Abuse for information about drug abuse problems. Your librarian can help you find the addresses of these agencies.

● Write to: Superintendent of Documents
Government Printing Office
Washington, DC 20402

Ask to be sent the latest issue of *U.S. Government Books*. This publication lists new booklets printed by the government on all kinds of topics. Some of the booklets are free; others are inexpensive.

● If your local newspaper has a health column, write to the columnist. Ask a specific health question.

Speakers at Work Doctors, nurses, and other health experts are concerned with physical fitness. They often try to persuade people to practice good health habits, eat well, and exercise to stay fit.

▶ Try it. Prepare a short talk to convince students your age that exercise is important for good health. You might suggest some specific exercises, games, and sports that would improve a person's physical fitness.

Building Bridges

161

Pronouns   *pages 130–139*

A. Write the pronoun in each sentence. Then write whether it is a *subject pronoun* or an *object pronoun*.

1. We spotted a beaver down by the pond.
2. Joel's loud voice frightened it away.
3. A large bullfrog sang us some croaking notes.
4. He sat on a log near the bank.
5. Lynda showed me two turtles in the mud.
6. They slowly crawled towards the water's edge.
7. In the tall grass I found four white eggs.
8. Carl wisely left them alone.
9. Three wild ducks allowed him to walk near.
10. You should come visit the pond sometime.

B. Write each sentence. Use the pronoun in parentheses (   ) that correctly completes the sentence.

11. I left (my, mine) records at Miguel's house.
12. Please turn off the light over (your, yours) desk.
13. Which two picnic baskets are (their, theirs)?
14. (Our, Ours) house is the last building on this street.
15. The bicycle with the flat tire is (her, hers).
16. My sister and (I, me) planned a surprise party.
17. Will Mrs. Rafael take (we, us) to the drive-in movie?
18. (She, Her) and Katrina started a baby-sitting service.
19. The dog brought (he, him) a chewed-up slipper.
20. (I and Tim, Tim and I) have been pen pals for two years.

Contractions   *pages 140–141*

C. Write the contraction for each pair of words.

21. I am
22. you will
23. she would
24. it has
25. they are
26. we have

Homophones   *pages 142–143*

D. Write each sentence. Use the homophone in parentheses ( )
that correctly completes the sentence.

27. Use (plain, plane) white cloth for the ship's (sale, sail).
28. (Its, It's) easy to finish this project in one (our, hour).
29. (They're, Their) going to (need, knead) funny costumes.
30. Did (you're, your) uncle (meet, meat) the Allens at
the grocery store?

Letters   *pages 152–155*

E. Write these items as if they were parts of friendly or business
letters. Punctuate and capitalize them correctly.

31. dear becky
32. your friend
33. october 7 1986
34. dairy foods company
35. sincerely yours
36. new york ny 10011
37. 312 south main street
38. dear sir or madam

Fact and Opinion   *pages 148–149*

F. Write *fact* or *opinion* for each statement.

39. Football is more fun to play than soccer.
40. Hal's Hardware Store has a supply of screens and
windows.
41. Center Street is the prettiest road in Lakeville.
42. My brothers are extremely talented and clever.
43. More than one billion people live in China.

G. Write an opinion that goes with each fact below.

44. Steaks can be broiled over charcoal.
45. Slip-on shoes do not have laces.

See also Handbook pages 344–349, 369–370, 382, 385.

Sentences *pages 4–17*

A. Write each declarative, interrogative, imperative, or exclamatory sentence. Begin each sentence correctly. Use correct punctuation at the end.

1. what a glorious day
2. do you have another pencil
3. bring a jacket with you
4. the school bell is ringing
5. where is the bus stop
6. how fast we ran
7. my new umbrella broke
8. fill the fish tank

B. Write each sentence. Underline the complete subject once. Underline the complete predicate twice.

9. Baby penguins are very funny birds.
10. Heather enjoys her dance lessons.
11. Seven students did experiments at the table.
12. A flash of lightning lit up the sky.
13. My father's cousin will visit me in June.
14. An elephant marched at the front of the parade.

C. Write the simple subject of each sentence. Write (*You*) if the subject is understood.

15. Jim plays soccer with us.
16. Put these clothes in the laundry basket.
17. Flocks of birds are flying south for the winter.
18. Make a map of your neighborhood.

D. Write the simple predicate of each sentence.

19. Mary had visited the Millers tonight.
20. My grandmother collects old magazines.
21. The stray dog has followed Lucy to her house.
22. Daniel is building a tree house in his yard.
23. A cool breeze blows through the leaves.

Nouns   *pages 48–53*

E. Write the plural form of each noun.

24. campfire
27. crocodile
30. eagle
25. wolf
28. life
31. chimney
26. church
29. cherry
32. story

F. Write *common* or *proper* for each noun.

33. Silver Lake
35. clock
37. America
34. daisy
36. Kansas
38. astronaut

Capital Letters and Periods   *pages 52–57*

G. Write each sentence. Capitalize the proper nouns.

39. Our class visited boston, massachusetts.
40. The freedom trail was an interesting place.
41. A guide showed us the home of paul revere.
42. We climbed the steps of the bunker hill monument.
43. The new england aquarium was our final destination.

H. Write each sentence. Abbreviate the underlined words.

44. Is Santa Cruz <u>Drive</u> a busy street?
45. <u>Mister</u> Levy is a police officer.
46. Sandy has soccer practice <u>Thursday</u> afternoon.
47. Jane moved to Harrison <u>Avenue</u> last month.
48. I will see the dentist on <u>November</u> 4.

Apostrophes   *pages 58–59*

I. Write the possessive form of each noun.

49. Gus
51. windows
53. ladies
50. year
52. dictionary
54. statue

Verbs *pages 88–107*

J. Write the verb from each sentence. Then write whether it is an *action verb* or a *linking verb*.

55. Matt climbed the ladder.

56. Rob is my best friend.

57. The baby seems sleepy.

58. Jan plays the trumpet.

K. Write each sentence. Draw one line under the main verb. Draw two lines under the helping verb.

59. Abe was looking for us.

60. We will mail this package.

61. She has locked the door.

62. The telephone is ringing.

L. Write the direct object of each sentence. Then write *what* or *whom* to show what question the direct object answers.

63. Denise reads the newspaper every day.

64. Mickey will ask Nathan for help.

65. Leon followed the path through the woods.

66. I invited six friends to my party.

M. Write the verb in each sentence. Then write *present, past,* or *future* to show what tense it is in.

67. Glen entered his drawing in the art contest.

68. My sister studies at the library.

69. Ned described his adventure to us.

70. Anna will attend the meeting this afternoon.

N. Write the past-tense form of each verb.

71. carry

72. slip

73. ring

74. freeze

75. wear

76. cover

77. take

78. bring

79. see

O. Write the verb in parentheses ( ) that correctly completes each sentence.

80. (Can, May) I borrow your skateboard?

81. Ann and Jo always (sit, set) in the back row.

82. Please (sit, set) the trunk down here.

83. (Can, May) you climb over this fence?

Pronouns *pages 128–139*

P. Write the pronoun in each sentence. Then write whether it is a *subject pronoun* or an *object pronoun*.

84. They took Sue's puppy to the veterinarian's office.

85. Andy gave her a tour of the city.

86. Linda's mother will drive us to the concert.

87. In Texas I visited some oil fields.

Q. Write each sentence. Use the pronoun in parentheses ( ) that correctly completes the sentence.

88. (We, Us) camped in the Rocky Mountains.

89. Darlene and (I, me) collect insects.

90. Did (they, them) enjoy the class field trip?

91. Look for (he, him) in the library.

R. Write each sentence. Underline the possessive pronoun.

92. These skates are hers.

93. Write to your pen pal.

94. I saw their apartment.

95. The cat licked its paw.

Contractions *pages 140–141*

S. Write the contraction for each pair of words.

96. we are

97. I shall

98. you will

99. he is

100. she would

101. they will

Grammar
Adjectives

Composition
Describing

Abraham Lincoln

Remember he was poor and country bred;
  His face was lined; he walked with awkward gait.
Smart people laughed at him sometimes and said,
  "How can so very plain a man be great?"

Remember he was humble, used to toil.
  Strong arms he had to build a shack, a fence,
Long legs to tramp the woods, to plow the soil,
  A head chuck full of backwoods common sense.

Remember all he ever had he earned.
  He walked in time through stately White House doors;
But all he knew of men and life he learned
  In little backwoods cabins, country stores.

Remember that his eyes could light with fun;
  That wisdom, courage, set his name apart;
But when the rest is duly said and done,
  Remember that men loved him for his heart.

—*Mildred Plew Meigs*

1 Adjectives

- An **adjective** describes a noun or pronoun.

An adjective tells something about a noun or pronoun. It can answer the question *how many* or *what kind*. Read the paragraph below. Some of the adjectives are shown in red, some are shown in blue, and some are underlined.

North Carolina is a southern state with fertile farms, thick forests, a long coastline, and many industries. Two products are furniture and cloth. The wooden furniture in many homes in the United States is from North Carolina. Textile production is an important industry, too. North Carolina leads all states and most countries in textile manufacturing.

The adjectives that tell *what kind* are in red. For example, *southern* describes the noun *state*, and *wooden* describes the noun *furniture*.

The adjectives that tell *how many* are in blue. *Two* describes the noun *products*, and *most* describes *countries*.

The words *a, an,* and *the* are underlined. *A, an,* and *the* are a special kind of adjective. They are called **articles.** Notice that *a* is used before a word that begins with a consonant sound. *An* is used before a word that begins with a vowel sound.

Skills Tryout

Name the adjectives in these sentences. Include articles.

1. Many people visit the historic sites in North Carolina.
2. The tourists enjoy the old mansions and villages.
3. One village is in an old section of Winston-Salem.
4. The colonial buildings and early clothing attract sightseers.
5. Some buildings are from 1766 and have interesting styles.

Practice

A. Write the adjectives in each sentence. Include articles.

1. A popular event in North Carolina is a historical play.
2. For two months in summer, the exciting drama is performed before a large audience.
3. It is staged at an old fort where early colonists lived.
4. The play shows the hard life the colonial settlers led.
5. The story tells about a lost colony and a strange word.
6. The colony was founded on an island called Roanoke thirty-three years before the Pilgrims landed.
7. Three years later all trace of the colonists was gone.
8. Some people searched for the lost colonists.
9. One word, *Croatoan*, was carved on a big post.
10. The mysterious disappearance has never been explained.

B. Write each sentence. Use *a* or *an* to complete it.

11. Pamela made _____ visit to Tryon Palace in New Bern.
12. It is _____ old North Carolina mansion.
13. The mansion was built by _____ colonial governor.
14. In 1774 _____ American revolutionary group met there.
15. The patriots made _____ pact against the British there.

C. Write each sentence. Underline the adjectives that tell *what kind* once. Underline the adjectives that tell *how many* twice. Do not include articles.

16. North Carolina's lovely capital, Raleigh, is an old city.
17. The original capitol was the big palace in New Bern.
18. The state flag has three colors and two dates.
19. Both dates stand for early Declarations of Independence.
20. It is a large state with a hundred counties.

Application WRITING SENTENCES

Write five sentences about the history of your state. In each sentence use an adjective that tells *what kind* or *how many*.

2 Adjectives Following Linking Verbs

- An adjective that follows a linking verb describes the subject of a sentence.

You know that adjectives often come before the nouns that they describe.

The new country chose Washington as President.

Adjectives can also follow the nouns or pronouns they describe. Look at the sentences below.

Washington was famous before the American Revolution.

The people felt secure with him as the President.

They were wise in their choice of a leader.

The adjectives *famous*, *secure*, and *wise* are predicate adjectives. A predicate adjective describes the subject of the sentence. The subject can be a noun like *Washington* or *people*. The subject can also be a pronoun like *they*.

A linking verb connects a predicate adjective with the subject. Remember the linking verbs that are forms of the verb *be*: *am*, *is*, *are*, *was*, and *were*. Some other linking verbs are *seem*, *look*, *feel*, *taste*, and *smell*.

Skills Tryout

Name the predicate adjective in each sentence. Tell which noun or pronoun in the subject each adjective describes.

1. George Washington was successful at farming.
2. For a long while he was loyal to Great Britain.
3. Great Britain was harsh toward its colonies.
4. Then war seemed unavoidable.
5. The colonies were ready to fight for freedom.
6. They felt prepared for war.

Practice

A. Write each sentence. Underline the predicate adjective once. Underline twice the noun or pronoun it describes.

EXAMPLE: That cherry pie smells wonderful!
ANSWER: That cherry pie smells wonderful!

1. George Washington is famous for his honesty.
2. According to legend, he was careless cutting trees.
3. Young George was guilty of ruining the cherry tree.
4. His father probably looked angry.
5. However, Washington was honest about his mistake.
6. George Washington was brave, too.
7. During the long winters of the war, he seemed fearless.
8. He was sensitive to the hardships of the soldiers.
9. They were ready to follow him anywhere.
10. Later Washington was also effective as President.

B. Write sentences from each of the following pairs of adjectives and nouns. Use a linking verb, and use the adjective as a predicate adjective.

EXAMPLE: brave soldiers
ANSWER: The soldiers were brave.

11. brilliant Thomas Jefferson
12. industrious John Adams
13. angry taxpayers
14. endless war
15. short supplies
16. weary colonists
17. delicious food
18. acceptable peace
19. independent country
20. happy people

Application WRITING SENTENCES

Write six sentences about America or Americans. Use the adjectives below as predicate adjectives following linking verbs.

busy   colorful   friendly   great   new   old

3 — Adjectives That Compare

- Use the *-er* form of an adjective to compare two persons, places, or things.
- Use the *-est* form of an adjective to compare three or more persons, places, or things.

Adjectives describe nouns. One way they can describe is by comparing persons, places, or things. When two nouns are compared, the *-er* form of the adjective is used. In the sentence below, two towers are compared.

One tower is <u>higher</u> than the other.

When three or more nouns are compared, the *-est* form of the adjective is used. In the sentence below, one tower is compared with all the towers in a group.

This tower is the <u>highest</u> of all.

Sometimes the spelling of an adjective must be changed when *-er* or *-est* is added.

Drop final <u>e</u>:	brav<u>e</u>	brav<u>er</u>	brav<u>est</u>
Change final <u>y</u> to <u>i</u>:	happ<u>y</u>	happ<u>ier</u>	happ<u>iest</u>
Double final consonant:	wet	wet<u>ter</u>	wet<u>test</u>

Skills Tryout

Tell which word in parentheses ( ) correctly completes each sentence.

1. A duck egg is (smaller, smallest) than an ostrich egg.
2. A hummingbird egg is the (smaller, smallest) of all.
3. A giraffe is the (taller, tallest) animal in the world.
4. It is even (taller, tallest) than an elephant.
5. Is that the (bigger, biggest) animal you can think of?

Practice

A. Write each sentence. Use the form of the adjective shown in parentheses ( ).

1. The (early + -est) bridges were fallen trees.
2. (Late + -er) bridges were copies of this design.
3. (Flat + -er) pieces of wood were laid across streams.
4. In the (wet + -er) weather they were washed away.
5. People looked for ways to cross (wide + -er) rivers.
6. Bridge builders started using (heavy + -er) materials.
7. A special design was used for the (large + -est) bridge.
8. A bridge crosses Australia's (busy + -est) harbor.
9. Some modern bridges look like (early + -er) designs.
10. The (late + -est) idea is to make bridges of concrete.

B. Write each sentence. Use the correct form of the adjective in parentheses ( ).

11. Bly is a (short) name than Donovan.
12. O is the (short) name in the world.
13. This tiger is the (big) cat in the zoo.
14. This leopard is (small) than that tiger.
15. The (long) worm of all is the bootlace worm.
16. It is (long) than 150 feet.
17. The cheetah is the (fast) animal on land.
18. The sailfish is even (fast) than the cheetah.
19. Is Mount Everest (high) than Mount McKinley?
20. Yes, it is the (high) mountain in the world.

Application WRITING SENTENCES

Have you ever stopped to think about how many kinds of animals there are? Think of the ways they differ—in how they look, where they live, and how they act. Write six sentences. Compare two or more animals in each one. Remember to use the *-er* or *-est* form of the adjective.

4 — Using *more* and *most* with Adjectives

> ● The words *more* and *most* are often used with adjectives of two or more syllables to make comparisons.

Some adjectives do not use the *-er* or *-est* form to compare.

One syllable:	stronger	strongest
Two or more syllables:	more splendid	most splendid

Many adjectives of two or more syllables use *more* and *most* to make comparisons. *More* is used with an adjective to compare two persons, places, or things. *Most* is used with an adjective to compare three or more persons, places, or things.

> This is a <u>more</u> <u>interesting</u> track meet than last week's.
> Today's meet is the <u>most</u> <u>important</u> event of the year!

Never use *more* before the *-er* form of an adjective.

> **Wrong:** Deron is more faster than you.
> **Right:** Deron is faster than you.

Never use *most* before the *-est* form of an adjective.

> **Wrong:** Alicia is the most smartest person I know.
> **Right:** Alicia is the smartest person I know.

Notice how the adjectives *good* and *bad* show comparison.

a <u>good</u> jump	a <u>better</u> jump	the <u>best</u> jump
a <u>bad</u> fall	a <u>worse</u> fall	the <u>worst</u> fall

Skills Tryout

For each adjective below, name the two forms used to compare persons, places, or things.

1. long　　**2.** admirable　　**3.** bad　　**4.** serious　　**5.** polite

Practice

A. Write each sentence. Use the correct form of the adjective in parentheses ( ).

1. These track shoes are (comfortable) than those.
2. The bar on the high jump is (low) now than it was before.
3. Pam is the (dependable) runner we have.
4. I'm (breathless) after running than after swimming.
5. Jim is a (careful) runner than Jake.
6. Nikki gave the (impressive) performance of her career.
7. That high jumper was (nervous) than Nikki was.
8. Pole-vaulting is the (hard) event of the whole meet.
9. Our team looked (cheerful) than their team.
10. Tripping was the (awkward) way to start.
11. Ours was the (high) score of the entire season.
12. The high jump was the (difficult) event of all.
13. The floor here is (slippery) than in our gym.
14. A good warm-up is the (helpful) way to prepare.
15. The coach's advice is (sensible) than Joe's.

B. Write the sentences. Use the correct form of *good* or *bad* to complete each sentence.

16. This is the (good) score Martin ever had.
17. Last season was (bad) than this one for us.
18. This year we have done (good) than Hill School.
19. Our (bad) event is the broad jump.
20. Next year we plan to have an even (good) team than we have this year.

Application WRITING SENTENCES

Write five sentences that compare people, places, or things. Use a form of one of these adjectives in each sentence.

good   bad   colorful   curious   beautiful

5 Using Commas in a Series

- Use a comma to separate words in a series.

I've never eaten salad corn.

We have salad corn and beans today.

Something is missing from the note on the chalkboard. Read the corrected note below. How has it been changed?

We have salad, corn, and beans today.

A comma (,) tells a reader to pause. This makes the meaning of a sentence clearer. The sentences below show how to use commas to separate words in a series. A series is made up of three or more items. The word *and* or *or* may come before the last word in a series. Note that no comma is used after the last item in a series.

Maria is <u>owner</u>, <u>cook</u>, and <u>dishwasher</u>.
She <u>fries</u>, <u>broils</u>, <u>steams</u>, or <u>bakes</u> fish.
<u>Hungry</u>, <u>thirsty</u>, and <u>tired</u> people eat here.

Skills Tryout

Tell where to add commas in the sentences below.

1. The tablecloths are red white and blue.
2. Ham beans salad and rice would make a good dinner.
3. You may drink cider milk or juice.
4. Who will buy clean chop and toss the vegetables?
5. A colorful healthful and delicious salad will be served.

Practice

A. Write the sentences. Add commas where they are needed.

1. The pictures on the menu are big bright and appealing.
2. What kinds of soups drinks and desserts do you have?
3. Try our fine fresh and tasty bread.
4. Maria mixes kneads and rolls her own biscuits.
5. Is this pie filled with custard apples or peaches?
6. We bake cool and slice our own pies.
7. Do you serve appetizers salads and casseroles?
8. Each day Dom orders eats and enjoys his breakfast.
9. The warm crisp and buttery toast smells wonderful.
10. Beans tortillas or tacos often appear on the menu.

B. Complete each sentence by adding two or more words to form a series. Add commas and the word *and*.

EXAMPLE: Are beef _____ your favorite meats?

ANSWER: Are beef, pork, and veal your favorite meats?

11. We have vanilla _____ yogurt.
12. Maria's helper Chuck stacks _____ the dishes.
13. Officer Hanlon always has soup _____ for lunch.
14. Be sure to put silverware _____ on the table.
15. Bacon _____ will be served for breakfast.

Application FILLING OUT FORMS

Copy the form below. It is a survey, or questionnaire. Use at least three words in a series for each item below your name.

SURVEY SHEET

Name: _____ Age: _____ Date: _____
Favorite colors: _____
Least favorite colors: _____
Hobbies that interest me: _____
Favorite sports: _____
Favorite animals: _____

6 — Adjective Suffixes

- A **suffix** is a letter or letters added to the end of a word.

You know that the meaning of a word can be changed by adding a prefix; for example, *agree* and *disagree*. The meaning of a word can also be changed if a suffix is added. The letters *-ful* in the word *careful* are a suffix. They add the meaning "full of" to the word *care*.

Remember that a base word is the simplest form of a word. Many adjectives are formed by adding a suffix to a base word. Here are some common suffixes and their meanings.

Suffix	Meaning	Example
-able	worthy of, able to be	honorable, breakable
-ful	full of, having qualities of	joyful, graceful
-less	without	tasteless
-y	having, being like	curly, bossy

Skills Tryout

Name the word in each sentence that ends with an adjective suffix. Then name the suffix.

1. Abraham Lincoln was a remarkable person.
2. He grew up in a chilly log cabin.
3. He used his sleepless nights for studying.
4. His great height made him noticeable.
5. This thoughtful boy later became President.

Practice

A. Write the sentences. Add one of the suffixes below to the word in parentheses ( ) to complete each sentence.

-able   -ful   -less   -y

1. Lincoln's early years were not always (comfort).
2. He slept on a (lump) mattress filled with cornhusks.
3. The walk to school was long and (dust).
4. He was usually a (play) young man.
5. His sense of humor made life more (agree).
6. He was (skill) with an ax and other tools.
7. Although he was shy, he was never (friend).
8. No one seemed to mind the rumpled and (care) appearance of his clothes.
9. Lincoln was (thank) for the books people loaned him.
10. Eager for city life, he grew (rest) on the farm.

B. Write a word for each definition. Use the suffixes and base words below to form the words.

Suffixes: -able   -ful   -less   -y
Base Words: box   depend   fear   hill
                    harm   respect   luck   manage

11. without fear
12. being like a box
13. able to be managed
14. full of fear
15. being like a slope

16. worthy of respect
17. without causing damage
18. having good fortune
19. able to be relied on
20. full of injury

Application USING LANGUAGE

Write a list of words that have suffixes. Include at least four words that end with each suffix below. Try to list words that were not used in this lesson.

-able   -ful   -less   -y

Adjectives   *pages 170–171*

A. Write the adjectives in each sentence. Include articles.

1. Joshua bought thick red paper for valentines.
2. Gemma made some lace from a white doily.
3. In two days the class would have a contest.
4. After six hours of hard work, Joshua finished.
5. There were pretty valentines and funny valentines.
6. Ms. Bolting opened the long envelope.
7. The pink and green valentine won a prize.
8. A huge blue heart with silver sprinkles won, too.
9. The grand prize went to Gemma and Joshua.
10. They took the two ceramic mugs home.

Adjectives Following Linking Verbs   *pages 172–173*

B. Write each sentence. Underline the predicate adjective.

11. Most people feel happy in the sunshine.
12. A warm day is comfortable.
13. Lightweight clothing is cool.
14. Barbecued chicken tastes terrific!
15. Of all the fruits, watermelon is the juiciest.

Adjectives That Compare   *pages 174–175*

C. Write each sentence. Use the correct form of the adjective in parentheses ( ).

16. That is the (dirty) puppy I've ever seen!
17. She is also the (frisky) one of the lot.
18. She's certainly the (cute) puppy here.
19. The spaniel is (calm) than the others.
20. He seems (sleepy) than the rest.

Grammar Review

Using more and most with Adjectives (pages 176–177)

D. For each adjective below, write the two forms used to compare persons, places, or things.

21. good **23.** bashful **25.** painful **27.** helpful **29.** slow
22. silly **24.** polite **26.** slippery **28.** unsure **30.** bad

Commas in a Series pages 178–179

E. Write each sentence. Add commas where they are needed.

31. George will bring bread butter and catsup.
32. Sausage hamburgers and chicken are on the menu.
33. Do you want lemonade punch or juice?
34. Everyone will help cook serve and clean up.
35. After dinner you can hike sleep or read.

Adjective Suffixes pages 180–181

F. Write the sentences. Add the suffix *-able, -ful, -less,* or *-y* to the word in parentheses ( ).

36. Is this seat (adjust)?
37. A (mist) fog rolled in.
38. Be (care) not to trip.
39. Running so fast made him (breath).
40. What a (dust) room this is!
41. A hammer is a (help) tool.
42. My dog's behavior is (predict).
43. This (noise) fan will not disturb your sleep.
44. Your rose garden is very (color).
45. An octopus escapes its enemies by squirting a black (ink) liquid in their faces.

See also Handbook pages 350–353, 382–385.

Grammar Review

Writing with Adjectives

Grammar and Writing Workshop

- Use adjectives to add detail to your writing.

Read the following sentences.

1. A noise awoke me from a dream.
2. A sudden noise awoke me from a scary dream.

The two sentences are similar, but sentence 2 gives more information. Sentence 1 gives the facts, but sentence 2 includes interesting details. An adjective describes each noun in sentence 2. We learn that the noise was *sudden* and that the dream was *scary*.

Adjectives can help to make your writing colorful and interesting. When nouns alone don't tell enough, use adjectives to add details!

The Adjective Game Choose a noun from the list below and write it. Think of adjectives that might describe the noun in a sentence. See how many adjectives you can write for your noun in two minutes.

cat	mountain	shoes
story	automobile	guitarist
horse	music	river

How many adjectives did you write? Find a classmate who chose the same noun. Did he or she think of any adjectives that are not on your list? Do you have any that are not on your classmate's list?

Choose a different noun and start again. You might form teams with one or more of your classmates.

Add-an-Adjective Read each sentence below. Think of adjectives that could describe the underlined noun. Then write the sentence twice, adding a different adjective each time.

EXAMPLE: The poodle trotted along the beach.
ANSWER: The poodle trotted along the sandy beach.
The poodle trotted along the crowded beach.

1. The band played a song.
2. The passengers waited for their luggage.
3. I took a swim just before dinner.
4. Douglas and I explored a house in our town.
5. Take that bicycle and put it in the garage.
6. We saw photographs of some machines.
7. The bird perched on the railing of the porch.

No-Clue Time Now add adjectives to sentences without using clues. Find two nouns in each sentence below. Think of an adjective that describes each noun. Write the sentence, adding two adjectives—one before each noun.

8. The cat sat on the fence.
9. The forest has secrets.
10. I have some ideas for the show.
11. The sweater is in the drawer.
12. These shelves can't hold so many books.
13. The chimp held the banana.
14. Do you have the tools to make this repair?

Using the Thesaurus

Some writers use the adjective *nice* too often. Write five sentences about an enjoyable day at the park, but don't use the word *nice*. Find five synonyms for *nice* in the Thesaurus. Use a different synonym in each sentence.

7 Reading Descriptions

- Writers use details to create clear descriptions.

Descriptions are word pictures. They help a reader picture what a writer has in mind. Writers create clear descriptions by using details. They use words that tell how something looks, smells, sounds, tastes, or feels.

Read these descriptions from the book *Secret of the Andes* by Ann Nolan Clark. In this story a boy and an old Indian live alone high in the Andes. Notice how the author uses details to help the reader picture this faraway place.

1. They lived in a hidden valley high up on the rock slope of a mountain. Mountain peak upon mountain peak, sheer and hard and glistening in frozen mantles of ice and snow, encircled them.

2. Morning clouds softened the tips of the mountain peaks. Here and there the cloud mists parted. Then patches of blue sky could be seen, and snow peaks, sharp and pointed and sparkling against the blue.

3. Hundreds of llamas were munching the moss-green ychu grass that covered the floor of the highland valley. They made spots of golden yellow against the soft green of the ychu and the glaring white of the glacier snow fields.

4. He saw the burned tree that lightning had struck, standing black and bold, a lone sentinel*. He crossed the trickling stream that bubbled along to join the mighty river. Everything was hot and still. The shadows had folded themselves beneath the trees and the shrubbery. The Great Sun was in mid-sky, looking down on the boy and the llamas.

*sentinel   A soldier or other person standing guard.

About the Descriptions

1. In description 1 what words help you see the mountains?
2. What words help you feel the mountains?
3. What does the first sentence in description 2 mean? How can clouds *soften* mountain peaks?
4. What words bring the peaks not hidden by the clouds into clear focus?
5. In description 3 what words describe or name colors?
6. How can you tell the scene is viewed from a distance?
7. In description 4 what does the burned tree look like?
8. What does the sun do that makes it seem human?

Activities

Write a paragraph that describes the tree in this photograph. Use details that tell about its color and size. Tell what it feels like when you touch it. Think of how it might move in the wind. Then give it a human action. For example, you might say it *groans* in the wind. Your paragraph should create a mental picture of the tree for whoever reads it.

8 Choosing Descriptive Details

- Writers choose descriptive details that work together to support a main idea.

Description starts with observation. You look. You notice details that make your subject unique—unlike any other of its kind. You may also need to listen or touch or smell or taste. When you have finished observing, you will probably have many details. You will want to keep some and discard others. Here are two methods writers use to sort out details. Each of these methods helps to organize a clear description.

Method 1

Choose one adjective that sums up your impression of what you are describing. Use that adjective in a topic sentence.

The kitchen was <u>cheerful</u>.

Select details that support the topic sentence.

The kitchen was cheerful. Its walls were painted a sunny yellow. A copper teakettle whistled merrily on the stove. The warm aroma of freshly baked bread lifted my spirits. I felt pleasantly contented.

Method 2

Choose one of the senses: seeing, hearing, tasting, smelling, or touching. Select details related to that sense. For example, George Selden focuses on hearing in this paragraph. It describes the sound of a single cricket in New York City.

It was like a quick stroke across the strings of a violin, or like a harp that had been plucked suddenly. If a leaf in a green forest far from New York had fallen at midnight through the darkness into a thicket, it might have sounded like that.

—*The Cricket in Times Square*

Skills Tryout

Answer these questions about the example paragraphs on page 188.

1. In the paragraph about the kitchen, what details tell what the kitchen looked like?
2. What kitchen sound was described?
3. What kitchen smell was described?
4. In the paragraph about the cricket, the sound of the cricket is compared to three sounds. What are they?

Practice

A. Read the topic sentence below. Then read sentences 1–5. Write *yes* if a sentence gives a detail that supports the topic sentence. Write *no* if it does not.

TOPIC SENTENCE: The playground is deserted.

1. The empty swings move slightly in the breeze.
2. A pair of chattering squirrels scamper up a tree.
3. A baseball mitt lies forgotten on a park bench.
4. There is a faint smell of burning leaves in the air.
5. Scraps of paper blow across the lonely baseball diamond.

B. Write a detail sentence for each topic sentence.

6. The faded photograph was fascinating.
7. In winter the beach is lonely.
8. Autumn has its special sounds.
9. Inside the chest was a dazzling array of gems!
10. The granite walls of the castle looked forbidding.

Application WRITING A PARAGRAPH

Write a paragraph about one of these topics. Use descriptive details in your paragraph.

a. morning sounds
b. an object in your classroom
c. a favorite possession
d. a mysterious place

9 — Using Space Order

> ● **Space order** is one way to arrange details in a paragraph.

You know that when you write a sentence, you write the words in an order that makes sense. In a similar way, when you write a paragraph, you need to list the details in an order that makes sense. There are a number of ways to do this. One way is to list details in space order.

Space order means "the way things are arranged in space." For example, picture a row of books on a shelf. You might describe the books in a left-to-right order. That is probably the order in which you would notice them. Here is a paragraph that describes a famous statue. The details are arranged in top-to-bottom order—from the headdress to the beard.

The colossal Sphinx has the body of a lion and the face of a man. The face is believed to be a likeness of an Egyptian king. At the top of the head, part of the royal headdress is gone. Gone, too, are the six-foot nose in the middle of the face and the eight-foot beard below. They were shot off long ago by soldiers who used the Sphinx for target practice.

Other examples of space order are front to back, near to far, bottom to top, and row by row. Some words and phrases that help to describe the location of things in space are listed below.

> across, opposite, in the center, on the left, on the right, behind, in back of, under, in front of, next to, above, below, farther away, closer, alongside of

Skills Tryout

Tell in what order you would arrange details describing the items below. Choose *top to bottom, bottom to top, left to right, near to far,* or *front to back*.

1. a totem pole
2. the cars in a train
3. a ski slope
4. trophies on a shelf
5. a highway disappearing into the distance

Practice

A. Write the topic sentence below. Under it write the five details in correct space order.

TOPIC SENTENCE: Five cars were parked in the driveway.

1. A 1984 station wagon was parked behind the taxicab.
2. A red convertible was parked at the head of the drive.
3. The black limousine was parked at the end of the drive.
4. In back of the convertible was a yellow taxicab.
5. An antique sedan was between the station wagon and a black limousine.

B. Write a paragraph describing this place setting. Try to include in your paragraph some words and phrases from the box on the opposite page.

Application WRITING A PARAGRAPH

Write a paragraph that describes where you sit in the classroom. Mention such details as who sits to the right of you, to the left of you, in front of you, in back of you, and so on. Also mention objects you sit near, such as a window, a closet, or a bulletin board. See how exactly you can describe the position you occupy in space.

10 — Writing a Descriptive Paragraph

Writing Project

- A **descriptive paragraph** paints a word picture of a person, a place, or a thing.

"A picture is worth a thousand words," says an old proverb. Have you ever thought that the reverse is also true? A description can help a reader "see" something the writer is telling about. In a description the writer uses words that create a picture in the reader's mind.

In this lesson you will draw a picture of a special place, and write a paragraph describing it. Then you and your classmates will make a travel book with your drawings and descriptions.

1. Prewriting

Look at the photograph. How would you describe this beach? First, name the things you see. They are the picture details.

ocean, sand, people, umbrellas

Next, describe each detail. Imagine what you would see, hear, feel, smell, or taste on this beach.

roaring, foamy, salty ocean
smooth, silky, warm sand
happy people laughing and shouting
bright, colorful umbrellas

It is easier for a reader to picture what you are describing when you compare it to something. What does this beach remind you of?

It is like a noisy, colorful parade.

▶ Think of some of your favorite places. They may be places near your home or far away. Look through magazines and books in your classroom to get three or four ideas. Read the ideas below. Then list your own ideas.

- a treehouse in the woods
- a busy street with shops and people
- an old barn
- a fishing pond
- a secret cave

Of the places you listed, circle the one you would most like to write about. Be sure it is a place you can describe well. This will be the topic for your paragraph.

▶ Draw a picture of the place you chose for your topic. If your idea came from a picture or photograph, make your own drawing. As you draw, try to imagine what you would see, hear, feel, smell, or taste.

2. Writing

Pretend you are in the place that you pictured. You want to write a note to a friend describing where you are. A good way to begin is to compare the place to something your friend knows. You might write, "The beach is like … ." Another way to begin is, "The beach reminds me of … ." The comparison will be your topic sentence. Read this topic sentence: "The beach is like a noisy, colorful parade."

▶ Write a topic sentence for your paragraph. Use the details from your picture to develop a description. Use colorful, varied adjectives that will help the reader form a mental picture of your place. Include all your ideas in your first draft. You will be able to check your writing and make changes later.

3. Revising

▶ Ask a classmate to work with you on revising your paragraph. Close your eyes and listen as the person reads your description. Are you able to form a mental picture from your description? Discuss the checklist questions with your classmate and think of ways to improve your paragraph.

Revision Checklist
- Did I write a topic sentence that compares a place to something my reader knows?
- Did I write details that tell about the place?
- Did I describe what I could see, hear, feel, smell, or taste?
- Did I use colorful, varied adjectives?
- Did I take out ideas that aren't related to my topic?

Read the sample and notice how it was improved by taking out ideas that aren't related to the topic.

> The beach is like a noisy,
> colorful ~~parad~~ *parade*. ~~I love the large~~
> ~~floats in a parade.~~ *Above the roar of the ocean,* You can
> hear the laughing sounds of
> people laughing and shouting, *but*
> ~~my sister does not like it when~~
> ~~it gets crowded.~~ Swimmers bob
> and dive in the *salty, foamy* water. Other

> *The beach is like a noisy, colorful parade. Above the roar of the ocean, you can hear the sounds of people laughing and shouting. Swimmers bob and dive in the salty, foamy water. Other people march along the warm, silky sand. The beach is dotted with bright umbrellas, like giant balloons floating in the crowd.*

EDITING MARKS

— cross out
∧ add
♂ move
≡ capital letter
/ small letter
¶ indent
◯ check spelling

▶ Revise your first draft, using the editing marks to make changes that will improve your paragraph.

4. Publishing

▶ Use the Proofreading Checklist in the Young Writer's Handbook on page 377 to check your paragraph. Make corrections, using the editing marks.

▶ Create a class travel book. Punch three holes in the sides of your drawing and description. Tie everyone's pages together with string or yarn. Use construction paper to make a cover for your book. Also, include a table of contents, listing each person's special place. Display your class travel book in the library for everyone to enjoy.

Writing Project

Detailed Drawings

Draw two very different pictures of the same scene or person. Use one basic sketch for both drawings, but change the details. Choose one of the ideas below, or use an idea of your own.

- A shoe on the day it was bought and after a year of wear
- Activities on a pond in Maine during October and during February
- A city street in the daytime and at night
- A person in street clothes and dressed for a party
- A cat when it's happy and when it's angry
- A park on a nice day and during a thunderstorm

Social Studies

As you did the lessons in this unit, you observed. You looked for details and used those details to write descriptions. As you observed closely, you probably saw details you had never noticed before.

Observing details is very important in social studies. If you know how to observe, you can "read" information in the pictures and photographs in your social studies book.

▶ Try it. "Read" this photograph. List five details you notice. Look for details that show what life was like in the past and how it was different from life in the present. Find details that tell about the life-style of the people in the photograph.

Writers at Work Archaeologists study the people, customs, and life of ancient times. They look at objects from the past. They describe them and try to figure out what their use was.

▶ Imagine you are an archaeologist in the future. Suppose you find a safety pin, a can opener, or some other object used in the twentieth century. Describe the object. Tell what you think its use was. (Perhaps you will invent a new use for the object!)

Adjectives   *pages 170–177*

A. Write each sentence. Underline the predicate adjective once. Underline twice the noun or pronoun it describes.

1. We felt exhausted after the twenty-mile canoe trip.
2. In the early morning those mountains look majestic.
3. Greg seems curious about the new student.
4. The garden was overgrown with weeds.

B. Write each sentence. Use the correct form of the adjective in parentheses ( ).

5. Cindy found the (tiny) seashell of all.
6. Kevin's watch seems (accurate) than mine.
7. Redwoods are the (tall) trees in North America.
8. The museum displayed its (valuable) painting.
9. My blouse was (expensive) than my skirt.
10. Is a cougar (fast) than a leopard?

Commas   *pages 178–179*

C. Write each sentence. Add commas where they are needed.

11. We went swimming on a hazy hot and humid day.
12. Boxes papers and books were piled high in the closet.
13. Jerry's job is to sort straighten and fold the laundry.
14. My dog can sit bark and heel on command.

Suffixes   *pages 180–181*

D. Read each definition. Then write a word that has the same meaning by adding the suffix *-able, -ful, -less,* or *-y* to the underlined word.

15. without <u>color</u>
16. having <u>health</u>
17. full of <u>doubt</u>
18. able to be <u>returned</u>

Describing   *pages 186–191*

E. Read the paragraph. Then write answers to the questions.

A cool wind rushed through the trees. Dry, brown leaves rustled and crackled. Two birds flitted lightly from branch to branch, chirping like crickets.

19. What words help you feel the wind?
20. What words describe the way the leaves look?
21. What are the birds doing that crickets do, too?

F. Read the topic sentence below. Then read sentences **22–25.** Write *yes* if a sentence gives a detail that supports the topic sentence. Write *no* if it does not.

The old, abandoned house seemed haunted.

22. The front stairs creaked in an eerie fashion.
23. The house stood next to the post office.
24. Strange shadows moved in the attic windows.
25. The house had a tall brick chimney.

G. Read the topic sentence below. Then write the four details in bottom-to-top space order.

TOPIC SENTENCE: Ten books sat on the library shelves.

Four math books were located above the dictionary.
A dictionary was on the bottom shelf.
Two green music books rested on the top shelf.
There were three spelling books above the math books.

H. Write the topic sentence below. Then write three sentences that add descriptive details.

A colorful butterfly fluttered in the warm breeze.

See also Handbook pages 350–353, 368, 382, 384.

Checkpoint: Unit 5

Grammar
Adverbs

Composition
Researching

Whistles

I never even hear
The boats that pass by day;
By night they seem so near,
A-whistling down the bay,
That I can almost understand
The things their whistles say.

I've waked sometimes all warm
In my bed, when eerily
I have heard them out of the dark
A-whistling cheerily
To tell the sleepy folk on land
All's well at sea.

—*Rachel Field*

1 Adverbs

- A word that describes a verb is an **adverb**.

You have learned that every sentence contains a verb, and that many verbs express action. Read the sentences below. The underlined words in the sentences are adverbs. Each of the adverbs describes a verb by telling *how, when,* or *where.*

The group accidentally found a cave. (found how?)

Marie entered the cave immediately. (entered when?)

They searched inside. (searched where?)

Here are some commonly used adverbs. Notice that adverbs often end in *-ly*, especially adverbs that tell *how.*

How?	slowly, carefully, gladly, quietly, well, fast
When?	often, lately, always, never, usually, now, today
Where?	here, there, everywhere, forward, outside, nearby

Skills Tryout

In the sentences below, the verbs are underlined. Name the adverbs that describe them.

1. The explorers quietly admired the cavern.
2. Outlaws sometimes hid in caves.
3. The tunnel sloped downward.
4. Tourists frequently visit Carlsbad Caverns.
5. Three children approached the cave cautiously.

Practice

A. In the sentences below, the verbs are underlined. Find the adverb in each sentence and write it.

1. Caves sometimes <u>contain</u> lakes.
2. Cave explorers <u>test</u> their equipment carefully.
3. Swarms of bats <u>flew</u> overhead.
4. Explorers ordinarily <u>carry</u> flashlight batteries.
5. She <u>marked</u> her trail clearly.
6. We <u>started</u> our journey early.
7. Water continually <u>follows</u> cracks in the rocks.
8. The water slowly <u>carves</u> the rock.
9. The cave's size always <u>amazes</u> tourists.
10. Beautiful rock formations <u>rise</u> upward.

B. Write each sentence and underline the adverb. Write *how*, *when*, or *where* to show what the adverb tells about the verb.

EXAMPLE: We never found the mysterious crystal cave.
ANSWER: We <u>never</u> found the mysterious crystal cave. (when)

11. Mike often brings a compass.
12. Alice studied the map closely.
13. The underground river flowed nearby.
14. He waited outside.
15. Our voices echoed strangely.
16. Cave explorers usually wear sturdy boots.
17. The walls of the cave plunged downward.
18. They gladly gave her a hand.
19. My favorite rock formation will appear soon.
20. We finally reached the end of the tunnel.

Application WRITING SENTENCES

Write five sentences about exploring. Use an action verb and one of the following adverbs in each sentence: *never, outside, quietly, secretly, today.*

2 Adverbs That Compare

- Adverbs have forms that are used to compare actions.

Adverbs can describe by making comparisons, just the way adjectives can. The *-er* form of an adverb is used to compare two actions. The *-est* form of an adverb is used to compare three or more actions.

Ed wakes early.
Ed wakes earlier than Don.
Ed wakes the earliest of all.

I walk fast.
I walk faster than you.
I walk the fastest of all.

Most adverbs use *more* and *most* to show comparison.

We climbed gradually at first.
We climbed more gradually the next day.
We climbed the most gradually at the end.

More and *most* are often used with adverbs that end in *-ly* and adverbs that have two or more syllables. Be careful not to use *more* with the *-er* form of an adverb or *most* with the *-est* form.

The adverbs *well* and *badly* have special forms that show comparison.

She swims well.
She swims better than you.
She swims the best of all.

I dive badly.
I dive worse than you.
I dive the worst of all.

Skills Tryout

For each adverb below, give the form that is used to compare two actions. Then give the form that is used to compare three or more actions.

1. often   2. well   3. densely   4. hard   5. neatly

Practice

A. Write the sentences. For each adverb in parentheses ( ), add *more* or use the *-er* form.

1. The Sacramento River flows (gently) in late spring.
2. The river valley opens (wide) between the Coast Ranges.
3. Flowers grow (thickly) during the rainy season.
4. The river overflows (frequently) in that season than now.
5. The valley turns green (soon) than the mountaintop.

B. Write each sentence. For each adverb in parentheses ( ), add *most* or use the *-est* form.

6. Trappers arrived (early) of all the explorers.
7. That area grew (fast) because gold was discovered there.
8. Which peak rises (high) in this range?
9. The mountains slope the (gradually) on the east side.
10. These are the (commonly) grown flowers in warm weather.

C. Write the sentences. Use the correct form of *well* or *badly* to complete each sentence.

11. This guide followed the trail (well) than that one.
12. Our party rode the (badly) of the three groups.
13. The horses managed (badly) than the mules on this trail.
14. We understood the map (well) than the scout did.
15. Who remembers this trip the (well) of all?

Application WRITING SENTENCES

Have you ever done the same outdoor activity in different seasons? Choose an activity. Write five sentences that compare how it differs in spring and winter. Use a form of one of these adverbs in each sentence.

clearly   easily   fast   hard   warmly

3 Adverbs Before Adjectives and Other Adverbs

- An adverb may describe a verb, an adjective, or another adverb.

You know that an adverb can describe a verb.

The Rocky Mountains rise majestically above the plain.

Adverbs can also describe adjectives or other adverbs by telling *to what extent*.

1. **The bighorn sheep is a very rare animal.**
2. **The sheep jumps so fast it is hard to see.**

Notice that in sentence **1** the underlined adverb *very* describes the adjective *rare*. In sentence **2** the underlined adverb *so* describes the adverb *fast*.

Here are some adverbs that are commonly used to describe adjectives and other adverbs.

rather	almost	very	quite
justly	fairly	totally	terribly
certainly	slightly	unusually	so
incredibly	remarkably	unbelievably	too

Skills Tryout

Name the adverb that describes each underlined adverb or adjective below.

1. The Rockies are incredibly <u>beautiful</u> mountains.
2. The temperature feels slightly <u>cooler</u> as you climb higher.
3. Even in early summer, snowstorms occur quite <u>suddenly</u>.
4. Unusually <u>cold</u> weather can be dangerous.
5. You can't be too <u>careful</u> in the mountains.

Practice

A. Write each sentence. Then write the adverb that describes the underlined adjective or adverb.

1. Idaho is justly <u>famous</u> for its sheep ranches.
2. Sheep are very <u>hardy</u> animals.
3. They can survive remarkably <u>cold</u> weather.
4. In summer the shepherds move their flocks rather <u>quickly</u>.
5. Fairly <u>often</u> they go from hot valleys to cool mountains.
6. These herders almost <u>always</u> use horses to move the sheep.
7. Cattle also graze in the unusually <u>lush</u> meadows.
8. Potato farms are certainly <u>common</u> in southern Idaho.
9. An incredibly <u>small</u> amount of the crop is eaten fresh.
10. Quite <u>often</u> the potatoes become frozen french fries.
11. Totally <u>vacant</u> towns dot the state's mining country.
12. Silver City was unbelievably <u>wealthy</u> at one time.
13. Now wind blows through the completely <u>empty</u> streets.
14. Skiing attracts a considerably <u>large</u> number of tourists.
15. Idahoans like their extremely <u>varied</u> way of life.

B. Write each sentence. Use the adverbs below to complete the sentences.

quite   so   too   terribly   wildly

16. Good weather is _____ important to a potato farmer.
17. _____ much rain in early spring can ruin the crop.
18. Tourism has become _____ successful in Idaho.
19. Rafting trips on the Snake River can be _____ exciting.
20. Stretches of _____ rolling white water are scary and fun.

Application WRITING SENTENCES

Write five sentences about your state. In your sentences use adverbs that describe adjectives and adverbs.

4 Using Adverbs and Adjectives

- Use adjectives to describe nouns and pronouns.
- Use adverbs to describe verbs, adjectives, and other adverbs.

In the sentences below, the underlined adjectives describe a noun and a pronoun. The adjective *hungry* describes the noun *gorilla,* and *remarkable* describes the pronoun *she.*

The gorilla feels hungry.   She is remarkable.

The adverbs below describe a verb, an adjective, and an adverb. *Hungrily* describes the verb *eats. Remarkably* describes the adjective *clever. Unusually* describes the adverb *fast.*

Koko eats the banana hungrily.   She is remarkably clever.

She learns unusually fast.

The words *good, bad,* and *well* may be used as adjectives. *Well* is an adjective when it means "healthy." The adjective *well* usually follows a linking verb such as *is, feel,* or *look.*

Koko ate a good meal.   She had felt bad.   Now she looks well.

Well and *badly* are often used as adverbs that tell *how.*

Koko behaves well.   Once in a while she behaves badly.

Skills Tryout

Tell which word correctly completes each sentence.

1. Koko's teacher is (extreme, extremely) patient.
2. Koko learns the language Ameslan (gradual, gradually).
3. Ameslan, or American Sign Language, is the hand speech (common, commonly) used by about 200,000 deaf Americans.
4. At first Koko made the signs (bad, badly).
5. Now she uses her fingers (good, well).

Practice

A. Write the word in parentheses ( ) that correctly completes each sentence.

1. Koko's fingers move (quick, quickly) to make the signs.
2. She is extremely (smart, smartly).
3. She (occasional, occasionally) signs two words at once.
4. Koko often is (playful, playfully).
5. Sometimes she gestures (angry, angrily).
6. She is distracted (fair, fairly) easily.
7. She cleans things with a (slight, slightly) damp sponge.
8. Afterwards she (usual, usually) rips up the sponge.
9. Koko has never seen a (real, really) alligator.
10. But toy alligators frighten her (terrible, terribly).
11. Koko likes sandwiches that are (thick, thickly).
12. She brushes her teeth (careful, carefully).
13. She often smiles (happy, happily) in the mirror.
14. The teacher is (proud, proudly) of Koko's success.
15. Koko refers to herself as a (fine, finely) gorilla.

B. Choose the word in parentheses ( ) that correctly completes each sentence. Write the sentence. Then write whether *good*, *well*, *bad*, or *badly* is an adjective or an adverb in the sentence.

EXAMPLE: Koko needs a (good, well) night's sleep.
ANSWER: Koko needs a good night's sleep. (adjective)

16. Koko stays (good, well) by getting plenty of sleep.
17. A substitute teacher does a (good, well) job.
18. Unfortunately Koko performs (bad, badly) for him.
19. They do not work (good, well) together.
20. The substitute teacher feels (bad, badly).

Application WRITING SENTENCES

Write five sentences about training an animal. Use adverbs and adjectives, including *good*, *bad*, *well*, and *badly*.

5 — Using Negative Words

> ● **Negative words** mean "no." Avoid using two negative words in the same sentence.

Mandy will <u>not</u> delay her science experiment.

"<u>No</u> extra equipment is needed," she said. "I've <u>never</u> done this before. It <u>doesn't</u> look hard, though."

The underlined words above are negatives. Negatives mean "no." Here is a list of some other common negatives.

nobody   nothing   no one   nowhere   none

Remember that a contraction is a shortened form of two words. The contractions listed below are negatives. Each is formed from a verb and *not*. The word *not* is an adverb.

isn't = is not   don't = do not   couldn't = could not
wasn't = was not   hasn't = has not   wouldn't = would not
doesn't = does not   haven't = have not   won't = will not

You need only one negative word to make a sentence negative. Avoid **double negatives**—two negatives in a sentence.

Wrong: In science Mandy doesn't never get lower than an A.

Right: In science Mandy never gets lower than an A.

Right: In science Mandy doesn't ever get lower than an A.

Skills Tryout

Name the negative word in each sentence. Tell which negatives are contractions.

1. Didn't anyone know what to do first?
2. Nobody answered Mandy's question.
3. She put salt in the water till no more dissolved.
4. Now she doesn't know where to put the container.
5. Nothing will happen unless she heats it up.

Practice

A. Write the sentences. Underline the negative words.

1. Couldn't anyone guess what would happen next?
2. We haven't seen anything in the glass.
3. Perhaps none of the water has evaporated.
4. Actually I have never seen crystals form.
5. You surely need no help with this!
6. Nobody could understand the directions.
7. Doesn't anyone know how to solve the problem?
8. No one can fold a piece of paper in this shape.
9. Hasn't anybody tried yet?
10. I could find nothing to use as a funnel.

B. Write the word in parentheses ( ) that correctly completes each sentence. Avoid double negatives.

11. There is no tubing here (nowhere, anywhere).
12. No one will (never, ever) be able to put this together.
13. There (was, wasn't) nowhere to work on my project.
14. Nothing (won't, will) happen if you change the water in the fish bowl.
15. Hasn't (no one, anyone) fed the fish yet?
16. None of this (isn't, is) visible without a microscope.
17. Couldn't (anyone, no one) see the blood vessels?
18. We haven't written down (any, none) of the steps.
19. We (won't, will) never be able to do this again.
20. There (was, wasn't) no need to check the results.

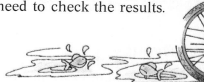

Application LISTENING

Listen to how negatives are used in the conversations of people around you and on television. Write five sentences you hear that contain negatives. If any of the sentences you hear contain double negatives, correctly rewrite them.

6 Compounds

- A **compound** is a word formed from two or more words.

Lucas and his family are on the way to the fair. They notice these words on the signs: *springtime*, *merry-go-round*, *hot dogs*, *homemade*, and *ice cream*. All of these words are compounds. Each one is made up of two or more words.

A compound may be written as one word, as separate words, or with a hyphen (-) or hyphens. Notice the examples below of the three kinds of compounds.

Ways to Form Compounds
One word: inside, suitcase, downtown, grandfather, weekday
Separate words: post office, city hall, no one, tape deck
Hyphen or hyphens: single-handed, four-sided, sister-in-law

Skills Tryout

Name the compound in each sentence.

1. Lucas, Ramona, and Miguel greet their grandmother.
2. All four of them live uptown.
3. They took a taxicab to the fair.
4. Ramona hopes to win a door prize.
5. Her brother-in-law made crafts for the fair.

Practice

A. Write the sentences. Underline the compounds.

1. The carnival was right near the high school.
2. Lucas could smell the sweet potatoes baking.
3. Mrs. Cortes bought lunch for her grandchildren.
4. Ramona and Miguel rode on the tilt-a-whirl.
5. It felt good to be outdoors in the warm sun.
6. The grass was turning green in the park playground.
7. The children rode through the fair on a fire truck.
8. The people smiled and gave the truck the right-of-way.
9. Ramona won a prize tossing beanbags.
10. After dinner the family had ice cream.

B. Match the words in column **A** with the words in column **B** to form compounds. Write each compound as one word.

A	B		A	B
11. day	paper		16. week	pole
12. news	bag		17. after	yard
13. hand	band		18. flag	fall
14. out	time		19. rain	end
15. head	side		20. back	noon

C. Use these ten words to write five compounds. The compounds will be written as separate words.

microwave	post	truck	tape	oven
tow	measure	officer	card	police

Application USING LANGUAGE

Write three compounds that begin with the word *side* and three compounds that begin with the word *up*. Then use each compound in a sentence.

Adverbs   *pages 202–203*

A. Write each adverb. Then write *how, when,* or *where* to show what the adverb tells about the verb.

1. Stella often swam in the pond.
2. Two raccoons washed their food carefully.
3. Stella watched quietly from the rocks.
4. She leaned forward when she heard the splash.
5. A beaver slapped its tail forcefully.
6. Mockingbirds and blackbirds sang everywhere.
7. The woods have been filled with wildlife lately.
8. Her camera was nearby.
9. She quickly took ten pictures.
10. After lunch she dozed peacefully on a rock.

Adverbs That Compare   *pages 204–205*

B. For each adverb write the two forms used to compare actions.

11. well   12. quickly   13. hard   14. badly   15. often

Adverbs Before Adjectives and Other Adverbs   *pages 206–207*

C. Write each sentence. Then write the adverb that describes the underlined adjective or adverb.

16. It has been unusually <u>wet</u> this spring.
17. I've never been so <u>cold</u>.
18. Last year the weather was quite <u>warm</u>.
19. We put away our winter clothes too <u>soon</u>.
20. I hope summer comes very <u>quickly</u>.

Using Adverbs and Adjectives *pages 208–209*

D. Write each sentence. Use the correct word in parentheses (   ).

21. Singing was (easy, easily) for Andrew.
22. Hours of practice help him sing (well, good).
23. Andrew is also a (good, well) pianist.
24. He (usual, usually) practices in the afternoon.
25. He never plays (bad, badly) at concerts.
26. Andrew enters contests (regular, regularly).
27. He (frequent, frequently) wins prizes.
28. Does he feel (bad, badly) when he loses?
29. One time he looked (sad, sadly).
30. Yet he (polite, politely) applauded the winner.

Using Negative Words *pages 210–211*

E. Write each sentence. Use the correct word in parentheses (   ).

31. Didn't (anybody, nobody) turn off the television set?
32. There are (never, ever) any light bulbs around.
33. Danny couldn't find (no, any) fuses.
34. No one can see (anything, nothing) at all.
35. Silvia (has, hasn't) no place to do her homework.

Compounds *pages 212–213*

F. Write the ten one-word compounds.

36. earth + quake
37. side + walk
38. card + board
39. flash + light
40. spring + time
41. touch + down
42. basket + ball
43. home + work
44. dragon + fly
45. egg + plant

See also Handbook pages 354–357.

Writing with Adverbs

Grammar and Writing Workshop

- Use adverbs to add detail to your writing.

Read the sentences below.

1. **The gymnast landed on the mat.**
2. **The gymnast landed gracefully on the mat.**

There is only a one-word difference between the sentences, but this slight change makes a big difference! The adverb *gracefully* in sentence 2 tells how the gymnast landed. This adverb makes sentence 2 more detailed and more interesting. It gives a very clear picture of the gymnast's landing.

A different adverb would give a different picture. See how one adverb can turn a superb athlete into a terrible athlete.

The gymnast landed clumsily on the mat.

Adverbs add important details to writing.

The Adverb Game Choose a verb from the list below and write it. How many adverbs can you think of that might describe that verb? Take two minutes to write as many adverbs as you can for your verb.

swim	fall	argue
sing	write	laugh
walk	talk	work

How many adverbs appear on your list? Find a classmate who chose the same verb and compare your lists.

Now choose a different verb from the list. Then write any adverbs that might describe this new verb.

Add-an-Adverb   Read each sentence below. Think of adverbs that could describe the underlined verb. Then write the sentence twice, adding a different adverb each time.

EXAMPLE: Hank stepped into the boat.
ANSWER: Hank stepped boldly into the boat.
              Hank stepped carefully into the boat.

1. I listened to the music.
2. Roxanne smiled when she walked into the surprise party.
3. The crowd cheered at the end of the game.
4. The acrobat moved along the high wire.
5. Maggie spoke about fire prevention to the audience.

No-Clue Time   Now add adverbs to sentences without using clues. Find the verb in each sentence below. Think of an adverb that describes the verb. Write the sentence, adding an adverb.

6. Louis tiptoed past the baby's crib.
7. The building swayed because of the earthquake.
8. Aunt Martha batted the ball.
9. Uncle George ran to third base.
10. The tall flowers danced in the breeze.
11. The children reached for the apples.
12. The wind blew last night.

Using the Thesaurus

"The photographer moved fast to the edge of the meadow. She raised her camera very fast. As fast as she could, she adjusted the lens...."

Any word used too often can become boring. Find the entry for *fast* in the Thesaurus. Then write four sentences. Use a different synonym for *fast* (meaning "hurriedly") in each sentence.

7 Choosing a Topic

- When you choose a topic for a report, select one that interests you.
- Narrow the topic to fit the size of your report.

There are several keys to writing a good report. The first is to choose a suitable topic.

- Choose a topic that interests you. If you write about something that bores you, it will be difficult to make your report sound interesting.
- Choose a topic that will interest your audience. Consider who will be reading or listening to your report.
- Choose a topic that is narrow enough for your report. Avoid broad topics such as *animals*. It would be impossible to cover that topic in a short report.

Narrowing a topic is simple when you know how to classify, or arrange things in groups. Notice how the topic *animals* is narrowed.

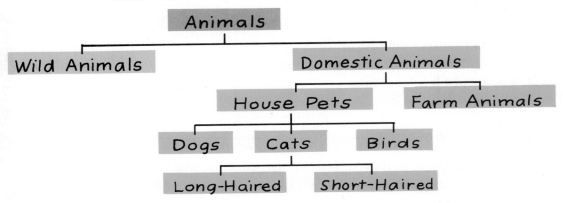

Once you have narrowed the topic to *short-haired cats*, you can still keep narrowing. You might choose *Siamese cats*. From there you might go on to *special markings on Siamese cats*. Or you might go on to *why many cat lovers prefer Siamese cats*. Any of these topics are narrow enough for a short report.

Skills Tryout

Tell which topic is the narrowest in each group.

1. clothing, pants, blue jeans
2. climate, tornadoes, storms
3. seasonings, cinnamon, spices
4. ice dancing, Olympic events, winter sports
5. plants, red oaks, trees of North America

Practice

A. Write the topic that is the narrowest in each group.

1. cabins, housing, homes
2. national parks, recreation areas, Grand Canyon
3. oysters, shellfish, sea animals
4. sporting goods, ski boots, ski equipment
5. school supplies, three-ring binders, notebooks

B. Narrow each topic below to one that could be covered in a short report.

EXAMPLE: machines
ANSWER: uses for home computers

6. games
7. countries
8. foods
9. pets
10. planets

11. music
12. plants
13. famous writers
14. summer activities
15. things that float

Application USING STUDY SKILLS

Choose one of these broad topics.

sports   entertainment   hobbies

Narrow the topic step by step. Make a diagram similar to the one on page 218.

8 — Using the Library

- Books in a library are listed by title, author, and subject in a card catalog or computer listing.

When you have chosen a topic for a report, where can you find information about it? For information on most topics, the first place to look is the library. In the library, books are divided into two main categories, fiction and nonfiction. Fiction books contain made-up stories. They are arranged alphabetically by the author's last name. Nonfiction books are books that give facts. They are arranged numerically. Each nonfiction book has a number printed on its spine. This is the **call number** of the book. The books are numbered in such a way that books about the same subject are grouped together.

When you want to find a book in the library, check the card catalog or computer listing. These sources list every book in the library by its title, its author, and its subject. Catalog cards are arranged in alphabetical order. Study the information given on each kind of card.

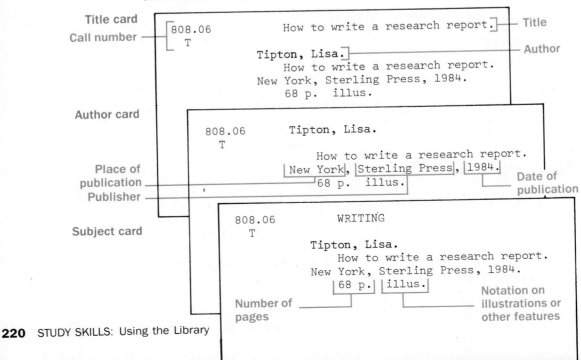

Skills Tryout

Use the catalog cards on page 220 to answer these questions.

1. What is the title of the book listed?
2. Who is the author?
3. Where and when was the book published?
4. Is this book illustrated?
5. What is the book's call number?

Practice

A. Write the word or words you would look up in the card catalog or computer listing to find the following items.

1. a book by Margery Sharp
2. the call number of the book *Westward by Canal*
3. the title of a book about eating good foods
4. the call numbers of books about volcanoes
5. the title of a book by P.L. Travers

B. Write *title, author,* or *subject* to tell what kind of catalog card you would use to answer these questions.

6. Who wrote *Kingdom of the Sun*?
7. What children's book did Ian Fleming write?
8. Does the library have any books about termites?
9. Did Isaac Asimov write any novels?
10. Did the same author write *This Is the Texas Panhandle* and *A Tree Grows in Brooklyn*?

Application USING STUDY SKILLS

Look up these subjects in a library card catalog or computer listing. Write the title, author, and call number of a book about each.

a. air pollution
b. the California gold rush
c. weather
d. Amelia Earhart

9 Using the Parts of a Book

- The **title page, copyright page, table of contents,** and **index** give valuable information about a book.

Certain parts of a book give important information about the book. These parts have special names.

In the front of the book is the title page. It shows the title, author, and publisher of the book. The copyright page is on the back of the title page. It tells the year in which the book was published. The copyright date can help to tell you how up-to-date the facts in the book are.

The table of contents usually comes next. It shows the major divisions of the book and lists each chapter. Use the table of contents to find out what broad topics a book covers.

Nonfiction books often have an index at the back. It alphabetically lists the topics covered in the book. Use the index to see if a book has the specific information you need.

TABLE OF CONTENTS

Chapters are listed in the order in which they appear.

The number of the first page of each chapter is given.

CONTENTS

	Page
Part I Folktales and Legends	4
Chapter 1 Johnny Appleseed	6
2 Evangeline	18
3 Joe Magarac	26
Part II Folk Songs	30
Chapter 4 Songs of the South	34
5 Songs of the West	48

INDEX

Topics are listed in alphabetical order.

A page number is given for every page that has information on the topic.

Bears
"Big Bear of Arkansas" (song), 35
Daniel Boone and, 392
"How the Bear Got Its Tail," 78-79
Big Foot, 19, 378
Brer Fox, 250-256, 311
Cajuns
festivals, 53
folklore, 50-51
food, 52

Skills Tryout

Tell whether you would use the title page, copyright page, table of contents, or index to answer these questions about a book.

1. Who is the author?
2. Does the book have any information on the folklore of Georgia?
3. On what page does Chapter 2 begin?
4. How up-to-date is the information in the book?
5. Which pages tell about Barbara Frietchie?

Practice

A. Use the sample table of contents and index on the opposite page to answer the following questions.
   1. How is the book organized?
   2. In which chapter would you expect to find cowboy songs?
   3. Which pages tell about the folklore of the Cajuns?
   4. Which page tells about Daniel Boone and bears?
   5. On which pages would you look to find out who wrote tales about Brer Fox?

B. Use the copyright page, table of contents, and index of this book to answer the following questions.

   6. When was this book published?
   7. On what page does the Young Writer's Handbook begin?
   8. In which unit will you learn about prepositions?
   9. On which pages will you find information on prefixes?
   10. On which pages will you find information on the encyclopedia?

Application USING STUDY SKILLS

Make up a title for a nonfiction book you would like to write. Then write a table of contents and at least two index entries for the book.

10 — Using an Encyclopedia

- Articles in an encyclopedia are arranged in alphabetical order.

How many times have you needed to find the answer to a specific question? The encyclopedia is often the place to look. You can find the answers to many questions if you know how to use an encyclopedia.

An encyclopedia is usually made up of several books, or volumes. It is a collection of articles about people, places, things, and ideas. The articles are arranged alphabetically. Notice the letters on the volumes of the encyclopedia below.

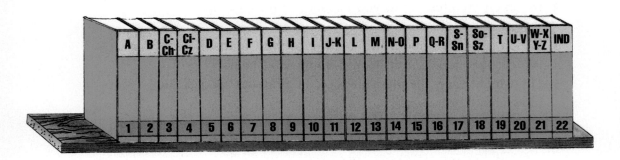

To find the answer to a question, first identify the key word in the question. For example, *aardvarks* is the key word in the question *What do aardvarks eat?* The next step is to find the book in which that topic can be found. The letters on the volumes of the encyclopedia will help you do that. The article on aardvarks can be found in book A, or Volume 1. Guide words on the pages will help you find the article.

Notice Volume 22 above. It is the index for the entire set of books. The index lists all the topics in the encyclopedia in alphabetical order. It gives the page number and the volume where the article on each topic can be found.

Skills Tryout

Take the first step in researching a topic. Identify the key words in these questions.

1. What is a quark?
2. How long is the Mississippi River?
3. Was Robin Hood a real person?

Practice

A. Write the key words in these questions.

1. How do fireflies make light?
2. What equipment is needed for scuba diving?
3. Why is the Bermuda Triangle famous?
4. How fast can a cheetah run?
5. Who discovered penicillin?

B. Write the key words in the questions. Then write the numbers of the volumes in which you would look up the words. Use the illustration on the opposite page to find the numbers.

6. Who invented the bicycle?
7. What are the rings of Saturn?
8. Who was Montezuma?
9. Can you really get water from a cactus?
10. What is the closest star?
11. Do all xylophones have the same number of bars?
12. What is the capital of Florida?
13. How big is an otter?
14. What form of government does Great Britain have?
15. What do giraffes feed on?

Application USING STUDY SKILLS

Write five questions you would like to know the answers to. Underline the key words in the questions. Then use an encyclopedia to find the answers.

11 — Using Other Reference Materials

- An **atlas** is a book of maps.
- An **almanac** is a book of current facts and figures.
- **Periodicals** are newspapers and magazines.

Libraries contain many other kinds of reference materials besides encyclopedias. These reference materials offer different kinds of information.

Atlases offer the largest selection of maps. Political maps show boundaries of countries. Relief maps show what the land looks like. Road maps show the major transportation routes.

Almanacs specialize in up-to-date information and are usually published every year. They contain many lists and tables. They do not devote as much space to background information as encyclopedias do.

High Peaks in United States, Canada, Mexico

Name	Place	Feet	Name	Place	Feet
McKinley	Alas	20,320	Crestone	Col	14,294
Logan	Can	19,850	Lincoln	Col	14,286
Citlaltepec (Orizaba)	Mexico	18,700	Grays	Col	14,270
St. Elias	Alas-Can	18,008	Antero	Col	14,269
Popocatepetl	Mexico	17,887	Torreys	Col	14,267
Foraker	Alas	17,400	Castle	Col	14,265
Iztaccihuatl	Mexico	17,343	Quandary	Col	14,265
Lucania	Can	17,147	Evans	Col	14,264
King	Can	16,971	Longs	Col	14,256
Steele	Can	16,644	McArthur	Can	14,253
Bona	Alas	16,550	Wilson	Col	14,246
Blackburn	Alas	16,390	White	Cal	14,246
Kennedy	Alas	16,286	North Palisade	Cal	14,242
Sanford	Alas	16,237	Shavano	Col	14,229

Periodicals are newspapers and magazines. Many libraries also have records, films, and videotapes.

By using different kinds of reference materials, you can gather a wide variety of information on a topic. For example, suppose you want to know about hot-air ballooning. An encyclopedia will give details about the history and construction of balloons. An almanac may have listings of yearly races and world records. An atlas can help you trace the routes of famous flights. A magazine article may give details of a recent race.

Skills Tryout

For each question below, tell whether you would look in an atlas, an almanac, or a periodical.

1. Where is Lake Tahoe?
2. What cities were hit by last month's hurricane?
3. Is Switzerland a coastal country?
4. Who won gold medals in the most recent Olympic games?
5. What is the tallest building in the United States?

Practice

Decide where you would look for answers to the questions below. Write *atlas, almanac,* or *periodical.*

1. Is Georgia near Florida?
2. Which new movies do the critics like?
3. What seas border Greece?
4. Who was the winner of last week's tennis tournament?
5. What was the total snowfall in Maine last year?
6. What countries are north of France?
7. Who is the governor of Indiana?
8. What are the names of the most famous comets?
9. How far is Houston from Dallas?
10. What is the population of your state's capital?
11. What is the highest temperature recorded in your state?
12. How does your mayor feel about the new state budget?
13. Which state has a town called Truth or Consequences?
14. How large is Death Valley?
15. Does Arizona have any mountains?

Application LIFE SKILLS

Look at a road map of the United States. Choose a town that you would like to visit. Follow the route from that town to yours. Then use the mileage scale to figure out how far the town is from your town.

12 — Taking Notes in Your Own Words

- Use your own words when taking notes on what you read.

There are many times when it is useful to take notes. Taking notes can help you remember what you read. It is also helpful to take notes on main ideas when gathering information for a report. When you take notes, be sure to use your own words. It is not always necessary to write complete sentences. Read this paragraph and the notes next to it.

The owner is the key to dog training.
— needs to be firm
— must be very patient
— should not punish —
*   reward instead*

What is the key to a well-trained dog? The owner's attitude! It's the owner's behavior, not the dog's intelligence, that makes the difference. The owner must be very firm—but kind. The dog must not be allowed to misbehave. The owner must have endless patience. Sometimes it takes weeks to teach one command to a dog. Most important, the owner must reward the dog often, not punish it. It's those rewards that keep the dog trying again and again.

Notice these things about the notes.

1. The notes are written on an index card. Later, cards can be sorted and grouped in logical order.
2. The main idea is stated at the top of the card. Supporting ideas are listed under it.
3. All the notes are in the notetaker's own words. They are not exactly the same as the author's words.

Skills Tryout

Restate these ideas in your own words.

1. No matter how large or small, all dogs require affection.
2. Dogs are among the most loyal of creatures.
3. Whether your dog has long hair or short, it is likely to shed hair at times.
4. There are more poodles in the United States than any other breed of dog.
5. Regular exercise is important for all dogs.

Practice

A. Write these statements in your own words.

1. Training elephants is a difficult task.
2. There are several dangers involved.
3. An elephant weighs enough to crush your bones.
4. Fortunately most elephants tend to be gentle.
5. They are also quite intelligent and learn easily.

B. Read the paragraph below and take notes on it. Note the main idea first, then add the supporting ideas.

Many animals are trained for specific jobs. Mules provide transportation on steep, narrow mountain paths because they are surefooted. Elephants help to clear forests by lifting and carrying logs. Sled dogs make it possible for people to travel on snow. Guide dogs act as eyes for blind people. Dogs in search-and-rescue parties locate people who are in danger.

Application ORAL REPORTING

Read a short article on a topic that interests you. Take notes in your own words. Then tell your class what you have learned, using your notes for reference.

13 — Outlining

- An **outline** organizes information into main ideas and supporting ideas.

An outline is the skeleton of a report. You can see at a glance how the pieces fit together. You can tell whether the main ideas are well supported by details.

The organization of an outline is simple. Each main idea becomes a main topic. Main topics are listed in logical order. Details, or supporting ideas, become subtopics. They are grouped under the proper main topic.

The form of an outline is standard. The title is centered at the top. Main topics begin at the left margin. They are labeled by Roman numerals followed by a period. Subtopics are indented. They are labeled by capital letters followed by a period.

Here is an outline of the paragraphs above. Notice how the parts line up. Notice that the first word on each line is capitalized.

Outlines

I. An outline as a skeleton
   A. Shows how pieces fit together
   B. Shows whether main ideas are well supported
II. Simple organization
   A. Main ideas become main topics
   B. Main topics listed in order
   C. Supporting ideas become subtopics
   D. Subtopics grouped under main topics
III. Standard form
   A. Title centered at top
   B. Main topics at left margin
   C. Roman numerals and periods for main topics
   D. Subtopics indented
   E. Capital letters and periods for subtopics

Skills Tryout

Use the outline on the opposite page to answer the questions.

1. How many main topics are in the outline?
2. How many subtopics belong to the second main topic?
3. Which main topic has the most subtopics?

Practice

A. Copy the outline below. Next to each part write *title, main topic,* or *subtopic.*

Australia
- I. Australia in the past
  - A. Discovery by Dutch
  - B. Settlement by British
- II. Australia today
  - A. People who live there
  - B. What the country is like
  - C. Type of government

B. Make an outline titled "An Interview" from the topics below. List the two main topics, and group the subtopics under them. Add Roman numerals and capital letters.

1. Making a list of questions
2. Preparation
3. The interview
4. Listening carefully
5. Making an appointment for the interview
6. Taking interview notes
7. Arriving on time
8. Studying the person's background
9. Thanking the person
10. Asking questions

Application USING STUDY SKILLS

Outline a selection that your teacher chooses from your social studies book. Compare your outline with those of your classmates. The outlines should be similar in structure even though the wording is different.

14 — Writing a Two-Paragraph Report

Writing Project

> • A **report** gives facts about a topic. It is based on research and is in the writer's own words.

In this unit you have been introduced to the tools of research. You have had practice in choosing a topic, using the library and reference books, taking notes, and outlining. Now you will have the opportunity to put all those research tools to work. You will write a two-paragraph report to share with the class. Through your research you can become the class expert on any topic you choose.

1. Prewriting

▶ Your first step is to select a topic. Begin by making a list of at least five possible topics. If you need ideas, look through an encyclopedia. You can also look at titles in the nonfiction section of a library.

Look at your list of topics and cross out your least favorites. Try out your remaining choices on some of your classmates. Ask them which topic they would like to hear more about. Put a check by the topic each person chooses. Circle the topic that was chosen most often. This list shows how one student decided to write about killer whales.

```
skydiving              √√
Grand Canyon
earthquake             √
(killer whales)        √√√
horse training
Loch Ness monster      √√√
```

▶ When you have chosen your topic, you can begin your research. A good place to start is an encyclopedia. An encyclopedia will give you an overall view of your topic and general facts about it. Next, check nonfiction books on your topic for more specific information. Remember to use the library's card catalog to locate the books you need. If your topic is current, you can find information in newspaper and magazine articles. Ask the librarian to show you how to find these sources.

Take notes on what you read, using your own words. That will make it easier to write your report later on. You can probably do all your research in one visit to the library.

Review your notes and group them in a logical order. Since you are going to write a two-paragraph report, look for two main ideas in your notes.

▶ Begin writing your outline. Your two main ideas will be the main topics in your outline. Label your two main topics I and II, as in the example. Look at your notes again. Find the most important details. These will be the subtopics in your outline. Label each subtopic with a capital letter.

> Killer Whales
> I. Largest, most beautiful dolphins
>   A. From 20-30 feet long
>   B. Weigh 10,000-18,000 pounds
>   C. Colored like penguins
> II. Bad reputation not deserved
>   A. Said to be vicious
>   B. Do not attack humans
>   C. Affectionate with keepers

2. Writing

▶ Writing the first draft of your report will not be difficult. Follow your outline and write a topic sentence for the first paragraph. Use the first main idea in your outline: "Killer whales are the world's largest and most beautiful dolphins."

Now add detail sentences to your first paragraph. Use the subtopics in your outline. You might write, for example, "A killer whale may be 20 to 30 feet long."

Follow the same steps to write the second paragraph of your report. Then complete your first draft by writing an interesting, informative title.

3. Revising

▶ Read your report to another person. See if your listener has any questions about what you wrote. Use this checklist to help you think about revising your first draft.

Revision Checklist

- Did I follow my outline?
- Did I begin each paragraph with a topic sentence?
- Do the detail sentences tell more about the topic sentences?
- Did I give the facts in my own words?
- Are my words and sentences in the best order?

Read the sample to see how it was improved. Notice the changes that were made to put the words and sentences in the best order.

Killer Whales are the largest and world's most beautiful dolphins. This very beautiful black and white animal is striking. A killer whale is 20 to 30 feet long and weighs 10,000 to 18,000 tons. It has the distinctive coloring pounds

> *Killer Whales*
> Killer whales are the world's largest and most beautiful dolphins. A killer whale is 20 to 30 feet long and weighs 10,000 to 18,000 pounds. This black and white animal is striking. It has the distinctive coloring of a penguin.
> The bad reputation of killer whales is not deserved. They are not vicious, and they do not attack humans. Actually, killer whales are affectionate with their keepers.

▶ Did you decide how you can improve your report? Use the editing marks to make your changes.

EDITING MARKS

——	cross out
∧	add
↰	move
≡	capital letter
/	small letter
¶	indent
◯	check spelling

4. Publishing

▶ You have worked hard to research and write a report that will interest others. You will want to share what you have done. First proofread your report for errors. Use the Proofreading Checklist in the Young Writer's Handbook on page 377. Make corrections, using the editing marks. Share what you have learned from your research by reading your report to the class. You may also wish to show the class pictures that illustrate your report.

Writing Project

A Library Poster

Make a poster to inform others about one of the world's greatest bargains—a library card. Go to your local library. Find out all the different kinds of materials that can be borrowed with a library card. Then plan and make your poster.

Social Studies

In social studies you are sometimes asked to summarize information. When you summarize, you tell only the main points. You leave out minor details. Summarizing is a good way to review what you have read. It forces you to think about what you have read and helps you to understand it.

▶ Try it. Read this encyclopedia article. Then summarize the article in your own words. Give its most important points in no more than five sentences.

SACAGAWEA, SAK uh juh WEE uh, SACAJAWEA, or SAKAKAWEA (1787?-1812?), was the interpreter for the Lewis and Clark Expedition to the Pacific Ocean in 1804 and 1805. Sacagawea's name means *Bird Woman*. She was born among the Shoshoni, or Snake, Indians of Idaho. Enemy Indians captured her, and sold her as a slave to a French-Canadian trader, Toussaint Charbonneau. Charbonneau and Sacagawea joined the Lewis and Clark Expedition as it passed up the Missouri River. Sacagawea was the principal guide of the expedition. While crossing the Continental Divide, the explorers met relatives of Sacagawea among the Shoshoni. She was able to get food and horses that the travelers needed to continue their journey to the Pacific Ocean and back (see LEWIS AND CLARK EXPEDITION).

Almost nothing was known of Sacagawea for a hundred years after the journey. According to one account, she died on the Missouri River in 1812. Others have contended that she died and was buried on the Wind River Reservation in Wyoming in 1884. An entry in Captain Clark's journal of 1825-1828 lists her as dead.

Sacagawea has been honored by having a river, a peak, and a mountain pass named after her. Monuments and memorials to her stand at Portland, Ore., Three Forks, Mont., Bismarck, N. Dak., Lewiston, Ida., and near Dillon, Mont.   WILLIAM H. GILBERT

Readers at Work Librarians help decide what new books a library will order each year. To do this, they read book reviews. A book review gives a summary and an evaluation of a book.

▶ List the kinds of books you would order for a library. For example, you might choose science fiction or biographies of famous athletes. For each kind of book, invent several book titles and authors.

Adverbs and Adjectives *pages 202–209*

A. Write the correct form of the adverb in parentheses ( ).

1. The logs burned (rapidly) than we had expected.
2. Jason swam (fast) of all during the championship meet.
3. Lisa can solve math problems (easily) than her brother.
4. This is the (carefully) tended garden in the park.
5. Gordon plays tennis (well) than I do.

B. Write the adverb that describes each underlined adjective or adverb.

6. The audience clapped very <u>loudly</u> at the play's end.
7. Kate is an extremely <u>talented</u> trumpet player.
8. Quite <u>often</u> chipmunks will eat out of your hand.
9. The space-shuttle flight was highly <u>successful</u>.
10. Spring was unusually <u>warm</u> this year.

C. Write the word in parentheses ( ) that correctly completes each sentence.

11. Frederick (easy, easily) completed the crossword puzzle.
12. Giraffes are especially (gently, gentle) animals.
13. A roller-coaster ride can be a (wild, wildly) experience.
14. The sun shone (radiantly, radiant) all afternoon.

Negative Words *pages 210–211*

D. Write the word in parentheses ( ) that correctly completes each sentence.

15. Nothing can (never, ever) keep Bill from reading books.
16. Hasn't (anyone, no one) seen Jo's yellow notebook?
17. There (was, wasn't) nowhere to sit in the auditorium.
18. I don't have (no, any) clean socks in my drawer.

Compounds *pages 212–213*

E. Write the sentences. Underline the compounds.

19. Every morning the newspaper arrives at seven o'clock.
20. Our neighbor's dog is a fox terrier.
21. My brother-in-law works as a waiter in a restaurant.
22. Last night's thunderstorm brought three inches of rain.

Library *pages 220–221*

F. Write *title, author,* or *subject* to tell what kind of catalog card would answer these questions.

23. Who wrote *A Wrinkle in Time*?
24. Does the library have any books about alligators?
25. What is the name of Marguerite Henry's latest book?

Reference Materials *pages 224–227*

G. Write the answer to each question about using encyclopedias, atlases, almanacs, and periodicals.

26. What is the key word in the question *How are candles made*?
27. What kind of information is contained in atlases?
28. What reference would you look in to find out about rainfall in the United States last year?
29. What reference would you look in to find yesterday's football scores?

Outlining *pages 230–231*

H. Make an outline entitled *Afternoon Activities.* Use *Indoor activities* and *Outdoor activities* as the main topics. Add at least three subtopics below each main topic. Remember to use Roman numerals to label main topics and capital letters to label subtopics.

See also Handbook pages 354–357, 372.

Cumulative Review

Sentences   *pages 10–17*

A. Write the complete subject of each sentence. Underline the simple subject. Write (*You*) if the subject is understood.

1. Our old rowboat needs some repairs.
2. Read two books for your report on dolphins.
3. Put those photographs in the scrapbook.
4. This winding path leads to Greta's house.

B. Write the complete predicate of each sentence. Underline the simple predicate.

5. Regina is planning the class picnic.
6. We played football in the park.
7. Russell has looked at the moon through a telescope.
8. Mr. Benjamin rested under the shady elm tree.

Capital Letters and Periods   *pages 52–57*

C. Write the sentences. Capitalize the proper nouns. Write the abbreviations correctly.

9. We followed rte 33 to hillside park.
10. During oct many tourists drive through new hampshire.
11. Call edward ross, jr, immediately.
12. The cortez library will close at 4 pm today.

Verbs   *pages 96–99, 102–103*

D. Write each sentence. Use the verb in parentheses ( ) that correctly completes the sentence.

13. Max will (finish, finishes) his exercises soon.
14. Yesterday two jets (flew, flown) over my house.
15. Aaron never (complain, complains) about his chores.
16. Elliot has (gave, given) us tickets to the game.

Cumulative Review

Cumulative Review

Pronouns   *pages 128–139*

E. Write each sentence. Use the pronoun in parentheses ( ) that correctly completes the sentences.

17. Did (they, them) follow the rabbit's footprints?
18. Leona introduced Amy and (I, me) to Mr. Romero.
19. Jack and Judy put on (their, theirs) roller skates.
20. Melissa entertained (we, us) with jokes and riddles.

Adjectives and Adverbs   *pages 170–171, 202–203, 208–209*

F. Write the word in parentheses ( ) that correctly completes each sentence. Then write whether the word is an *adjective* or an *adverb*.

21. Karla saw a (real, really) dinosaur bone at the museum.
22. The audience listened (polite, politely) to the speaker.
23. Marty (usual, usually) begins his homework after dinner.
24. We are expecting a (bad, badly) snowstorm tomorrow.

Commas   *pages 178–179*

G. Write the sentences. Add commas where they are needed.

25. We run swim and bicycle during the summer.
26. Sara arranged violets daisies and ferns in the vase.
27. I must wash dry and iron my new shirt.
28. An apple is a tasty healthy and delicious snack.

Negative Words   *pages 210–211*

H. Write each sentence. Use the correct word in parentheses ( ).

29. No one will (never, ever) find my secret hiding place.
30. Wouldn't (anyone, no one) help you with your packages?
31. Nobody knew (nothing, anything) about the broken window.
32. There (was, wasn't) no gasoline in the car.

Cumulative Review

Grammar
Prepositions

Composition
Creating

The Bridge

A bridge
by day
is steel and strong.
It carries
giant trucks that roll along
above the waters
of the bay.
A bridge is steel and might—
till night.

A bridge
at night
is spun of light
that someone tossed
across the bay
and someone caught
and pinned down tight—
till day.

—Lilian Moore

1 Prepositions

- A **preposition** relates a noun or pronoun to another word in the sentence.

In the poem below, the underlined words are prepositions.

The boot was <u>over</u> the door.
The clock was <u>under</u> the tray.
The chair was <u>off</u> the floor.
It happened <u>on</u> April Fools' Day.

A preposition relates the noun or pronoun that follows it to another word in the sentence. The noun or pronoun that follows the preposition is called the **object of the preposition.** In the poem, for example, the preposition *over* relates *door* to *boot. Door* is the object of the preposition.

The boot was <u>over</u> the <u>door</u>.

Thirty Common Prepositions

about	at	by	in	on	to
above	before	down	inside	out	under
across	behind	during	near	outside	up
after	below	for	of	over	with
around	beside	from	off	through	without

Skills Tryout

Name the preposition in each sentence. The object of the preposition is underlined in each sentence.

1. April Fools' Day falls on <u>April 1</u>.
2. This was once the date of <u>New Year's Day</u>.
3. The date changed, but some people forgot about <u>it</u>.
4. Each April 1 they still exchanged gifts with their <u>friends</u>.
5. Only now they gave joke gifts placed in pretty <u>boxes</u>.

Practice

A. Write each sentence. Underline the preposition.

1. April Fools' Day is celebrated in many countries.
2. Many tricks are played on this day.
3. Three hundred years ago it began in France.
4. The holiday soon spread across Europe.
5. The French call it "The Day of the Fish."
6. Children surprise each other with paper fish.
7. "April fish" is the French name for an April fool.
8. Friends learn each other's tricks over the years.
9. Most pranks are planned before April 1.
10. Few people can spend the whole day without a smile.

B. Write each sentence. Underline the preposition once. Underline the object of the preposition twice.

EXAMPLE: She plays jokes on her friends.
ANSWER: She plays jokes on her friends.

11. People play practical jokes during this day.
12. You might find a dollar by a tree.
13. Someone is hiding behind a bush.
14. He holds a long thread in his hand.
15. The other end is attached to the dollar.
16. He pulls on the thread.
17. The dollar disappears when you reach for it.
18. Don't be angry about the joke.
19. Get back at him.
20. Tell him a spider is crawling up his back.

Application WRITING SENTENCES

Write five sentences about April Fools' Day. In each sentence use at least one preposition from the list on the opposite page. Underline the prepositions.

2 — Prepositional Phrases

- A **prepositional phrase** includes the preposition, the object, and all the words that come between them.

Read this nonsense poem. Then read just the seven prepositional phrases in the blue boxes.

O my agèd Uncle Arly!
Sitting on a heap of Barley
Through the silent hours of night,
Close beside a leafy thicket.
On his nose there was a Cricket,
In his hat a Railway-Ticket;
(But his shoes were far too tight).
—*Edward Lear*

Every prepositional phrase starts with a preposition and ends with the object of the preposition. It also contains any words that come between. Look at these examples.

Prepositional Phrases		
Prepositions	Words Between	Objects
on	a	heap
of		barley
through	the silent	hours

Skills Tryout

Name each prepositional phrase. The prepositions are underlined.

1. Kate was reading <u>about</u> some humorous poets.
2. She found some poems <u>by</u> the famous Edward Lear.
3. Kate read his poems <u>at</u> the public library.
4. She showed them <u>to</u> her friend Gerald.

Practice

A. Write each sentence. Underline the prepositional phrase.

1. Gerald and Kate had smiles on their faces.
2. They were both reading a poem by Edward Lear.
3. It was a limerick, a poem in a special form.
4. The name *limerick* comes from Ireland.
5. Supposedly it is named after an Irish city.
6. Lear wrote poems about silly subjects.
7. His poems are filled with wonderful nonsense.
8. People enjoyed his sense of humor.
9. Sometimes his writing poked fun at other poets.
10. Friends sometimes recited his poems through the night.

B. Write the prepositional phrase in each sentence. Underline the preposition once. Underline the object of the preposition twice.

EXAMPLE: We read poems from a large book.
ANSWER: from a large book

11. Kate and Gerald read Lear's nonsense poems for fun.
12. There is often a serious message behind the nonsense.
13. He loved writing about people's habits.
14. One book had funny drawings above the limericks.
15. Gerald paused after his favorite poems.
16. He copied these poems in his notebook.
17. Kate kept a poetry collection beside her bed.
18. Sometimes she memorized a poem at bedtime.
19. Their teacher read some limericks before lunch.
20. Their favorite began, "We went to the animal fair."

Application WRITING SENTENCES

Write five nonsense sentences using prepositional phrases. For example, you might write, "We found an elephant inside our refrigerator." Underline the prepositional phrases.

3 — Prepositions and Adverbs

- Some words can be either prepositions or adverbs.

Some words, such as *off*, *up*, and *inside*, can be prepositions or adverbs. There is an easy way to tell how such words are being used. The word is a preposition if it begins a prepositional phrase and has an object. It is an adverb if it describes a verb and stands alone, without an object.

Prepositions	Adverbs
Get <u>off</u> the subway. Go <u>up</u> the steps. Go <u>inside</u> the museum.	Get <u>off</u>. Go <u>up</u>. Go <u>inside</u>.

There are many words that can be used as prepositions or adverbs. Twelve of them are listed below.

along	below	in	near	out	under
around	down	inside	off	outside	up

Skills Tryout

For each sentence below, tell whether the underlined word is a preposition or an adverb.

1. Are we getting <u>near</u>?
2. We are <u>near</u> the Museum of Natural History.
3. Let's walk <u>around</u>.
4. Observe the dinosaurs and walk <u>around</u> them.
5. To see the blue whale, look <u>up</u>.

Practice

A. Write each sentence. Then write whether the underlined word is a preposition or an adverb.

1. Rachel was <u>in</u> the subway car.
2. Leo was still standing <u>outside</u>.
3. Just before the door closed, he stepped <u>in</u>.
4. It was their first ride <u>below</u> the ground.
5. Rachel looked <u>down</u> the subway tunnel.
6. No one seemed to mind being so far <u>under</u> the city.
7. The train seemed to fly <u>along</u>.
8. At Seventy-seventh Street, they got <u>out</u>.
9. They saw that the museum was just <u>outside</u> the subway.
10. The doors were opening as they hurried <u>up</u> the walk.

B. Write each sentence. If the underlined part is an adverb, change it to a prepositional phrase. If it is a prepositional phrase, change it to an adverb.

EXAMPLE: Their friends were waiting <u>inside</u>.
ANSWER: Their friends were waiting inside the door.

EXAMPLE: Please put a donation <u>in the box</u>.
ANSWER: Please put a donation in.

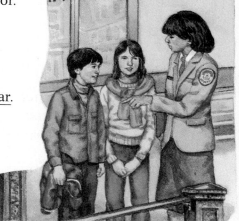

11. They took their coats <u>off the bench</u>.
12. A guard gave them directions as she came <u>near</u>.
13. To see the Eskimo masks, go <u>up one floor</u>.
14. Rachel looked <u>around the gift shop</u>.
15. She waited for me <u>inside</u>.

Application WRITING SENTENCES

Write six sentences about a trip you took. Use each of the following words twice—once as a preposition, once as an adverb.

around   inside   out

4 — Using Prepositional Phrases

- Use object pronouns in prepositional phrases.
- Use the prepositions *between* and *among* correctly.

When the object of a preposition is a pronoun, an object pronoun must be used. The following are the object pronouns.

me   you   him   her   it   us   them

The prepositional phrases are underlined in the following three sentences.

1. Will you work <u>with us</u>?   2. Show the plans <u>to me</u>.
3. I am planting a garden <u>with Cassie and her</u>.

Notice that in sentence 3 the preposition has two objects, a noun and a pronoun.

In the sentences below, the prepositions *between* and *among* are underlined.

The tomatoes were shared <u>between</u> the two families.
Divide the peaches <u>among</u> Julie, Li, and Armand.

The prepositions *between* and *among* are sometimes confused. Use *between* when you refer to <u>two</u> persons, places, or things. Use *among* with <u>three or more</u> persons, places, or things.

Skills Tryout

Name the word that correctly completes each sentence.

1. Cassie showed the garden book to (they, them).
2. The community garden was started by Alice and (him, he).
3. I divided my time (among, between) digging and planting.
4. Delsin planted six kinds of fruit for Pam and (she, her).
5. The tools were shared (between, among) Pat, Mona, and Ed.

Practice

A. Choose the pronoun in parentheses ( ) that correctly completes each sentence. Write the sentence.

1. Carla went to the garden center with (we, us).
2. Joan dug a strawberry bed beside Todd and (I, me).
3. Ms. Florio gave some seedlings to (she, her).
4. We planted sweet corn for Jesse and (her, she).
5. I borrowed tools from the Carons and (they, them).
6. The wheelbarrow and hose belong to Carrie and (me, I).
7. Leave a space in the garden for Robbie and (he, him).
8. Did you share the parsley plants with Leo and (she, her)?
9. Will the biggest tomatoes be grown by Gerry or (us, we)?
10. This area was donated by my parents and (they, them).
11. Give the rake and hoe to Alonzo and (he, him).
12. The weeding was done by Martha and (I, me).
13. Shira put in a fence with the Florios and (we, us).
14. We fertilized an area for (them, they).
15. Carrie sprayed water at Luana and (he, him).

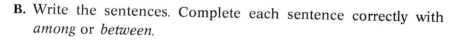

B. Write the sentences. Complete each sentence correctly with *among* or *between*.

16. Walk carefully (among, between) the two rows of lettuce.
17. I must decide (between, among) melon and squash.
18. Divide the fruits (among, between) Pam, Chen, and Jo.
19. Choose your favorite vegetable (between, among) carrots, peas, string beans, and broccoli.
20. (Among, Between) Arlo and Edith, who works harder?

Application WRITING SENTENCES

Spring is usually the season for starting work on a garden. Write five sentences about growing your own favorite fruits, vegetables, or flowers. Use prepositions followed by object pronouns. Include the words *between* or *among* in at least two of your sentences.

5 — Using Commas

- Use a comma after *yes, no,* or *well* at the beginning of a sentence.
- Use a comma to set off the name of a person spoken to.
- Use a comma to separate a last name from a first name when the last name is written first.

Read this letter from Harmony Publishers. Notice the commas.

Franklin, you're probably wondering what this letter is about. Well, you've been a good customer, Franklin. That's why, Franklin, we'd like to give you a chance to join our Nature Book Club...

Franklin decided to join. He wrote his name on the book club application.

NAME (last name first): *Miller, Franklin*

The letter and application above show three uses of the comma:

1. To set off words such as *yes, no,* or *well* at the beginning of a sentence
2. To set off the name of someone who is spoken to
3. To separate a last name from a first name when the last name is written first

Skills Tryout

Tell where commas belong in these sentences.

1. Yes class has started.
2. *Zinn Ann* was called last.
3. Is Ann Zinn here Billy?
4. No Mr. Wu she's absent.
5. Can you Meg give her this?
6. Yes I'll see her tonight.

Practice

A. Write the sentences. Use commas where they are needed.

1. Nancy did you see the letter I got today?
2. Yes I got one just like it.
3. Well are you going to send away for this offer?
4. I don't know Mrs. Novak what I'm going to do.
5. Is there anything else for me in the mail Nancy?
6. No there isn't.
7. What were you expecting Marta?
8. I was hoping Nancy that Tim's letter would be there.
9. Well maybe it will be in tomorrow's mail.
10. Marta let's take a look at the rest of our mail.

B. Write the sentences. Use commas where they are needed.

11. Well do you really think Marta I might win a prize?
12. Yes I do think Nancy that you might win.
13. Well have you ever won a contest like this Mrs. Novak?
14. No Marta but a friend of mine won third prize.
15. Well in that case Mrs. Novak I'll fill out this form.

Application FILLING OUT FORMS

The following people volunteered to take part in a walkathon for a local charity: Nate Brown, Jane Kowalsky, Suzanne Bailey, Pierre Renard, Kira Chernow. Copy the form shown below. First, enter their names on the form. Then enter your own name.

WALKATHON ON APRIL 15			
Last Name	First Name	Last Name	First Name
1. _____		4. _____	
2. _____		5. _____	
3. _____		6. _____	

6 Context Clues

- A **context clue** helps you understand the meaning of an unfamiliar word.

Sometimes you may hear or read words that are unfamiliar. Often the context, or words around the unfamiliar word, will give a clue to the new word's meaning. Such clues are called context clues.

Study the different kinds of context clues below.

Kinds of Clues	Examples
A *synonym*, or word that has almost the same meaning	A running dog has <u>kinetic</u>, or *moving*, energy
An *antonym*, or word that has an opposite meaning	Air must be <u>vibrating</u>, not *still*, to produce sound.
A *definition* of the new word	The rock was moved by <u>force</u>, *that is, by a push or a pull.*
Further information about the new word's meaning	<u>Condensation</u> occurred. *Steam changed to ice.*

Skills Tryout

Say the words that give you a clue to the meaning of the underlined word.

1. Energy is <u>mutable</u>, always changing.
2. Draw an <u>isosceles</u> triangle, that is, one with two equal sides.
3. Matter can be <u>transformed</u> into energy. For example, water can be changed into steam.
4. The earth <u>rotates</u>, or spins, on its axis.
5. Symphony orchestras should produce <u>euphonious</u> sounds, not unpleasant ones.

Practice

A. Write each sentence. Then use the words in parentheses ( )
to write the correct meaning of the underlined word.

1. An amplifier <u>amplifies</u>, or increases, sounds. (makes bigger, makes smaller)
2. Some animals <u>communicate</u> with each other. They make sounds to signal danger. (be common, give messages)
3. The <u>larynx</u> is the upper part of the windpipe that contains the vocal cords. (part of the nose, part of the throat)
4. <u>Acoustic</u> tiles help to lower noise in a room. (ceramic, sound-absorbing)
5. A screwdriver can be used as a <u>lever</u> to lift off the lid of a paint can. (cover, tool)
6. Energy should be <u>conserved</u>, not wasted. (saved, spent)
7. The skater cut down <u>friction</u>. She sharpened her skates so that they would move more smoothly. (ice, rubbing)

B. Use the context clue to find the meaning of each underlined word. Write the underlined word. Then write what you think the word means.

8. Sound travels 1235 kilometers per hour. A <u>supersonic</u> plane travels at least 1236 kilometers per hour.
9. Scientists tested the ability of humans to <u>endure</u> noise. They made people listen to jet planes.
10. Many lakes that used to be clean are now <u>polluted</u>.
11. Sound can be <u>reflected</u> off ceilings or walls.
12. Sound can be <u>absorbed</u>. Heavy drapes can trap noise.

Application USING LANGUAGE

Use a dictionary to find a meaning for each word below.
Then write a sentence that gives a context clue for the meaning.
Underline the part that gives the clue.

sonorous   molten   tempo

Prepositions *pages 244–245*

A. Write each sentence. Underline the preposition once. Underline the object of the preposition twice.

1. The cast often forgot their lines during rehearsals.
2. The director gave a speech before the opening.
3. She talked about the prompter.
4. The cast was worried over nothing.
5. The prompter would stand offstage behind the curtain.
6. If they forgot their lines, they could look at her.
7. The play began after eight.
8. Rodney's dog barked at the wrong time.
9. The telephone didn't ring in the second act.
10. Everything went well after the intermission.

Prepositional Phrases *pages 246–247*

B. Write each sentence. Underline the prepositional phrase.

11. Alligators were very common in prehistoric times.
12. An alligator is part of the reptile group.
13. Its skin is like a sheet of overlapping scales.
14. The long snout is a covering for the very sharp teeth.
15. Only the nostrils show when the reptile is under the water.

Prepositions and Adverbs *pages 248–249*

C. Write *adverb* if the underlined word is an adverb. Write *preposition* if it is a preposition.

16. Let's go <u>inside</u>.
17. Skis are <u>down</u> those stairs in the sports department.
18. Wilma wants more time to look <u>around</u>.
19. Karen is waiting <u>outside</u> the store.
20. She wants us to come <u>out</u>.

Using Prepositional Phrases   *pages 250–251*

D. Write each sentence. Use the correct word in parentheses (   ).

21. My family is having a party for Julie and (I, me).
22. They've asked me to choose (between, among) hamburgers, a Chinese dinner, and a pizza party.
23. I can't decide (between, among) pizza and hamburgers.
24. Invitations were sent to Manuel and (she, her).
25. Carl gave invitations to Roberto and (he, him).

Using Commas   *pages 252–253*

E. Write each sentence. Add commas where necessary.

26. Shirley Lewis you can be a member of a special club.
27. Yes the Kite-Fly Guild wants YOU to join.
28. All you have to do Shirley is print your name below.
29. No you don't have to send any money now.
30. Write your name (last name first): Lewis Shirley.

Context Clues   *pages 254–255*

F. Write the underlined word. Then write the word in parentheses (   ) that gives its meaning.

31. A bird's feathers <u>insulate</u> it against the heat or cold. (protect, disguise)
32. Many birds <u>migrate</u> to the south in the winter. (travel, stay)
33. The Locust Glen Bird Watchers were <u>despondent</u> because the severe winter storm had killed so many songbirds. (happy, very unhappy)
34. Todd wants to be an <u>ornithologist</u> and study birds for a living. (bird scientist, fish scientist)
35. The hawk swooped down at its <u>prey</u>, but the mouse got away. (victim, nest)

See also Handbook pages 358–361, 382, 384.

Writing with Prepositions

Grammar and Writing Workshop

- Use prepositions to make your writing more exact.

Read the sentences below.

1. **Susan found her lost ring.**
2. **Susan found her lost ring under the sink.**

Clearly, sentence 2 gives more information. It not only tells that Susan found her ring, it tells <u>where</u> she found it.

What if sentence 2 had been written differently? Susan might have found the ring *over* the sink. She might have found it *near* the sink. A preposition can completely change the meaning of a sentence.

You can use prepositions to make your writing more exact and more interesting.

The Preposition Game **Box A** below is filled with prepositions. They can be used with the words in **Box B** to form prepositional phrases.

Choose a preposition from **Box A** and write it. Now look in **Box B** for words to use to complete prepositional phrases. For example, the preposition *on* can be used with *the beach*. Write as many prepositional phrases as you can that might be used in sentences.

Box A		
on	for	under
by	in	above
to	near	about

Box B		
a mile	the people	the house
the end	the bridge	a dollar
an hour	the winter	the beach

How many prepositional phrases did you write? You might wish to write a sentence for each of your prepositional phrases.

Add-a-Phrase Use prepositional phrases to complete the sentences below. Write each sentence.

EXAMPLE: We heard about the accident.
ANSWER: We heard about the accident at the school.

1. Samantha sold her radio _____.
2. Jeff composed a song _____.
3. We traveled to New York City _____.
4. The fire fighters _____ are trained to handle emergencies.
5. Laura saw several robins _____.
6. Miguel practiced his typing _____.

No-Clue Time Now add prepositional phrases to sentences without using clues. Write each sentence below, adding a prepositional phrase.

7. Larry met the inventor.
8. Lucy left the house.
9. Harvey held the umbrella.
10. The plane departed.
11. Take a seat.
12. Who left this book?
13. We met each other.
14. The button rolled.
15. We stayed indoors.
16. Kyle wrote stories.
17. She enjoyed movies.
18. Did you find paper?
19. The fish swam.
20. Jo read a poem.

Using the Thesaurus

Some prepositions, such as *after* and *during*, relate to <u>times</u>. Other prepositions, such as *beside* and *under*, relate to <u>places</u>.

Find the entry for *before* in the Thesaurus. Five synonyms are given for *before*. Use each synonym in a sentence.

Notice that *before* may relate to either time or place.

7 — Listening for the Sounds of Poetry

> • Sounds of poetry include rhyme, rhythm, and alliteration.

In poetry the sounds of words are very important. Poets use word sounds to create certain effects. Rhyme, rhythm, and alliteration are three important ways that poets use the sounds of words.

You know how to recognize rhyme and rhythm when you hear them. Words that **rhyme** end with the same sounds. **Rhythm** is a certain pattern of stressed syllables. But what is alliteration? **Alliteration** is the repetition of the same sound at the beginning of words. The sentence below shows alliteration.

<u>P</u>eter <u>P</u>iper <u>p</u>icked a <u>p</u>eck of <u>p</u>ickled <u>p</u>eppers.

Read these poems aloud. Listen for the sounds of poetry.

Weather

Dot a dot dot   dot a dot dot
Spotting the windowpane.
Spack a spack speck   flick a flack fleck
Freckling the windowpane.

A spatter a scatter   a wet cat a clatter
A splatter a rumble outside.
Umbrella umbrella umbrella umbrella
Bumbershoot barrel of rain.

Slosh a galosh   slosh a galosh
Slither and slather a glide
A puddle a jump a puddle a jump
A puddle a jump puddle splosh
A juddle a pump aluddle a dump a
Puddmuddle jump in and slide!

—*Eve Merriam*

Wind Noises

Rumbling in the chimneys,
Rattling at the doors,
Round the roofs
    and round the roads
The rude wind roars;
Raging through the darkness,
Raving through the trees,
Racing off again
    across the great gray seas.

—*Unknown*

Swift Things Are Beautiful

Swift things are beautiful:
Swallows and deer,
And lightning that falls
Bright-veined and clear,
Rivers and meteors,
Wind in the wheat,
The strong-withered horse,
The runner's sure feet.

And slow things are beautiful:
The closing of day,
The pause of the wave
That curves downward to spray,
The ember that crumbles,
The opening flower,
And the ox that moves on
In the quiet of power.
　　　　　—Elizabeth Coatsworth

Alone by the Surf

There is no world sound–
Only stillness of stars,
Silence of sand,
A single shell,
By the sliding sea.
　　　—Leila Kendall Brown

About the Poems

1. Which poems have words that rhyme?
2. Which poems have a definite rhythm pattern?
3. Which words in "Alone by the Surf" begin with the sound of *s* or *sh*?
4. Which poem uses many words that begin with the sound of *r*? What are those words?
5. Which poem has words that rhyme *within* a line?

Activities

A. Beat out the rhythm of "Weather" as you read it aloud. For the first stanza show a light rain by tapping out the rhythm with a pencil. Show a heavier rain by clapping the rhythm of the second stanza. For the third stanza show the sloshing of the rain by slapping the rhythm with your hands on the top of your desk.

B. Choose one of the poems that has rhyme. List the rhyming words. Then list other words that rhyme with those words.

8 — Writing Similes and Metaphors

- Two unlike things that have something in common can be compared by a simile or a metaphor.

Writers can create vivid pictures in the reader's mind by comparing unlike things. Read the comparisons below. Notice the two things being compared.

The jungle <u>birds</u> were like bright, chattering <u>flowers</u>.

This type of comparison is called a **simile**. It uses the word *like* to make a comparison of two different things. Birds and flowers are very different. Yet jungle birds and flowers have one thing in common. They are colorful. The comparison helps you picture the birds.

The comparison below is also a simile. It uses the word *as* to compare two unlike things.

The <u>idea</u> was as fresh as a <u>garden after a rain</u>.

You can also compare two different things without using *like* or *as*. Just say that something *is* something else. This type of comparison is called a **metaphor**.

The singing <u>whales</u> are an undersea <u>chorus</u>.

Similes and metaphors can make your writing more vivid. The key is to be creative. Avoid old, worn-out expressions like *as cold as ice* or *as sweet as sugar*.

Skills Tryout

Tell what is being compared in each sentence. Then tell whether the comparison is a simile or a metaphor.

1. The skater twirled like a spindle of yarn.
2. The boulders were guards at the cave's entrance.
3. A favorable outcome is as unlikely as snow in July.

Practice

A. Write what is being compared in each sentence. Then write *simile* or *metaphor*.

1. The thought was like a puppy nipping at my heel.
2. The tuba sounded as gruff as an old bear.
3. The clowns on stilts were giraffes in the crowd.
4. The conversation was as lively as a pillow fight.
5. Dolphins are water children.

B. Complete each sentence to make a simile. Write the sentences.

6. His words were as rough as _____.
7. The news was as welcome as _____.
8. The music was like _____.
9. The party was as noisy as _____.
10. Water-skiers are like _____.

C. Complete each sentence to make a metaphor. Write the sentences.

11. Her baby brother is a _____.
12. Dreams are _____.
13. Sometimes my room is a _____.
14. Ladybugs are _____.
15. The old shoes were _____.

D. Write a simile or a metaphor for each topic.

16. a picnic
17. a roller coaster ride
18. the first day of spring
19. snowdrifts
20. a campfire

Application WRITING SIMILES

Create fresh comparisons from these overused expressions.

a. as quiet as a mouse
b. as rough as sandpaper
c. as smooth as glass
d. as sour as a lemon

9 — Using the Senses in Poetry

> • Poems often describe the way things look, smell, sound, taste, or feel.

Read these poems. As you read each one, think about which of your senses the poem appeals to—sight, smell, hearing, taste, or touch. A poem may appeal to more than one sense.

Knoxville, Tennessee

I always like summer
best
you can eat fresh corn
from daddy's garden
and okra
and greens
and cabbage
and lots of
barbecue
and buttermilk
and homemade ice-cream
at the church picnic
and listen to
gospel music
outside
at the church
homecoming
and go to the mountains with
your grandmother
and go barefooted
and be warm
all the time
not only when you go to bed
and sleep
　　　　　—Nikki Giovanni

Slippery

The six-month child
Fresh from the tub
Wriggles in our hands.
This is our fish child.
Give her a nickname: Slippery.
　　　　—Carl Sandburg

Coolness

*Translated by
Harold G. Henderson*

How cool the breeze:
　The sky is filled with voices–
　Pine and cedar trees.
　　　　—Onitsura

This Is Just to Say

I have eaten
the plums
that were in
the icebox

and which
you were probably
saving
for breakfast

Forgive me
they were delicious
so sweet
and so cold.
—William Carlos Williams

Kansas Boy

This Kansas boy who never saw the sea
Walks through the young corn rippling at his knee
As sailors walk; and when the grain grows higher
Watches the dark waves leap with greener fire
Than ever oceans hold. He follows ships,
Tasting the bitter spray upon his lips.
For in his blood up-stirs the salty ghost
Of one who sailed a storm-bound English coast.
Across wide fields he hears the sea winds crying,
Shouts at the crows—and dreams of white gulls flying.
—*Ruth Lechlitner*

About the Poems

1. What senses does the poem "Knoxville, Tennessee" appeal to?
2. In "Slippery" what does the child feel like?
3. In "This Is Just to Say" what adjectives does the poet use to describe the plums? What senses do these words appeal to?
4. In "Coolness" what sound does the poet hear? What does the poet feel?
5. In "Kansas Boy" what does the poet think the field of corn looks like? What taste is named? What sound?

Activities

A. Write the name of a season. Under it list all the sights, sounds, smells, tastes, and "touches" that you think are special about that time of year.

B. Use the poem "Coolness" as a model. Write a poem or a sentence or two of your own. Write about something like smoothness, roughness, loudness, or softness.

C. Illustrate one of the poems in this lesson. Draw a picture or use one from a magazine. Then copy the poem and attach it to the illustration.

10 — Writing a Poem

Writing Project

- A **poem** may describe an experience.

Have you ever thought very hard about just one thing? About one experience you have had—something you did or something you saw? Have you ever tried to choose just the right words to express that experience to someone else? That is what a poet does.

In this unit you have thought about sounds in poetry. You have practiced describing by telling how one thing is like another. You have practiced describing how things look, sound, and feel. Now you can use some of those ideas to write a poem you will share with your classmates.

1. Prewriting

Read these two poems.

A Dragon-Fly

When the heat of the summer
Made drowsy the land,
A dragon-fly came
And sat on my hand,
With its blue jointed body,
And wings like spun glass,
It lit on my fingers
As though they were grass.
—*Eleanor Farjeon*

Snow Toward Evening

Suddenly the sky turned gray,
The day,
Which had been bitter and chill,
Grew intensely soft and still.
Quietly
From some invisible blossoming tree
Millions of petals cool and white
Drifted and blew,
Lifted and flew,
Fell with the falling night.
—*Melville Cane*

Each poet expressed an experience. One wrote about a dragonfly alighting on her fingers. The other wrote about a snowfall. Think about the words the poets used to describe what they could see, hear, and feel, and how things moved. Look at the chart for Melville Cane's poem.

See	Hear	Feel	Move
sky turned gray	soft and still	bitter and chill	drifted and blew
blossoming tree	quietly	cool	lifted and flew
millions of petals			fell
white			

▶ Look around your classroom or out the window and make a list of objects you see. Here are some objects you might list.

- sneaker
- flower
- clock
- ball
- pencil
- sidewalk

Look at the list you made. Think about an experience each object reminds you of. For example, a sneaker might remind you of running in a race. A flower may make you think about working in the garden. After you think about each object, circle the one that reminds you of a happy experience. You will describe this experience in your poem.

▶ Make a chart like the example with these headings: See, Hear, Feel, Move. Under each heading write down words and phrases that describe your experience. Use your memory to think about what the experience was like. Fill in the chart with all of your ideas.

2. Writing

▶ Turn the headings from your chart into questions, like those on the next page. As you write an answer to each question, you will notice that your words almost make a poem.

Question	Answer
What did I see?	Dust flying
	Yellow ribbon at the finish line
What did I hear?	Silence followed by a bang
	Cheering, shouting, clapping
What did I feel?	Hot sun
	Tired legs
How did something move?	Runners moving swiftly and gracefully

▶ Use the answers to your questions to write your poem. What do you remember most about your experience? Use that thought to begin your poem. Then write other words and phrases to describe your experience. Add comparisons to your poem to describe how one thing is like another: *Runners moving swiftly and gracefully like frightened deer.*

3. Revising

▶ Write each line of your poem on a separate strip of paper. Rearrange the strips until your poem is in the best order. You may add new strips with new lines, or you may decide to throw some strips away. Copy the lines of your poem after you have decided on the best order. Then revise your poem, using this checklist as a guide.

Revision Checklist
- Did I begin by telling what I remember most?
- Did I tell what I could see, hear, and feel?
- Did I use comparisons?
- Are the lines of my poem in the best order?
- Did I add descriptive words to make my writing interesting?

Read the sample and notice how descriptive words were added to make the poem more interesting.

Hot
Sun burning like a fire. *blazing*
clapping
Cheering, and shouting, and (claping)!

Silence followed by a startling bang.
Dust flying.
Hopeful runners moving swiftly, gracefully
like frightened deer.
Hot sun burning like a blazing fire.
Cheering, shouting, clapping!
Tired legs reaching for
the yellow ribbon at the finish line.

EDITING MARKS

——	cross out
∧	add
↰	move
═	capital letter
╱	small letter
¶	indent
◯	check spelling

▶ Use the editing marks to revise your poem. With each change, read your poem aloud to hear how it sounds.

4. Publishing

▶ Use the Proofreading Checklist in the Young Writer's Handbook on page 377 to proofread your poem. Use the editing marks to make corrections. Remember, you do not have to indent the first line of a poem. Begin each new thought with a capital letter, and use punctuation at the end of a complete thought.

▶ Join your classmates to make a poetry mural. Cover an empty wall in your classroom with wrapping paper. Illustrate your poem, and glue your picture and poem on the wrapping paper. Then enjoy reading all of the poems on the mural.

Writing Project

A Collection of Poems

Make a collection of poems as a gift for a special person. Begin by selecting your favorite poems from those you have written and those you have read. Then make a book to hold them.

Choose several sheets of colored paper. Fold each sheet in half. Next, place the sheets inside each other. Punch two small holes in the seam. Then thread a string or a ribbon through the two holes. Tie the ends together.

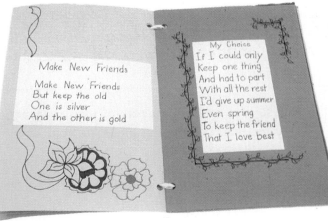

Copy the poems onto plain white cards. Write the author's name under each poem. Glue each card onto an inside page of your book. Decorate the colored borders if you wish.

Finally, write a title and your name on the cover of your book of poems.

270

Mathematics

Mathematics is a serious subject, but it can inspire humorous thoughts. Poetry can help you enjoy the lighter side of math.

▶ Try it. Read this poem. See if it expresses your thoughts about mathematics. Notice that one of the verses is about memorizing multiplication tables. Choose a verse from the poem that you especially like and memorize it.

Arithmetic

Arithmetic is where numbers fly
   like pigeons in and out of
   your head.
Arithmetic tells you how many
   you lose or win if you know
   how many you had before you
   lost or won. . . .
Arithmetic is numbers you squeeze
   from your head to your hand
   to your pencil to your paper
   till you get the answer.
Arithmetic is where the answer
   is right and everything is
   nice and you can look out
   the window and see the blue
   sky–or the answer is wrong
   and you have to start all over
   and try again and see how it
   comes out this time. . . .

Arithmetic is where you have
   to multiply–and you carry
   the multiplication table in
   your head and hope you won't
   lose it. . . .
If you ask your mother for one
   fried egg for breakfast and
   she gives you two fried eggs
   and you eat both of them,
   who is better in arithmetic,
   you or your mother?
                    —*Carl Sandburg*

Writers at Work Writers for children's TV programs often write jingles to help children learn important facts.

▶ Try it. Write a jingle to help a younger child learn a number fact. Here is an example: *Four plus four is eight.*
                              (Child's name), don't be late!

Prepositions   *pages 244–251*

A. Write each sentence. Underline the preposition once. Underline the object of the preposition twice.

1. You'll certainly get wet without an umbrella.
2. Two bronze statues stand in the park.
3. Many pioneers traveled across the prairie.
4. Our windows give us a view of the forest.
5. We rested during the afternoon.

B. Write each sentence. Underline the prepositional phrase.

6. Gil rested under the shady elm tree.
7. A snowy owl flew through the air.
8. How many sailboats are on the lake?
9. The detective hid behind a parked car.
10. The space shuttle landed after a safe flight.

C. Write *adverb* if the underlined word is an adverb. Write *preposition* if it is a preposition.

11. For two hours last night the rain poured <u>down</u>.
12. Dawn is waiting <u>inside</u> the train station.
13. We put the soccer balls <u>in</u> the closet.
14. Several bright yellow fish swam <u>around</u>.
15. The sign on the door says the doctor is <u>out</u>.
16. A hot-air balloon landed <u>near</u> the football field.

D. Write each sentence. Use the word in parentheses ( ) that correctly completes the sentence.

17. The three boys shared a joke (among, between) themselves.
18. Our school gave sports awards to Maria and (she, her).
19. Two silver jets passed directly over (we, us).
20. Who won the checkers game (between, among) Carl and May?

Checkpoint: Unit 7

Commas *pages 252–253*

E. Write each sentence. Add commas where necessary.

21. Yolanda come home soon.
22. Yes you might be right.
23. No the plane is late.
24. Shall we sing now Nat?
25. Well I am surprised!
26. I know Al that you are ten.

Context Clues *pages 254–255*

F. Write the underlined word. Then write the word in parentheses ( ) that gives its meaning.

27. There was a beautiful <u>array</u> of flowers at the flower show. (display, photograph)
28. The spy was sent on a <u>confidential</u> errand. He couldn't tell anyone about it. (useless, secret)
29. A wrecking crew will soon <u>demolish</u> the old building. (repair, destroy)
30. Lu showed her <u>gratitude</u> by giving me a present. (thanks, hope)

Poetry *pages 260–265*

G. Write the two things that are compared in each sentence. Then write whether the sentence is a *simile* or *metaphor*.

31. The baby's laughter chimed like bells.
32. This delicate teacup is as thin as an eggshell.
33. The pond was a mirror in the bright moonlight.
34. The breeze feels like feathers on my cheek.

H. Write these headings in a row: *See, Hear, Feel/Touch, Move.* Then think about the experience of walking in the rain. Under each heading, write down words and phrases that describe the experience.

See also Handbook pages 358–361, 382, 384.

Checkpoint: Unit 7

UNIT

8

Grammar
Sentences

Composition
Reasoning

The Cobbler

Crooked heels
  And scuffy toes
Are all the kinds
  Of shoes he knows.

He patches up
  The broken places,
Sews the seams
  And shines their faces.

—*Eleanor A. Chaffee*

1 Parts of Speech in Sentences

- A **part of speech** tells how a word is used in a sentence.

The following chart reviews six parts of speech.

	Definition	Example
noun	A **noun** names a person, place, thing, or idea.	May Day is a holiday.
pronoun	A **pronoun** takes the place of a noun or nouns.	It began long ago.
verb	An **action verb** shows action. A **linking verb** shows being.	The Romans honored the goddess Flora. May Day was her day.
adjective	An **adjective** describes a noun or pronoun.	Cold days were gone. The weather was warm.
adverb	An **adverb** describes a verb, an adjective, or another adverb.	The sun rose very early. Days were long now.
preposition	A **preposition** relates a noun or pronoun to another word.	May 1 used to be the first day of summer.

A noun can follow a linking verb: *May Day is a holiday*. A noun that follows a linking verb renames or identifies the subject.

Skills Tryout

Tell whether each underlined word is a noun, a pronoun, a verb, an adjective, an adverb, or a preposition.

1. The Romans picked flowers.
2. They made lovely bouquets.
3. The flowers were for Flora.
4. They decorated her statue.
5. Everyone danced merrily.
6. It was her holiday.

Practice

A. Write each sentence. Draw a line under the noun that follows a linking verb. Draw two lines under the subject that it renames or identifies.

EXAMPLE: On May Day in Sweden, actors are warriors.
ANSWER: On May Day in Sweden, actors are warriors.

1. One fighter is Summer.
2. The other is Winter.
3. Of course, Summer is always the winner.

B. Write each underlined word. After the word, write *noun, pronoun, verb, adjective, adverb,* or *preposition.*

4. The ancient Celts believed in a sun god.
5. During the winter the sun god disappeared.
6. They thought he was a prisoner.
7. Evil spirits had captured him.
8. They lit fires to chase the spirits away.
9. Some ancient peoples were believers in tree gods.
10. The people got up early on May Day.
11. They went into the woods to cut tree branches.
12. The branches were supposed to bring good luck.
13. In England, May Day became a big holiday.
14. People were always glad to see warm days again.
15. They cut down a tall tree.
16. Then they decorated it to make a Maypole.
17. Everyone danced around the Maypole.
18. Colorful Maypoles can still be seen on this holiday.

Application WRITING SENTENCES

Write the sentences below. Then write the part of speech of each word that is underlined.

Victoria Day occurs in May.   Queen Victoria was a powerful ruler.
It honors a queen, Victoria.   She was queen in the 1800s.

2 Compound Subjects

- A **compound subject** is two or more simple subjects that have the same predicate.

You know that the simple subject is the main word in the complete subject of a sentence. In the sentences below, the complete subjects are shown in blue, and the simple subjects are underlined.

The <u>principal</u> of our school announced a clean-up contest.
The art <u>teacher</u> for our class announced a clean-up contest.

Some sentences contain more than one main word in the complete subject. The sentences below have more than one simple subject.

The <u>principal</u> and our <u>teacher</u> announced a clean-up contest.
<u>Mrs. Colucci</u> or my <u>father</u> will be our block captain.

Two or more simple subjects that have the same predicate are called a compound subject. Here are some more sentences that have compound subjects.

<u>Cities</u>, <u>towns</u>, and <u>villages</u> will take part.
<u>Reiko</u> and <u>I</u> will plant flowers in a window box.

Notice that the simple subjects are joined by the conjunction *and* or *or*. A **conjunction** joins words.

Skills Tryout

Each sentence below has a compound subject. Name the simple subjects in each compound subject.

1. Our school and the newspaper will print advertisements.
2. The police and fire fighters will help us.
3. Brooms, bags, and cartons will be used.
4. Noreen and he are good sweepers.
5. Kenny and Tamar can clean the steps, too.

Practice

A. Write the complete subject of each sentence. If the subject is compound, write *compound*.

1. Sidewalks and steps will be swept clean.
2. You and Jonathan can collect the fallen branches.
3. One of the cleanest streets in our town is Davis Avenue.
4. The storekeepers and residents care about how their street looks.
5. A cousin of mine lives there.
6. Her family and my family planted trees there last spring.
7. We put up fences to protect the young trees.
8. Lew, Ira, or I will care for the trees.
9. Davis Avenue doesn't need a contest to look neat.
10. Sonia and I hope our street will look as nice.
11. Mrs. Colucci and my father made a work plan.
12. Everyone on our block will work four hours a week.
13. Today and tomorrow are my clean-up times.
14. The decorations committee helped repaint Town Hall.
15. Davis Avenue and our street will help our town win.

B. Write each sentence. Underline the compound subject.
EXAMPLE: Asheville and our town tied for the award.
ANSWER: <u>Asheville</u> and our <u>town</u> tied for the award.

16. The mayor and the governor will award the prizes.
17. Antonia and she have painted their front door.
18. Carl or you should win a special award.
19. The drugstore and the supermarket displayed posters.
20. Friday and Saturday were the busiest clean-up days.

Application WRITING SENTENCES

How would you clean up your neighborhood? Write five sentences about what you would do. Use a compound subject in each sentence.

3 Subject-Verb Agreement

- Compound subjects joined by *and* use the form of a verb that is used with a plural noun.

The correct verb form must be used in a sentence in order for the subject and verb to agree. The singular form of a verb must be used with a singular subject. The plural form must be used with a plural subject. Study the chart below.

	Singular	Plural
action verbs	Jo <u>likes</u> fairs.	We <u>like</u> fairs.
linking verbs	I <u>am</u> busy. She <u>was</u> a winner.	They <u>are</u> busy. The games <u>were</u> fun.

You know that a compound subject is two or more simple subjects that have the same verb. When the parts of a compound subject are joined by *and*, the verb is plural.

Nancy and Oliver <u>make</u> posters.
The trophy and the ribbons <u>are</u> prizes.
The races and the games <u>were</u> fun last year.
The students, parents, and teachers <u>sell</u> tickets.
My classmates and I <u>are</u> busy.
The adults and the children <u>like</u> fairs.

Skills Tryout

Name the verb in parentheses ( ) that correctly completes each sentence.

1. Jo, Dan, and Marjorie (finds, find) some boards.
2. Cathy and her friends (nail, nails) them together.
3. The triangles and a circle (are, is) blue.
4. Mr. Gerber and Ms. Danoff (paint, paints) the boards gold.
5. The posters and the flags (was, were) ready.

Practice

A. Write the verb in parentheses ( ) that correctly completes each sentence.

1. Juice and peanuts (is, are) popular snacks at the fair.
2. Mr. Healy and his daughter (cook, cooks) the chicken.
3. The Boy Scouts and Girl Scouts (serve, serves) the food.
4. The corn, fruit, and potatoes (taste, tastes) great.
5. Coleslaw and salads (completes, complete) the meal.
6. After lunch the blue team and the gold team (plays, play) tug-of-war.
7. Randy and Serena (are, is) captains of their teams.
8. Parents and teachers (cheers, cheer) both sides.
9. Serena and her team (pull, pulls) Randy over the line.
10. The winning team and the losing team (looks, look) tired.

B. Write each sentence. Use the correct form of the verb in parentheses ( ).

11. Boris and Heather (make, makes) kites for the fair.
12. Two students and Boris (plans, plan) a kite contest.
13. The kite contest and the soccer game (begin, begins).
14. The Blues and the Golds (play, plays) for the soccer cup.
15. All the soccer players and kite fliers (run, runs) onto the field.
16. Boris and the Blues (crash, crashes) into each other.
17. The Golds and Heather (are, is) a tangle of string.
18. The principal and the coaches (come, comes) to help.
19. Other students and parents (helps, help), too.
20. Boris, Heather, and the soccer players (laughs, laugh) at themselves.

Application WRITING SENTENCES

Write five sentences about something funny. Use *and* to connect compound subjects in your sentences.

4 — Compound Predicates

- A **compound predicate** is two or more verbs that have the same subject.

You know that the simple predicate is the main word in the complete predicate of a sentence. It is the verb.

Ms. Doyle bought the morning newspaper.
Ms. Doyle read the morning newspaper.

The words in green are the complete predicate of each sentence. The underlined word is the simple predicate, or verb.

Some sentences contain two or more verbs in the complete predicate.

Ms. Doyle bought and read the morning newspaper.

Notice that *Ms. Doyle* is the subject of both *bought* and *read*. The two verbs are joined by *and*.

A predicate with two or more verbs that have the same subject is called a compound predicate. Here are some more sentences that have compound predicates.

She opened the paper and read the headline.
Then she stopped, nodded, and smiled.

Skills Tryout

Name the verbs in the complete predicate of each sentence.

1. The class planned and wrote a class newspaper.
2. The students chose and edited the articles.
3. Ms. Doyle read and approved each story.
4. Mr. Cortes typed and proofread everything.
5. Sandra photocopied, sorted, and stapled the pages.

Practice

A. Write the complete predicate of each sentence. If the predicate is compound, write *compound*.

1. Everyone helped with the newspaper.
2. Paul sat and thought of ideas.
3. Diane revised and corrected articles.
4. Ms. Doyle stayed after school every day.
5. She explained things and answered questions.
6. Matt planned and designed the front page.
7. He arranged all the articles and pictures.
8. He pasted everything into place.
9. The newspaper surprised and pleased the other classes.
10. Everyone read and enjoyed it.

B. Write each sentence. Underline the compound predicate.

EXAMPLE: For weeks we hammered and sawed.
ANSWER: For weeks we <u>hammered</u> and <u>sawed</u>.

11. We stopped, rested, and talked.
12. The auditorium sparkled and shone.
13. The curtain opened and closed.
14. We danced and sang.
15. The audience cheered and clapped.

Application WRITING SENTENCES

How would you start a class newspaper, theater club, or other project? Write five sentences about what you would do. Use a compound predicate in each sentence. You may use one of the ideas listed below.

Organize a class trip to your state capital.
Start a pen-pal club with students in another state.
Invent a new sport or game.

5 Compound Sentences

> ● A **compound sentence** contains two or more simple sentences joined by a conjunction.

A simple sentence expresses one complete thought. It has one complete subject and one complete predicate.

Mercury is a small planet.
Jupiter is a large planet.

A compound sentence contains two or more simple sentences. The simple sentences are joined by *and, or,* or *but.*

Mercury is a small planet, and Jupiter is a large planet.
Jupiter is very far away, but you can often see it.
That light might be a star, or it might be a planet.

Notice that a compound sentence has at least two complete subjects and two complete predicates. It is different from a simple sentence that has a compound subject or a compound predicate.

Compound Sentence: Jupiter has sixteen moons, and Pluto has one moon.
Compound Subject: Saturn and Neptune have moons, too.
Compound Predicate: I looked at the sky and saw red Mars.

Skills Tryout

Tell whether each sentence is simple or compound.

1. Mercury was the name of a Roman god.
2. Mercury is nearest the sun, and Venus is second closest.
3. Each planet moves around the sun.
4. Mercury's year lasts 88 days, but Mars's year is 687 days.
5. Venus can be seen at dawn, or you might see it at night.

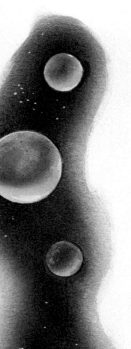

Practice

A. Write the sentences below. Then underline the two simple sentences in each.

1. We see stars and planets at night, and we see other bright lights, too.
2. Some lights are comets, and some are meteors.
3. Meteors are often seen, but comets are rare.
4. Comets are balls of frozen gas, and they orbit the sun.
5. Meteors are called shooting stars, and they travel fast.
6. Meteors burn up in space, or they fall to Earth as meteorites.
7. Some meteorites are stony, and some are balls of metal.
8. Sometimes very large meteorites hit Earth, and they make big holes in the ground.
9. The largest meteorite was found in Africa, and the second largest was found in Greenland.
10. People sometimes find meteorite holes, but the meteorites are usually gone.

B. Write *simple* or *compound* for each sentence.

11. The sun is a star, and it supplies heat for Earth.
12. It is only a medium-sized star, but it is the star closest to Earth.
13. Our sun and the other stars are giant balls of gas.
14. The sun is very bright, but it has some dark spots.
15. Scientists call these areas sunspots and study them closely.

Application WRITING SENTENCES

Write five sentences about the sun, the moon, the stars, or the planets. Write three compound sentences and two simple sentences with compound subjects or predicates.

6 Writing Compound Sentences

- A comma is used before the conjunction *and, or,* or *but* in a compound sentence.

- A **run-on sentence** is two or more sentences not separated by correct punctuation or connecting words.

You know that a compound sentence is formed from two or more simple sentences joined by a conjunction. Notice that a comma is used before the conjunction in the sentence below.

Memorial Day is in May, and Flag Day is in June.

A run-on sentence strings sentences together incorrectly. The sentence below is a run-on sentence.

One holiday honors people the other honors the flag.

You can correct a run-on sentence by making two simple sentences. You can also make one compound sentence by adding a comma and a conjunction.

One holiday honors people. The other honors the flag.
One holiday honors people, and the other honors the flag.

Skills Tryout

Tell whether each is a compound sentence or a run-on sentence.

1. Memorial Day was first called Decoration Day many people still call it that.
2. It was originally a day to honor Civil War soldiers, but now it honors soldiers from every war.
3. Parades are held in most towns, and a special ceremony takes place in Arlington, Virginia.
4. People honor the Unknown Soldier a bugle plays.
5. Our town has a parade a memorial service is held.

Practice

A. Write each sentence. Add a comma before the conjunction.

1. Flag Day was first officially celebrated in 1877 and it became a national holiday in 1916.
2. Before the Revolution colonists flew the British flag but later they had their own flag.
3. It was called the Grand Union and it had thirteen stripes with the British flag in the corner.
4. The colonists showed their loyalty to Great Britain but they also showed their love for America.
5. The Grand Union flag flew over Boston and it could be seen for miles.
6. After July 4, 1776, the colonists needed a new flag but they had trouble deciding on one.
7. Each colony had its own flag and each thought its flag was best.
8. Virginia's flag had a rattlesnake and it had the words "Don't Tread on Me."
9. Betsy Ross may have sewn the first flag or she may not have.
10. She lived in Philadelphia and she did make flags.

B. Correct these run-on sentences. Write each as a compound sentence by adding a comma and a conjunction.

11. A flag was chosen on June 14, 1777 it was soon flown.
12. In 1814, Francis Scott Key wrote a poem about the flag he called it "The Star-Spangled Banner."
13. He saw a flag with fifteen stars it had fifteen stripes.
14. Stripes were added for new states the flag got too large.
15. Today's flag has fifty stars it has only thirteen stripes.

Application WRITING SENTENCES

Describe your state's flag. Write five compound sentences.

7 Homographs

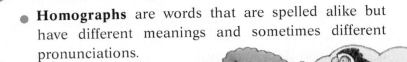

- **Homographs** are words that are spelled alike but have different meanings and sometimes different pronunciations.

The bird's owner and the doctor are having trouble understanding each other. They have forgotten that the word *bill* has more than one meaning. A bill can be the beak of a bird or the record of money a person owes.

Words like *bill* are called homographs. *Homograph* comes from Greek and means "written alike." Some homographs look and sound alike but have different meanings.

My parents play <u>bridge</u>.   **A truck drove across the <u>bridge</u>.**

Other homographs look alike but have different pronunciations as well as different meanings.

Tie <u>lead</u> weights to the fishing line. (led)
Can you <u>lead</u> us out of here? (lēd)

Skills Tryout

Name the pair of homographs in each sentence. In your own words tell what each homograph means.

1. We shed our knapsacks and put them in the shed.
2. The swallow will swallow that worm.
3. I would never desert anyone in the desert.
4. There was a tear in his eye when he saw the tear in his favorite shirt.
5. We had to wind up the game after the wind started blowing.

Practice

A. Write each pair of sentences. Underline the two homographs.

1. Don't tear your sweater. Onions make my eyes tear.
2. Plant a row of peas. Our friendly argument became a row.
3. Wind the string into a ball. What makes the wind blow?
4. Farmer Jones's sow had piglets. Liam will sow the beans.
5. She plays a bass fiddle. Tom caught three bass.

B. Write each sentence. Then write 1 or 2 to show which meaning of the underlined homograph is used.

fleet: 1. swift   2. a group of ships
pile: 1. a heap   2. fibers on the surface of a rug
sink: 1. to go beneath the surface of water   2. a basin
shed: 1. to take something off   2. a small building
light: 1. a lamp   2. not heavy

6. The child watched her toy boat sink.
7. Is that package light enough for you?
8. The tugboats and fireboats welcomed the American fleet.
9. What kind of snake shed this skin?
10. This rug has a very thick pile.
11. Please put the lawn mower in the shed.
12. Don't forget to turn off the light.
13. Are your clothes in that pile of laundry?
14. The antelope is a fleet animal.
15. Wash your hands in the sink.

Application USING LANGUAGE

Choose three of the homographs given below. Write two sentences for each. Show the two meanings of each word.

bark   pen   might   fly   club   squash   lap

Parts of Speech   *pages 276–277*

A. Write the part of speech of each underlined word.

1. Our country <u>is</u> a <u>land</u> of immigrants.
2. Many immigrants <u>came</u> <u>in</u> the nineteenth century.
3. It was a time of <u>great</u> unrest.
4. People <u>were</u> <u>sad</u> to leave their homelands.
5. Cities were <u>soon</u> filled with <u>new</u> Americans.

Compound Subjects and Compound Predicates   *pages 278–279, 282–283*

B. Write each sentence. Draw one line under any compound subject. Draw two lines under any compound predicate.

6. The Kolbas and the Crowells made a movie.
7. They planned and talked.
8. Tom and Barbara designed the set.
9. They hammered and sawed.
10. They sanded and painted.
11. Jugglers, magicians, and dancers were needed.
12. The cameras and lights went into action.
13. A knight and a villain were seen.
14. Barbara watched and waited.
15. The audience clapped and shouted.

Subject-Verb Agreement   *pages 280–281*

C. Write the correct form of the verb in parentheses (   ).

16. Spring and summer (is, are) my favorite seasons.
17. May and June (seem, seems) to pass very quickly.
18. Teachers and students (enjoy, enjoys) vacations.
19. Chuck and Janet (visit, visits) cousins in Canada.
20. Hot days and cool nights (make, makes) July pleasant.

Compound Sentences *pages 284–285*

D. Write *simple* or *compound* for each sentence.

21. The parade started, but the band wasn't there.
22. They were supposed to be there at noon.
23. The mayor spoke, but the governor didn't speak.
24. The band arrived, and the parade began.
25. For hours the sounds of fife and drums were heard all over our little town.

Writing Compound Sentences *pages 286–287*

E. Write each run-on sentence as a compound sentence.

26. The pitcher threw a fastball the batter did not swing.
27. The umpire called it a strike the batter complained.
28. The catcher signaled the pitcher shook her head.
29. The pitcher may have thrown the ball too slowly the batter may have timed it perfectly.
30. The ball went over the fence our team won.

Homographs *pages 288–289*

F. Write the homographs in each sentence.

31. We played bridge on the bridge.
32. The snake shed its skin in the shed.
33. Sow the seeds and feed the sow.
34. The bill for the birdseed was in the parrot's bill.
35. The crows had a row in the row of corn.
36. I dropped my ball-point pen in the pig's pen.
37. The light from that light is bright.
38. A fly can fly through that window.
39. The passage will lead through a lead door.
40. Stick this price tag on the stick.

See also Handbook pages 362–367.

Sentence Combining

- Sentences with ideas that go together can be combined.

Grammar and Writing Workshop

Read the sentences below.

A. Dan looked for flying saucers.
B. I went along with him. (, and)
A + B. Dan looked for flying saucers, and I went along with him.

Sentence B adds to the facts given in sentence A. We can combine the two sentences. Sentence A + B includes all the facts from the two shorter sentences. Only a comma and the word *and* have been added. The compound sentence A + B shows <u>how</u> the ideas in sentence A and sentence B go together. They are separate, equally important ideas joined by the word *and*.

In the example below, the two shorter sentences go together in a different way. Both sentences are about the same topic. But sentence D gives an unexpected fact that contrasts with the fact in sentence C. The contrasting sentences can be combined into one strong sentence. Sentence C + D shows how it is done. A compound sentence is formed by adding a comma and the word *but*.

C. We waited for hours.
D. No flying saucers appeared. (, but)
C + D. We waited for hours, but no flying saucers appeared.

Sometimes two sentences give two possible choices. Such sentences can be joined with a comma and the word *or*. Sentence E + F shows how it is done.

E. Those saucers have to arrive soon.
F. I'm going home. (, or)
E + F. Those saucers have to arrive soon, or I'm going home.

Combine-a-Pair Combine each pair of sentences below. Use the clues in parentheses ( ) the way they were used on page 292. Write each new sentence.

1. Dorothy doesn't believe in flying saucers.
   Sharon agrees with her. (, **and**)
2. The Air Force studied the question for many years.
   They found no proof that flying saucers exist. (, **but**)
3. Some scientists think there is life on other planets.
   They don't think space creatures have visited Earth. (, **but**)
4. Flying saucers are often just ordinary airplanes.
   They might be distant stars. (, **or**)
5. Read a variety of books.
   You will get only one side of the story. (, **or**)
6. Get enough reliable information.
   Make your own decision about flying saucers. (, **and**)

No-Clue Time Combine each pair of sentences without clues. Think about how the ideas in each pair of sentences go together. Use a comma and the word *and, but,* or *or* to join the sentences. Write each new sentence.

7. Andy likes science fiction.
   He keeps his favorite books by his bed.
8. His favorite authors know a lot about science.
   They are good storytellers.
9. The hero of one story traveled to the future.
   He could not return.
10. The hero of another story traveled back in time.
    She met Dolley Madison.
11. Andy would like to visit the future.
    I would rather visit the past.
12. I might journey to ancient Egypt.
    I might shake hands with Benjamin Franklin.

8 Listening to and Analyzing Proverbs

- A **proverb** is a popular saying that expresses a general truth or a bit of wisdom.

You can't judge a book by its cover.

A penny saved is a penny earned.

Don't count your chickens before they hatch.

The longest journey begins with a single step.

You can't teach an old dog new tricks.

Too many cooks spoil the broth.

You have probably heard most of these statements many times. They are proverbs. Proverbs are popular sayings that comment on everyday happenings. They say something true about daily life.

Proverbs are usually short, direct statements. The meaning of a proverb, however, often goes beyond the simple or obvious meaning of its words. For example, the proverb *You can't judge a book by its cover* does not only say something about books. Its broader meaning is that outward appearances can sometimes be deceiving. Proverbs say in a clever way what many people believe is true.

Skills Tryout

Tell what you think each of the proverbs below means.

1. All's well that ends well.
2. You cannot make footprints in last winter's snow.
3. One good turn deserves another.
4. What can't be cured must be endured.
5. Two heads are better than one.

Practice

A. Write the proverb suggested by each situation below. Choose from the following proverbs.

> Haste makes waste.
> The early bird catches the worm.
> You can't judge a book by its cover.
> Where there's a will, there's a way.
> Where there is smoke, there is fire.

1. Jean's cat came home with a mouthful of feathers. Jean was sure she knew what had happened.
2. When I saw the dog, I thought it was friendly. I was really surprised when it bit me.
3. Fred did ten math problems in five minutes, but nine of them were wrong.
4. Jerry waited until the last minute to start his report on scuba diving. By the time he got to the library, Sue had already borrowed all the books on that subject.
5. No one believed Mary would finish the race after her fall, but she knew she could do it.

B. Write at least two proverbs that are suggested by this cartoon.

Application SPEAKING AND LISTENING

Ask older family members or friends to tell you some proverbs they know. Ask for explanations of sayings that you do not understand. Share your collection with the class. Explain the meanings of the proverbs you have collected.

9 Following and Giving Directions

- Listen to and follow directions carefully.
- When giving directions, be specific and arrange the steps in order.

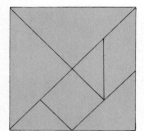

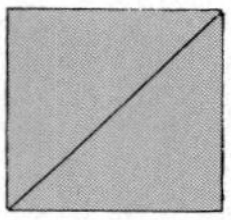

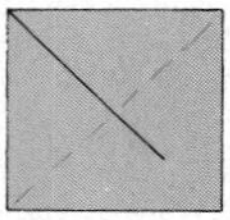

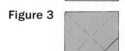

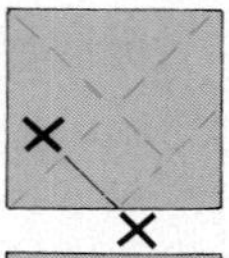

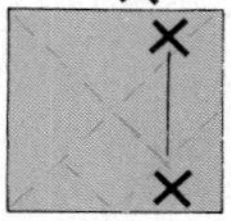

The figure shown on the left is a tangram. A tangram is a very old Chinese puzzle. A tangram is made by dividing a square into seven parts. The parts can be put together in different ways to form different pictures.

To make your own tangram, you must follow directions carefully. To tell someone else how to make a tangram picture, you must give clear, step-by-step directions.

Figure 1

Figure 2

Figure 3

Figure 4

Figure 5

Skills Tryout

Make your own tangram. Start with a square that is four inches on each side, and follow these directions.

1. Draw a line that divides the square into two triangles. Start in the upper right corner and end in the lower left corner.

2. Draw a line that almost divides the square into four triangles. Start in the upper left corner and end at a point 1½ inches from the lower right corner.

3. Make a dot at the end of the second line. Use it as the center point of a third line. The third line turns the lower right corner into a triangle.

4. Make a diamond in the lower center of the square. Do this by connecting the two points shown in Figure 4.

5. Your last line will make a small triangle to the right of the diamond. Draw the line between the two points shown in Figure 5.

Practice

A. Now make a tangram picture. First, number the pieces of your tangram as shown in the diagram and cut them out. Then follow the directions below to make a tangram house.

  1. Use pieces 1 and 2 to form a large square.
  2. Use pieces 4 and 6 to make a small square.
  3. Place piece 5 above the small square.
  4. Place the large square to the left of the two small squares.
  5. Use pieces 3 and 7 to make a roof.

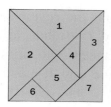 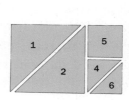 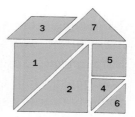

B. Practice giving oral directions. Tell someone else how to make the tangram swan shown on this page. Use words such as *up, down, above, below, to the left,* and *to the right* in your directions.

  6. Start with the swan's head. Tell how piece 4 should be joined to piece 5.
  7. Tell how piece 5 should be joined to piece 3.
  8. Tell how piece 3 should be joined to piece 7.
  9. Tell how piece 7 should be joined to pieces 2 and 1.
  10. Explain how to add piece 6 to make a tail for the swan.

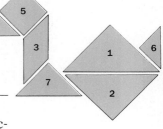

Application WRITING DIRECTIONS

Make an original tangram picture. Then prepare written directions that tell someone else how to put the picture together. Exchange papers with a classmate and see how well you can follow each other's directions.

10 — Solving Analogies

- **Analogies** show relationships between things.

Word puzzles are challenging and fun. One kind of word puzzle is an analogy. Analogies help you to see relationships between apparently different things. They do this by comparing the things.

Can you supply the missing word in this analogy?

<u>Rocket</u> is to <u>fast</u> as <u>turtle</u> is to _____.

To complete the analogy, you must understand the relationship between the words given. How does the word *fast* relate to the word *rocket*? *Fast* tells the rocket's rate of speed. The missing word must relate to the word *turtle* in the same way. It must tell about the turtle's speed.

<u>Rocket</u> is to <u>fast</u> as <u>turtle</u> is to <u>slow</u>.

Now look at this analogy.

<u>Wheel</u> is to <u>automobile</u> as _____ is to <u>ship</u>.

To solve the analogy, study the first two items. How are they related? A wheel steers an automobile. What steers a ship? A rudder steers a ship.

<u>Wheel</u> is to <u>automobile</u> as <u>rudder</u> is to <u>ship</u>.

Skills Tryout

Complete these analogies. Explain how you solved each one.

1. *Broccoli* is to *vegetable* as *apple* is to _____.
2. *Dark* is to *light* as *high* is to _____.
3. *Red* is to *stop* as _____ is to *go*.
4. *Hammer* is to *carpenter* as *hoe* is to _____.
5. *Fur* is to *cat* as _____ are to *bird*.

Practice

A. Supply the missing word in each analogy. Write the analogy.

1. *Up* is to *down* as *in* is to _____.
2. *Georgia* is to *state* as *United States* is to _____.
3. *Dog* is to *collie* as _____ is to *robin*.
4. *Happy* is to *laugh* as *sad* is to _____.
5. *Bird* is to *fly* as *fish* is to _____.
6. *Day* is to *Tuesday* as _____ is to *September*.
7. *Branch* is to *tree* as *petal* is to _____.
8. *Puppy* is to *dog* as *calf* is to _____.
9. *Long* is to *short* as _____ is to *dry*.
10. *Egypt* is to *country* as *Nile* is to _____.

B. Complete each analogy by adding the second pair of words. Add two items that have the same relationship as the first two items in the analogy.

11. *Hot* is to *cold* as _____ is to _____.
12. *Elephant* is to *big* as _____ is to _____.
13. *Hat* is to *head* as _____ is to _____.
14. *Bark* is to *dog* as _____ is to _____.
15. *Mountain* is to *hill* as _____ is to _____.

Application WRITING ANALOGIES

Use the suggestions below to make up your own analogies. Then have a classmate try to solve your analogies.

a. Create an opposite analogy. Each pair of words should be opposites.
   EXAMPLE: Night is to day as black is to white.
b. Create a child-and-adult analogy.
   EXAMPLE: Kitten is to cat as cub is to bear.
c. Create a mathematical analogy. Base it on a multiplication fact.
   EXAMPLE: Five is to fifteen as six is to eighteen.

11 Presenting Information in a Bar Graph

Writing Project

> ● A **bar graph** compares information in a diagram.

Information can be presented in many ways. Sometimes it is easiest to show a reader information in a diagram. A bar graph is one kind of diagram that can be used. Your teacher might make a bar graph to show class members' heights or test scores. A bar graph makes it easy for a reader to compare information.

In this lesson you will take a survey and show your results in a bar graph. Then you will write a paragraph explaining the information to your classmates.

1. Prewriting

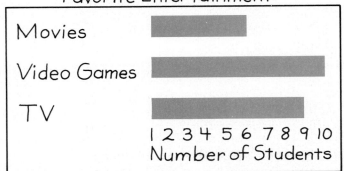

Favorite Entertainment

Movies

Video Games

TV

1 2 3 4 5 6 7 8 9 10
Number of Students

Look at the bar graph. It compares the number of students who prefer three kinds of entertainment. The kinds are listed on the side of the graph. The numbers across the bottom tell how many students prefer each one.

Point to *movies* on the graph. Follow the bar next to it until it ends. Look below the bar to the number 6. This number tells you that six students prefer movies. Read the graph to find out how many students prefer video games and TV. Compare the lengths of the three bars on the graph. This is how you know that the largest number of students prefer video games.

▶ Take a survey of your classmates to obtain information that you can show in a bar graph. Make a list of several "favorites" you would like to ask your classmates about. Here are some suggestions:

- Do you like books of fact, fiction, or biography best?
- Which season of the year do you like best?
- Do you like dogs, cats, or guinea pigs best?
- What is your favorite breakfast food?
- What is your favorite hobby?

Choose one idea you would like to use for your survey. This will be your topic. Tell your classmates what your topic is and ask for volunteers to be in your survey.

▶ Make a card for each student in your survey. As each classmate answers your question, record the answer and any comments on a card. When your survey is complete, group the

Name: Teresa Ramos
Favorite kind of
entertainment:
　　　video games
Comments:
　　I think video
games are the best because
they are challenging.

cards by students who gave the same answer. Count the number of students in each group.

▶ Use the information from your survey cards to make a bar graph. Write numbers across the bottom of your graph. Begin with number *1*. End with the number of students who gave the most popular answer. List the answers classmates gave to your question on the side of your graph. Now fill in the information from your survey cards to complete your bar graph.

2. Writing

Begin your paragraph with a topic sentence that states the purpose of your survey. In your topic sentence tell who you surveyed and what you were trying to find out. For example, "I surveyed the fifth-grade class to find out what kind of entertainment they like best." You might say, "I asked twenty-seven students what their favorite breakfast food is."

▶Write the topic sentence of your paragraph. Follow the topic sentence with sentences that give the results of your survey. Report the results, using the information from your bar graph. Conclude your paragraph with a summary of your survey results, like this: "The results of my survey show that video games are the most popular form of entertainment among fifth-graders."

3. Revising

▶Compare your paragraph to your bar graph. Check to be sure you have reported information correctly in your paragraph. Read your paragraph aloud and listen for words and sentences that can be improved. Use this checklist as a guide for revising your paragraph.

Revision Checklist
- Did I begin with a topic sentence that states the purpose of my survey?
- Did I follow the topic sentence with sentences that give the results of my survey?
- Did I conclude with a summary of my survey results?
- Are the facts from my survey correct?
- Did I use a variety of words instead of repeating words?

Read the sample and notice how a variety of words is used instead of repeating words.

prefer
ten students, like video games (to play).
classmates favor and _others_
Nine students like television, Six students

I surveyed the fifth-grade class to find out what kind of entertainment they like best. Ten students prefer to play video games. Nine classmates favor television, and six others enjoy movies most. The results of my survey show that video games are the most popular form of entertainment among fifth-graders.

EDITING MARKS

──	cross out
∧	add
♂	move
═	capital letter
/	small letter
¶	indent
◯	check spelling

▶ Now use the editing marks to change your paragraph.

4. Publishing

▶ Before you share the results of your survey, proofread your paragraph, using a ruler. Place the ruler under each line as you are reading. Concentrate on one line at a time. Use the Proofreading Checklist in the Young Writer's Handbook on page 377. Make corrections, using the editing marks.

▶ Hang your paragraph with your bar graph on a bulletin board. Add pictures, poems, and books to your display. For example, if the class picked summer as their favorite season, find pictures and poems about summer for your display. If you asked the class to choose among books of fact, fiction, and biography, display books of their favorite type.

Writing Project

A Puzzle Collection

Make a class collection of puzzles.

1. Make hidden-word puzzles. Write a few words on graph paper, one letter in each square. Use words naming things that belong to a group. Then fill in the free spaces with extra letters. (Notice the 15 animals in this puzzle.)

2. Make part-to-whole analogy puzzles. Think of something that is part of a whole. For example, a cow is a part of a herd, and a lion is a part of a pride. That statement becomes an analogy when you say: *Cow is to herd as lion is to pride.* Make puzzles by leaving out one part of the analogy.

Cow is to herd as _____ is to pride.

Grain is to sand as _____ is to water.

Room is to house as classroom is to _____.

Toe is to foot as finger is to _____.

○ is to ● as _____ is to ■

8 is to 8 as _____ is to ⊠

◪ is to ◪ as _____ is to ◑

3. Make shape-and-shade analogy puzzles. Use shapes and shadings to show likenesses and differences.

When you finish, ask your classmates to solve the puzzles.

Building Bridges

Mathematics

In this unit you have used word analogies to show relationships between things. Numbers can show relationships, too. Look at these relationships.

- If 1 foot = 12 inches and 3 feet = 36 inches, then 3 feet > 30 inches.
- If 0°C = 32°F and 100°C = 212°F, then 88°C < 212°F.

▶ Try it. Use the information above to solve these problems.

1. Water freezes at 32°F. Jeanette's thermometer shows that it is 5°C outside. Is it freezing outside?

2. Mario is making a collar and leash for his dog. The dog's neck is ten inches around. Mario wants the leash to be three feet long. He has sixty inches of cord. Does he have enough cord for both the collar and the leash?

Writers at Work Cooking for a family is not easy. Imagine cooking for a restaurant full of hungry people! That is the responsibility of a chef.

▶ Try it. Imagine that you are the chef for a large restaurant. You want to use this recipe. Rewrite the recipe so it will serve 60 people. Be sure to keep the steps in order. (The oven temperature and baking time will remain the same.)

Popovers for 6 People

1 cup flour   2 eggs
1 cup milk   1 teaspoon salt

1. Heat the oven to 400°F.
2. Grease 6 popover cups with butter.
3. Beat the eggs well.
4. Mix in the flour, milk, and salt.
5. Bake at 400°F for 50 minutes, or until popovers are golden brown.

Building Bridges

Checkpoint: Unit 8

Sentences *pages 276–287*

A. Write each underlined word below. After the word write *noun, pronoun, verb, adjective, adverb,* or *preposition.*

1. Alex <u>came</u> to the party.
2. Please pass <u>me</u> a pen.
3. I have a pet <u>mouse</u>.
4. Jane wore a <u>straw</u> hat.
5. We drove <u>across</u> the bridge.
6. Run <u>quickly</u> to the store.

B. Write each sentence below. Underline the compound subject or compound predicate.

7. The new bakery and pet store will both open tomorrow.
8. The chickens scratched, pecked, and squawked.
9. The excited football fans clapped and cheered.
10. Mr. Levy and a neighbor repaired an old fence.
11. A group of schoolchildren laughed and played.
12. Scott, June, or Alan can carry those trunks to the attic.
13. The wind howled and whistled.
14. Students, parents, and teachers attended the school play.

C. Write the verb in parentheses ( ) that correctly completes each sentence.

15. Mrs. Santos and Rose (swim, swims) together at the pool.
16. Tomatoes, carrots, and lettuce (goes, go) into the salad.
17. My sister and I (like, likes) books about science.
18. Ten boys and girls (dances, dance) the Virginia reel.

D. Write each sentence. Underline the two simple sentences in each.

19. Do you enjoy playing baseball, or do you prefer soccer?
20. Many snakes are harmless, but some are poisonous.
21. The potato soup is ready, and it tastes delicious.
22. Lucie found a fossil, but I discovered two arrowheads.

E. Write *compound* or *run-on* for each sentence.

23. These shiny pebbles may be valuable they may not be.
24. Tim and Miko are neighbors, and they have fun together.
25. Kelly went to the library she forgot her card.
26. The boat will leave soon, but we can still get on.

Homographs   *pages 288–289*

F. Write each pair of sentences. Underline the two homographs.

27. Don't tear your coat. A tear rolled down my face.
28. Grandpa will wind the yarn. A brisk wind is blowing.
29. Gather sticks for the fire. That glue sticks well on paper.
30. Runners are fleet. An admiral commands this fleet.

Reasoning   *pages 294–299*

G. Write what you think each proverb means.

31. A stitch in time saves nine.
32. Every cloud has a silver lining.

H. Write the correct word in parentheses ( ) to complete each analogy.

33. *Inch* is to *height* as *pound* is to (weight, ruler).
34. *Strong* is to *weak* as *early* is to (fast, late).
35. *Beef* is to *meat* as *peach* is to (fuzz, fruit).

I. Read the directions for touching your toes. Then write the steps in the correct order.

Bend forward from the waist.
Raise your arms above your head.
Return to a standing position, arms at your sides.
Do not bend your knees, though.

See also Handbook pages 362–367.

Cumulative Review

Sentences   *pages 10–17, 278–285*

A. Write the complete subject of each sentence. Underline the simple subject. Write (*You*) if the subject is understood.

1. My friend Lori ran in a race last Saturday.
2. Come to my house for dinner tonight.
3. The weary hikers rested on the mountaintop.
4. Take some pears home to your brother.

B. Write the complete predicate of each sentence. Underline the simple predicate.

5. My sister solves crossword puzzles on rainy days.
6. The musicians were practicing for a performance.
7. Scott's mother built a bookcase for his room.
8. Our basketball team has won every game.

C. Write each sentence. Underline the compound subject or compound predicate.

9. Erica and Rosemary planned their Halloween costumes.
10. The seals swam and splashed in the chilly ocean waters.
11. Singers, actors, and dancers bowed to the audience.
12. We stopped and waited on the busy street corner.
13. A police officer and a firefighter spoke to our class.

D. Write the verb in parentheses ( ) that correctly completes each sentence.

14. Ducks and geese (fly, flies) in flocks.
15. Terry and Paul (make, makes) wooden toys.
16. Doctors and nurses (care, cares) for sick people.
17. Children and adults (enjoy, enjoys) a colorful parade.
18. Trucks and cars (rumble, rumbles) across the bridge.
19. Sunshine and rain (is, are) good for a garden.

Cumulative Review

E. Write *simple* or *compound* for each sentence.

20. Sandy's bicycle had a flat tire, but I fixed it.
21. Marilyn wrote a report about stars and planets.
22. Pat and Mickey will mail your letters.
23. Kyle skated across the pond, and Billy watched him.

Capital Letters and Periods   *pages 52–57*

F. Write the sentences. Capitalize the proper nouns. Write the abbreviations correctly.

24. Did albert banks, sr, open a restaurant on rte 31?
25. Last aug we visited the grand canyon.
26. On wed we are having a surprise party for ms dow.
27. Will dr martinez be in his office at 11 am today?

Verbs   *pages 88–93, 96–97, 100–105*

G. Write each sentence. Underline the verb. Then write whether it is an *action verb* or a *linking verb*.

28. The cool summer breeze feels refreshing.
29. The chipmunk hides its food in the tree.
30. Alan and I are classmates this year.
31. The plane flew swiftly from Boston to Chicago.
32. Eleanor plays the flute and the trombone.

H. Write each sentence. Draw one line under the main verb. Draw two lines under the helping verb.

33. Clara is making a poster for our science fair.
34. Richard has lost his new glasses.
35. You will enjoy a trip through the Great Smoky Mountains.
36. Some students have finished the lesson already.

I. Write the past-tense form of each verb.

37. fall   **41.** drink   **45.** wear
38. rub   **42.** ride   **46.** do
39. think   **43.** carry   **47.** see
40. give   **44.** sip   **48.** dry

Pronouns   *pages 128–137*

J. Write whether each pronoun is a *subject pronoun* or an *object pronoun*.

49. she   **50.** I   **51.** him   **52.** we   **53.** me   **54.** us

K. Write each sentence below. Use the correct pronoun in parentheses ( ).

55. The dog is (their, theirs).   **57.** That is (my, mine) pen.
56. Diane cut (hers, her) hair.   **58.** Is this hat (yours, your)?

Adjectives and Adverbs   *pages 170–177, 202–205, 208–209*

L. Write each sentence. Underline the predicate adjective once. Underline twice the noun or pronoun it describes.

59. Michael felt pleased with his report card.
60. I was interested in your seashell collection.
61. The leopard looked restless in its cage at the zoo.
62. Pam seems tired after her long swim.
63. Many students were hungry just before lunch.

M. For each adjective write the two forms used to compare persons, places, or things.

64. sensible   **65.** bad   **66.** dark   **67.** good

N. For each adverb write the form used to compare two actions. Then write the form used to compare three or more actions.

68. quickly   **69.** well   **70.** badly   **71.** early

O. Write each sentence. Use the correct word in parentheses ( ).

72. The waves (gentle, gently) rocked the canoe.
73. This banana bread tastes (sweet, sweetly).
74. The music club sang the songs very (good, well).
75. Too much water is (bad, badly) for the geranium plant.

Prepositions   *pages 244–249*

P. Write each sentence. Then write whether the underlined word is a *preposition* or an *adverb*.

76. I live <u>near</u> the lake.   **78.** Jeff was <u>outside</u> the barn.
77. The top spun <u>around</u>.   **79.** Hold the picture <u>up</u>.

Q. Write each sentence. Underline the preposition once. Underline the object of the preposition twice.

80. Hang your jacket in the closet.
81. Stan and Molly are members of our club.
82. We played volleyball on the beach.
83. Take some flowers to Mrs. McGregor.

Commas   *pages 178–179, 252–253*

R. Write the sentences. Add commas where they are needed.

84. Well are you coming to my house on Saturday Kevin?
85. Robin swept washed and waxed the floor.
86. Yes Stacy you will need a raincoat today.
87. Would you like rice potatoes or noodles?

Acknowledgments continued from page ii

PERMISSIONS: We wish to thank the following authors, publishers, agents, corporations, and individuals for their permission to reprint copyrighted materials. Page 2: "Late summer evening..." from *More Cricket Songs: Japanese Haiku*, translated and © 1971 by Harry Behn. Reprinted by permission of Harcourt Brace Jovanovich, Inc. Page 18: "Sing a Song of People" by Lois Lenski. Reprinted by permission of The Lois Lenski Covey Foundation, Inc. Page 26: This Key to Pronunciation is adapted from *Scott, Foresman Intermediate Dictionary*, by E.L. Thorndike and Clarence L. Barnhart. Copyright © 1983 by Scott, Foresman and Company. Reprinted by permission. Page 46: "Old Log House" from *A World to Know* by James S. Tippett. Copyright © 1933 by Harper & Row, Publishers, Inc. Renewed 1961 by Martha K. Tippett. Reprinted by permssion of the publisher. Page 86: "The Three Horses" from *I Rode the Black Horse Far Away* by Ivy O. Eastwick. Copyright © 1960 by Abingdon Press. Used by permission. Page 88: "Cat" from *Menagerie* by Mary Britton Miller. Reprinted by permission of the Estate of Mary Britton Miller. Page 142: "Nym and Graph" from *It Doesn't Always Have to Rhyme* by Eve Merriam. Copyright © 1964 by Eve Merriam. Reprinted by permission of the author. Page 168: "Abraham Lincoln: by Mildred Plew Meigs. From *Child Life Magazine*. Copyright 1936, 1964 by Rand McNally & Company. Reprinted by permission of C. Walter Ruckel. Pages 186–187: Excerpts from *The Secrets of the Andes* by Ann Nolan Clark. Copyright 1952, renewed © 1980 by Ann Nolan Clark. Reprinted by permission of Viking Penguin, Inc. Page 188: Excerpt from *The Cricket in Times Square* by George Selden. Copyright © 1960 by George Selden Thompson and Garth Williams. Reprinted by permission of Farrar, Straus & Giroux, Inc., and Laurence Pollinger Limited. Page 200: "Whistles" from *Poems* by Rachel Field (New York: Macmillan, 1957). Reprinted by permission of Macmillan Publishing Company. Page 226: Excerpt from *The World Almanac and Book of Facts*, 1982 edition, copyright © Newspaper Enterprise Association, Inc., 1981, New York, NY 10166 Page 237: "Sacagawea" from *The World Book Encyclopedia*. © 1983 World Book, Inc. Page 242: "The Bridge" in *I Thought I Heard the City* by Lilian Moore. Copyright © 1969 by Lilian Moore. Reprinted with the permission of Atheneum Publishers. Page 274: Eleanor Chaffee and *Junior Red Cross News* for "The Cobbler." Page 260: "Weather" from *Catch a Little Rhyme* by Eve Merriam. Copyright © 1966 by Eve Merriam. Reprinted by permission of the author. Page 261: "Alone by the Surf" by Leila Kendall Brown from *A Little Child Looking*, copyright © 1956 by Pageant Press. "Swift Things Are Beautiful" from *Away Goes Sally* by Elizabeth Coatsworth. Copyright © 1934 by Macmillan Publishing Co. Inc., renewed 1962 by Elizabeth Coatsworth Beston. Reprinted by permission of Macmillan Publishing Company. Page 264 "Knoxville, Tennessee (17 May 68)" from *Black Feeling, Black Talk, Black Judgement* by Nikki Giovanni. Copyright © 1968, 1970 by Nikki Giovanni. By permission of William Morrow & Company. "Slippery" from *Smoke and Steel* by Carl Sandburg. Copyright © 1920 by Harcourt Brace Jovanovich, Inc.; renewed 1948 by Carl Sandburg. Reprinted by permission of the publisher. "This Is Just to Say" from *Collected Earlier Poems of William Carlos Williams* by William Carlos Williams. Copyright © 1938 by New Directions Publishing Corporation. Reprinted by permission of New Directions. "Coolness" by Onitsura from *An Introduction to Haiku* translated by Harold G. Henderson. Copyright © 1958 by Harold G. Henderson. Reprinted by permission of Doubleday & Company, Inc. Page 265: "Kansas Boy" by Ruth Lechlitner, from *Poetry Magazine* (November 1931). Reprinted by permission of the author. Page 266: "A Dragon-Fly" from *Eleanor Farjeon's Poems for Children*, p. 145 (J.B. Lippincott). Copyright 1933, renewed 1961 by Eleanor Farjeon. Reprinted by permission of Harper & Row, Publishers, Inc. "Snow Toward Evening" from *So That It Flower* by Melville Cane. Copyright 1926 by Harcourt Brace Jovanovich, Inc.; renewed 1954 by Melville Cane. Reprinted by permission of the publisher. Page 271: "Arithmetic" in *The Complete Poems of Carl Sandburg*, Copyright 1950 by Carl Sandburg; renewed 1978 by Margaret Sandburg, Helga Sandburg Crile, and Janel Sandburg. Reprinted by permission of Harcourt Brace Jovanovich, Inc.

Contributors to the Teacher's Edition: James J. Alvino, gifted notes; Nancy S. Bley, learning disabled notes; Claudia Campbell, translation of Parent Letters into Spanish; Contemporary Perspectives, Inc., marginal notes, Reinforcement Masters, and Practice Masters; Rita M. Deyoe-Chiullán, English as a Second Language notes; Anthony D. Fredericks, Parent Letters; National Evaluation Systems, Inc., tests; Rita Steinglass, Unit Sparkler language games.

SCHOOL ADVISORY PANEL

CLASSROOM TEACHERS
Levels 5 and 6
Louise Carson, Sunset Elementary School, Issaquah, Washington; Judy Dawson, Birch Run Elementary School, Birch Run, Michigan; Doug Dillon, Madoux Elementary School, Cincinnati, Ohio; Ronnie Fassberg, Bluefield Elementary School, Spring Valley, New York; James Knox, Thomasboro Elementary School, Charlotte, North Carolina; John Manalili, Sachem Central School District, Holbrook, New York; Laima Stede, Taft School, Ferndale, Michigan; Carolyn Wilson, New Monmouth School, Middletown, New Jersey

SPECIAL CONSULTANTS
Betty Gould, Patchogue, New York; Barbara Todd, Los Angeles, California

Teacher Focus Group, New Jersey Public and Parochial Schools: Marie Antieri, Phyllis Mordente Farese, Constance B. Fenner, Maureen Fulop, Carole Guild, Linda Larner, Eileen C. Molloy, Annette Rauscher, Eileen St. André, Barbara M. Silvernale, Barbara Verian
Thesaurus Lessons Consultant: Rosemary Cooke, Southern Boulevard School, Chatham Township, New Jersey

Review and Practice Handbooks

Grammar Handbook

Young Writer's Handbook

Sentences

sentence
- A **sentence** is a group of words that expresses a complete thought. *page 4*

  The audience cheered loudly for the home team.

declarative sentence
- A **declarative sentence** makes a statement and ends with a period (.). *page 6*

  The homecoming parade begins at noon on Saturday.

interrogative sentence
- An **interrogative sentence** asks a question and ends with a question mark (?). *page 6*

  When did this special-delivery letter arrive?

imperative sentence
- An **imperative sentence** gives a command or makes a request. It ends with a period (.). *page 8*

  Look in both directions before stepping off the curb.

exclamatory sentence
- An **exclamatory sentence** expresses strong feeling. It ends with an exclamation mark (!). *page 8*

  I can't believe you ate the whole pizza!

MORE PRACTICE 1 Sentences

Write *sentence* or *not a sentence* for each group of words below.

1. My parents bought a new washing machine.
2. The delicate vase smashed into hundreds of pieces.
3. An extremely warm climate.
4. Washing the dishes.
5. The canyon walls are very steep.
6. Baked apples with cinnamon and cream.
7. They remembered every detail of the story.
8. Hawaii has many lagoons and waterfalls.
9. In the days of the dinosaurs.
10. Finished writing the report.

MORE PRACTICE 2 Sentences

A. Write the group of words in each pair that is a sentence.

1. **a.** The road crews have been working day and night.
   b. Clearing away the huge drifts of snow.
2. **a.** Sanded and stained a rocking chair.
   b. Major Thomas refinishes antique furniture.
3. **a.** The technician at the city hospital.
   b. Ms. Halley works in a large laboratory.
4. **a.** My father likes to enter recipe contests.
   b. Baking chicken twelve different ways.
5. **a.** Renata has trained the dog to shake hands.
   b. Holds up its left front paw.
6. **a.** Difficult to locate the small squash plants.
   b. The weeds in the garden multiplied quickly.
7. **a.** Waving my hand in all directions.
   b. An annoying fly buzzed around my head.
8. **a.** With a huge splash.
   b. The canoe tipped over in the middle of the lake.

B. Write each sentence. Then write *declarative, interrogative, imperative,* or *exclamatory* to show what kind of sentence it is.

9. On special occasions we eat dinner in a nice restaurant.
10. Send in four boxtops today for a free exercise guide.
11. What a thrilling ride we had on that roller coaster!
12. How did you find your paper in that pile on the desk?
13. The pan is too hot to lift without a potholder.
14. Lock the gate when you leave.
15. That is a terrific idea!
16. Where is the nearest ticket office?
17. Laura fell asleep during the last part of the movie.
18. Remember to speak clearly into the microphone.
19. Raul had a cold and sore throat for almost two weeks.
20. Would you like another glass of lemonade?

MORE PRACTICE 3 Sentences

A. Write each sentence. Then write *declarative, interrogative, imperative,* or *exclamatory* to show what kind of sentence it is.

1. I just won first prize in the raffle!
2. We met last evening at the photography club meeting.
3. How much does one slice of cheesecake cost?
4. Fold your sweater before you put it in the drawer.
5. The bandleader pointed at the drummer.
6. Help me carry these books to the library.
7. How much does that leg of lamb weigh?
8. It can't be time to leave already!

B. Write each declarative or interrogative sentence. Begin each sentence correctly. Use correct punctuation at the end.

9. do you have change for a dollar
10. we carried canteens of cold water on the hike
11. when does the next bus leave for Grand Rapids
12. we often eat toasted bagels or muffins at breakfast
13. where did you get your new purple socks
14. how many votes does she need to be elected
15. he works at least twelve hours a week at the market
16. the team has not lost a game in six weeks
17. when was the last time you watered these ferns
18. our teacher selected three students to present reports

C. Write each imperative or exclamatory sentence. Begin each sentence correctly. Use a period or exclamation mark at the end.

19. i am too hungry to wait
20. show Ricardo the post cards
21. that new hat looks great
22. take another piece of paper
23. i really loved that story
24. wait for Leslie after school
25. stretch your muscles first
26. he will never try that again
27. sharpen these pencils for me
28. the game is tied
29. what a super magic show that was
30. let me know when lunch is ready

MORE PRACTICE 4 Sentences

A. Write each sentence. Then write *declarative, interrogative, imperative,* or *exclamatory* to show what kind of sentence it is.

1. Why did you change your mind so suddenly?
2. The chef added some spices to the spaghetti sauce.
3. This is absolutely the best book I've read all year!
4. Bring an extra sweater in case it gets chilly.
5. Do you speak any foreign languages?
6. These hot peppers are burning my tongue!
7. Did I miss the beginning of the show already?

B. Write each declarative or interrogative sentence. Begin each sentence correctly. Use correct punctuation at the end.

8. when will the next full moon appear
9. the Scouts had a car wash last weekend
10. does he always wear that funny hat
11. has Dr. Pacino been your dentist a long time
12. the magician pulled a rabbit out of a hat
13. my sister delivers newspapers early each morning
14. have you met the new neighbors yet
15. would you lend me money for lunch today
16. the tiger watched the other animals from high in the tree

C. Write each imperative or exclamatory sentence. Begin each sentence correctly. Use a period or exclamation mark at the end.

17. i can't decide what to wear tonight
18. set the alarm for seven o'clock sharp
19. today is the hottest day in five years
20. save me some of those walnuts and raisins
21. turn on the light in the staircase
22. i smell something burning
23. choose your favorite flavor for dessert
24. put a sign for the sidewalk sale on the bulletin board
25. that is the worst movie of the season

Subjects and Predicates

complete subject

- The **complete subject** is all the words in the subject part of a sentence. The subject part names someone or something. *page 10*

  Electronic games fascinate many people.

complete predicate

- The **complete predicate** is all the words in the predicate part of a sentence. The predicate part tells what the subject is or does. *page 10*

  The fallen tree blocked traffic for hours.

simple subject

- The **simple subject** is the main word in the complete subject. *page 12*

  The hot weather makes me tired.

simple predicate

- The **simple predicate** is the main word or words in the complete predicate. *page 14*

  Alicia organized the class picnic this year.

subject of imperative sentence

- *You* (understood) is the subject of an imperative sentence. *page 16*

  (You) Hide the gift under your bed for now.

MORE PRACTICE 1 Subjects and Predicates

Write each sentence. Underline the complete subject once. Underline the complete predicate twice.

1. His sprained ankle began to swell.
2. A barrel cactus survives with very little water.
3. A woolen sweater feels very nice on a windy day.
4. The state of California is quite long and narrow.
5. The frightened deer disappeared into the forest.

MORE PRACTICE 2 Subjects and Predicates

A. Write each sentence. Underline the complete subject once. Underline the complete predicate twice.

1. Two friends visited the art museum together.
2. Our science teacher pointed to a model of a heart.
3. Her hobby is collecting antique foreign coins.
4. The spotted mare pushed the wooden gate open with her nose.
5. Mrs. Winters has a new pair of contact lenses.
6. A chameleon blends in with the colors around it.
7. The football team practiced the new play for an hour.
8. The secretary wrote the telephone message in shorthand.
9. The glass was filled with freshly squeezed orange juice.
10. Ralph ate some fresh figs for dessert.

B. Add a complete subject or a complete predicate to each group of words below. Write the complete sentence.

EXAMPLE: _____ crawled along the sandy beach.
ANSWER: A large tortoise crawled along the sandy beach.

11. The team captain _____.
12. _____ always sings in the shower.
13. _____ leaped over the high fence.
14. The bold chimpanzee _____.
15. An ocean liner _____.
16. _____ ate too much dinner.
17. Her ten-speed bicycle _____.
18. Two frisky kittens _____.
19. _____ entered the poetry contest.
20. _____ studied for the exam.
21. A stubborn mosquito _____.
22. _____ hid beneath a chair.
23. _____ ordered a pepperoni pizza.
24. An avalanche of snow _____.
25. _____ burned down last week.

MORE PRACTICE 3 Subjects and Predicates

A. Read each sentence below. A line has been drawn between the complete subject and the complete predicate. Write each complete subject. Draw a line under the simple subject.

1. Many tropical fruits | grow in the Hawaiian Islands.
2. The dancers' costumes | sparkle in the bright lights.
3. Hummingbirds | are perhaps the tiniest birds in the world.
4. The sticky glue | was all over my fingers.
5. A few scraggly bushes | grew on the empty lot.
6. My older sister | prefers to use her nickname.
7. Grandma Moses | began her painting career in her seventies.
8. My favorite flavor | is a mixture of chocolate and coffee called mocha.
9. Some frightening creatures | appeared at our door on Halloween.
10. Dr. Barberis | attended medical school in Chicago, Illinois.
11. The fierce lion | growled threateningly at the zoo keeper.
12. The gardener | planted three varieties of rose bushes.

B. Read each sentence below. A line has been drawn between the complete subject and the complete predicate. Write each complete predicate. Draw a line under the simple predicate.

13. My mother | bought a new lamp for the living room.
14. My best friend | laughs at all my corny jokes.
15. Minestrone soup | contains many delicious vegetables.
16. A gigantic blimp | carried a big banner across the sky.
17. The daring skier | went down the highest slope.
18. A rainbow | had appeared after the brief summer shower.
19. The careless driver | was given a ticket by the officer.
20. Our class | built an igloo from papier-mâché.
21. Glenda | reads science-fiction stories constantly.
22. The chef | has prepared a tasty casserole of broccoli and cheese.
23. Their shaggy dog | chases every passing car.
24. The ringing of the telephone | startled me.
25. The fire fighter | climbed up the ladder to the twelfth floor.

MORE PRACTICE 4 Subjects and Predicates

A. Write each sentence. Underline the simple subject. Write *(You)* if the subject is understood.

EXAMPLE: Water these plants once a week.
ANSWER: Water these plants once a week. (You)

1. Six silly monkeys made funny faces at us.
2. Praise your pet when it behaves nicely.
3. Give my pencil back after the test.
4. Peel some carrots for the stew.
5. Leslie Hall sent me a free ticket for the school play.
6. Turn left at the second stoplight.
7. The sleepy baby dropped the plastic bottle.
8. A baseball shattered our front window.
9. Wait for me in the theater lobby after the show.
10. Take an umbrella along in case of rain.
11. Mr. Tanaka walked to the office today.
12. Lend me the money to call home please.

B. Write the simple predicate of each sentence.

13. Ellen played the flute.
14. A helicopter landed nearby.
15. The wind blew the door shut.
16. My cousins have moved to Ohio.
17. The pony has injured its leg.
18. A volcano in Italy erupted.
19. We sent it by mail.
20. The crowd was cheering loudly.

C. Write each sentence. Then write *declarative* or *imperative* to show what kind of sentence it is. Underline the simple subject in each declarative sentence. Write *(You)* for each imperative sentence.

21. Return these books to the library before Tuesday.
22. The pilot signaled to the control tower.
23. Tell us about your last trip to the mountains.
24. Keep a record of the plant's growth.
25. My parents have asked me to sweep the front steps.

Nouns

noun
- A **noun** names a person, place, thing, or idea.   *page 48*

  My cousin studies chemistry at a university.
  Jeannie wants to be a veterinarian.

common noun
- A **common noun** is the general name of person, a place, or thing.   *page 52*

  The hiker climbed a steep trail.

proper noun
- A **proper noun** names a particular person, place, or thing.   *page 52*

  Dale Gordon camped at Rocky Mountain National Park.

possessive noun
- A **possessive noun** shows ownership.   *page 58*

- Add 's to form the possessive of a singular noun.

  Carl's house is next door.   The man's car stalled.

- Add ' to form the possessive of a plural noun ending in -s.

  The teachers' meetings always last for hours.

- Add 's to form the possessive of a plural noun not ending in -s.

  The children's singing filled the rooms.

MORE PRACTICE 1   Nouns

Write the following sentences. Underline all the nouns in each sentence.

1. Many people crowded onto the subway.
2. The wooden cabinet contained an old set of encyclopedias.
3. The clown at the circus carried a tiny striped umbrella.
4. My blue raincoat has a broken zipper.
5. My grandmother likes to paint pictures of animals.
6. The pitcher threw the ball to the catcher.
7. Roberta sat in the first row of the theater.

MORE PRACTICE 2 Nouns

A. In each sentence below, the nouns are underlined. Write each noun on your paper. Then write *common* or *proper* to show what kind of noun it is.

1. Lorenzo read a biography of Robert Louis Stevenson.
2. The family ate a delicious dinner.
3. T.R. Williams is on the staff at a large university.
4. The violinist from Austria performed.
5. They rode the ferry to Emerald Island for a picnic.
6. The Phoenix Suns played basketball at the Oakland Coliseum.
7. A sunset over Diamond Head is a beautiful sight.
8. We had a marvelous view from the overlook.
9. Uncle Henry fished in Oak Creek for trout.
10. Josefina washed all the windows.

B. Write each sentence. Draw one line under the common nouns. Draw two lines under the proper nouns.

11. Gail Karlen traveled on the bus to Seattle from Sacramento.
12. Their computer is from a store called Homeworks.
13. Willie hopes to visit Europe.
14. Dr. Casey and his daughters visited the Whitney Museum.
15. Richard Drake started a new job at First Central Bank.
16. Grant Junior High School is on Lake Street near Fourth Avenue.
17. The magician asked Debra to be an assistant on Saturday.
18. The Golden Gate Bridge goes from San Francisco to Marin County.
19. During vacation our relatives will visit from Tennessee.
20. Maria Mitchell was a famous astronomer who discovered a comet.

C. Write the possessive noun in each sentence below. Then write *singular* or *plural* to show which it is.

21. Our school's symbol is an eagle.
22. The joggers' faces looked tired after climbing the hill.
23. The women's scarves were bright and colorful.
24. Those glasses' lenses turn dark in the sunlight.
25. I borrowed John's bicycle to deliver my papers yesterday.

MORE PRACTICE 3   Nouns

A. Write the sentences. Draw one line under each possessive noun that is singular. Draw two lines under each possessive noun that is plural.

1. The horses' hooves sounded like thunder on the wooden bridge.
2. We enjoyed ourselves at the twins' birthday party.
3. My cat loves to play with an ostrich's feather.
4. The babies' crying kept everyone in the nursery busy.
5. This dress's sleeve has a tear near the elbow.
6. Dan works in the men's shoes department.
7. We saw the boat's sails from across the bay.
8. The players' uniforms are maroon and white.
9. The passengers' suitcases were placed on the wrong airplane.
10. This watch's crystal has a crack in it.
11. These knives' blades need sharpening.
12. The telephone's sudden ringing startled him.
13. Several girls' bicycles had bright flags.
14. At the hotel all the guests' rooms were cleaned in the morning.

B. Write the possessive form of each noun given.

15. balloon
16. mice
17. nurses
18. sheep
19. faces
20. Mr. Lucas
21. grandchildren
22. kittens
23. friend

C. Write each sentence. Draw one line under the common nouns. Draw two lines under the proper nouns.

24. Karen Corelli is a sophomore at Harvard University.
25. The mechanic drove to Front Street for the stalled car.
26. Jesse Taylor sailed on a ship named the Queen Elizabeth.
27. The Rio Grande is a river bordering Texas and Mexico.
28. Carmen ordered a cheeseburger from Hamburger Heaven.
29. The bridge crosses over the Delaware Water Gap.
30. Many sea lions and birds live on Seal Rock near the Cliff House Restaurant.

MORE PRACTICE 4 Nouns

A. Write the sentences. Draw one line under each possessive noun that is singular. Draw two lines under each possessive noun that is plural.

1. The boss's announcement appeared on the bulletin board.
2. My cousin sews women's dresses for a large fashion company.
3. The roses' buds opened overnight.
4. The ambulance's siren warned other drivers to pull over.
5. The orchestra's conductor arrived late for the performance.
6. Goldilocks sat in the bears' chairs.
7. Several dentists' offices are on the twelfth floor.
8. All the stores' windows displayed winter clothing.
9. The bird's nest held two tiny blue eggs.
10. By October the trees' branches have dropped most of the leaves.

B. Write each noun from the sentences below. Then write *common* or *proper* to show what kind of noun it is.

11. Mount Vesuvius is an active volcano in Italy.
12. The tournament will be held at Washington High School.
13. The parachute came down near the New Jersey Turnpike.
14. Bugs Bunny has a very famous voice.
15. Old Faithful is a geyser at Yellowstone National Park.
16. Joey tasted delicious pink grapefruit from Florida.
17. Christopher Columbus sailed with three tiny ships.
18. Patricia Garcia received a letter from Albuquerque.

C. Write the following sentences. Complete each sentence with one of the nouns below. Use the noun that best fits the sentence.

19. My _____ played backgammon for hours.
20. We watched the _____ at the zoo.
21. Kevin tripped on the _____.
22. The _____ needs to be repaired.
23. Some _____ ordered two salads.
24. The weary _____ rested for a while.
25. Kay walked to the new _____.

dishwasher
customers
supermarket
monkeys
hikers
relatives
escalator

Singular and Plural Nouns

singular noun ● A **singular noun** names one person, place, thing, or idea. *page 50*

plural noun ● A **plural noun** names more than one person, place, thing, or idea. *page 50*

The lion roars. The monkeys chatter.

spelling plural nouns ● Add *-s* to form the plural of most nouns.

dog, dogs   tower, towers   lake, lakes

● Add *-es* to form the plural of nouns that end in *s, x, ch,* or *sh.*

glass, glasses   fox, foxes
dish, dishes   lunch, lunches

● If a noun ends in a consonant and *y,* change the *y* to *i* and add *-es* to form the plural.

party, parties   strawberry, strawberries

● If a noun ends in a vowel and *y,* add *-s* to form the plural.

trolley, trolleys   day, days

● Some nouns ending in *f* or *fe* form the plural by changing the *f* to *v* and adding *-s* or *-es.*

shelf, shelves   life, lives

● Some singular nouns change their spelling to form the plural.

foot, feet   goose, geese   woman, women

● Some nouns have the same form for the singular and plural.

moose, moose   sheep, sheep   deer, deer

MORE PRACTICE 1 Singular and Plural Nouns

A. Write the underlined noun in each of the sentences below. Then write *singular* if the noun is singular. Write *plural* if it is plural.

1. I need two airmail <u>stamps</u> for these letters.
2. Laura made a bacon, lettuce, and tomato <u>sandwich</u>.
3. The flood left many <u>families</u> homeless.
4. Four elephants have sixteen <u>feet</u> between them.
5. A sly <u>fox</u> watched the chickens hungrily.
6. The cow led her <u>calves</u> to the meadow.
7. The <u>donkey</u> stubbornly refused to move another inch.
8. We picked several pails of fresh <u>blackberries</u>.
9. A <u>woman</u> drove the tractor through the fields.
10. Many <u>cities</u> grew up along the river's edge.
11. We cut all the apples into <u>halves</u> and baked them.
12. I made three <u>wishes</u> at the carnival wishing well.

B. Write the plural of each of these nouns.

13. patch
14. country
15. goose
16. grocery
17. rash
18. scarf
19. beach
20. play
21. surprise

C. Write each sentence. Use the plural form of the noun in parentheses ( ).

22. San Francisco still uses its old (trolley) for public transportation.
23. The bean plants grew at least three (inch) last week.
24. Representatives from six (county) attended the meeting.
25. There are many beautiful (valley) in the New England states.
26. All the beds in our house have firm (mattress).
27. Aunt Edith misplaced the (key) to her car.
28. Our city zoo has several different kinds of (deer).
29. Morse code uses a system of dots and (dash).
30. The circus ringmaster announced, "Ladies and (gentleman)."

MORE PRACTICE 2   Singular and Plural Nouns

A. Write the underlined noun in each of the sentences below. Then write *singular* if the noun is singular. Write *plural* if it is plural.

1. Harold waited on a bench at the park until we arrived.
2. Eight tiny reindeer pulled the sleigh over the snow.
3. The boys helped paint the fence and the shed.
4. We heard strange noises in the yard at midnight.
5. That man works in the pharmacy at the hospital.
6. I drank three glasses of water after mowing the lawn.
7. This book is about the life of Helen Keller.
8. Norman looked through the boxes of old magazines.
9. Noreen used a crutch while her leg healed.
10. The bunny nibbled on some lettuce leaves.

B. Write the plural of each of these nouns.

11. splash
12. moose
13. guppy
14. wrench
15. ax
16. victory
17. toy
18. alley
19. penny
20. torch
21. activity
22. calf

C. Write each sentence. Use the plural form of the noun in parentheses ( ).

23. The harvesters picked many (bunch) of grapes.
24. Many towns along the Pacific coast have (wharf) for fishing boats.
25. The Marines collected (toy) for the children's hospital.
26. Esteban raises (guppy).
27. The dancer blew (kiss) to the cheering audience.
28. Our two (canary) whistle all day long.
29. Walter wears special shoes for his fallen (arch).
30. That bakery is famous for its (loaf) of sourdough bread.
31. Many (actress) competed for the starring role.
32. The dog helped the rancher herd the (sheep).
33. The manager of the hardware store ordered a dozen (ax).
34. It is very important to do muscle (stretch) before exercising.
35. Our collie had six (puppy).

MORE PRACTICE 3   Singular and Plural Nouns

A. Write the plural of each of these nouns.

1. crash
2. foot
3. fly
4. army
5. branch
6. volley
7. suffix
8. boss
9. sheep
10. handle
11. witness
12. stitch

B. Write the underlined noun in each of the sentences below. Then write *singular* if the noun is singular. Write *plural* if it is plural.

13. How many days will you be on vacation?
14. We baked fifteen batches of cookies for the bake sale.
15. I just felt a splash of rain on my head.
16. The monkeys at the zoo are always entertaining.
17. A flock of wild geese flew over the lake.
18. Robert Frost wrote a famous poem about birches.
19. Jerry raked all the leaves into a big pile.
20. The clerk was given a raise in salary.
21. The cartoon was about a flying squirrel and a moose.
22. The recipe called for a dozen eggs.
23. Aunt Linda told exciting stories about her rafting trip.
24. Let's use paper plates at the picnic.

C. Write each sentence. Use the plural form of the noun in parentheses ( ).

25. The carpenter added a set of (bookshelf) to the library.
26. Sylvia has a huge jar filled with (penny).
27. In school we studied about (prefix) last week.
28. Two of my (hobby) are photography and bird watching.
29. Two (woman) rode at the head of the parade on palomino horses.
30. Many (company) are hiring part-time workers this month.
31. Some neighborhoods in my town have (alley) behind the houses.
32. The school buildings are closed on four (holiday) this spring.
33. We packed the crystal (glass) carefully in newspapers.
34. My (shoe) are full of mud after hiking near the lake.
35. Everyone seems to be wearing digital (watch) these days.

Verbs

action verb • An **action verb** shows action. *page 88*

The magician <u>pulls</u> a dove out of an empty box.

linking verb • A **linking verb** shows being. It links the subject with a word or words in the predicate. *page 90*

am, is, are	Jan <u>is</u> an artist.
was, were	My throat <u>was</u> sore.
look, seem, feel	This sweater <u>feels</u> scratchy.
taste, smell	Pineapples <u>taste</u> sweet.

helping verb • A **helping verb** works with the main verb. *page 92*

am, is, are, was, were	He <u>was</u> <u>cooking</u>.
have, has, had	I <u>have</u> <u>finished</u>.
will	They <u>will</u> <u>agree</u>.

direct object • The **direct object** receives the action of the verb *page 94*

Dianne rode a <u>bicycle</u>. I see my <u>neighbor</u>.

MORE PRACTICE 1 Verbs

Each sentence below contains an action verb. Write the sentence and underline the verb.

1. Darla reached the finish line first.
2. The rice boiled over the top of the saucepan.
3. The ice cream melted all over the counter.
4. Philip changes the radio station too often.
5. The high school band presents a free concert once a month.
6. The gymnast flipped twice in the air.
7. Roger delivers groceries for Supersave Market.
8. The timid deer darted out of sight among the trees.
9. Grandpa repairs antique clocks in the basement.
10. The student recited the entire poem from memory.

MORE PRACTICE 2 Verbs

A. Write the sentences. Use an action verb to complete each sentence.

1. The horses _____ across the field.
2. My best friend _____ butterflies.
3. Conrad _____ mystery novels.
4. The restaurant owner _____ blueberry cheesecake.
5. Several rabbits _____ the lettuce plants in the garden.
6. The furniture movers _____ the heavy piano.
7. The pilot _____ another jumbo jet in the air.
8. David _____ comedians from silent movies.

B. Write each sentence. Underline the linking verb. Use an arrow to connect the two words that the verb links.

EXAMPLE: Marie was very sleepy at school.

ANSWER: Marie was very sleepy at school.

9. The runners felt exhausted after the race.
10. This package is a gift for Larry's sister.
11. The lake looks cold.
12. Last year Nina was the catcher on our neighborhood baseball team.
13. These sausages are extremely spicy.
14. Sometimes my cat seems unfriendly to strangers.
15. I am the youngest child in my family.

C. Write the sentences. Choose the correct form of *be* to complete each sentence.

EXAMPLE: Lonnie _____ the winner of the raffle. (is, are)

ANSWER: Lonnie is the winner of the raffle.

16. Sunday _____ the hottest day in five years. (was, were)
17. I _____ the new president of the Computer Club. (is, am)
18. The scenes from that new movie _____ thrilling. (was, were)
19. Jan's relatives _____ very happy about her coming visit. (is, are)
20. A sandwich with peanut butter and raspberry jam _____ my idea of the perfect lunch! (is, are)

MORE PRACTICE 3 Verbs

A. Write each sentence. Draw one line under the main verb. Draw two lines under the helping verb.

1. The teacher had scolded the student.
2. My family is painting the kitchen.
3. The mayor will dedicate the new library tomorrow.
4. Forest fires have destroyed thousands of trees this year.
5. I am helping at the garage sale.
6. The committee had chosen Pierre as its leader.
7. Many famous people are writing their biographies.
8. Eric has recovered nicely.

B. Write each sentence. Draw one line under the action verb. Draw two lines under the direct object.

9. Our family always eats dinner at six o'clock sharp.
10. The hikers carried their supplies in knapsacks.
11. She set the table.
12. Ken added the vinegar.
13. The lifeguard rescued the swimmer.
14. The kitten scratched my hand.
15. I pried the lid off the jar.
16. Katrina wore bright red suspenders with her jeans.
17. Dr. Swenson removed the cast from the patient's arm.

C. Write the sentences. Use the helping verb *are, have,* or *will* to complete each sentence.

18. The twins _____ invited twenty people to the party.
19. The two candidates _____ meeting for a discussion tonight.
20. The sun _____ set soon.
21. Astronomers _____ discovered several new stars in recent years.
22. Brian and Gail _____ directing the talent show at school.
23. The teacher _____ assign a report topic to each student.
24. Three new movies _____ opening downtown this weekend.
25. We _____ earned enough money to pay for the tickets.

MORE PRACTICE 4 Verbs

A. Write each sentence. Underline the linking verb. Use an arrow to connect the two words that the verb links.

1. She is my favorite teacher this year.
2. This bread tastes stale.
3. Our supplies are quite low.
4. The mailbox was completely empty for a week.
5. He is our representative to Congress.
6. I am a beginner at playing the piano.
7. Your forehead feels rather warm to me.
8. My parents were upset about the closing of the park.

B. Write the direct object of each sentence. Then write *what* or *whom* to show what question the direct object answers.

9. I wrapped the gift with red, white, and blue paper.
10. Lisa changes her hairstyle every other week.
11. I finished the assignment as quickly as possible.
12. Eduardo invited the police chief to our meeting.
13. The frisky kitten chases its tail all the time.
14. We notified the principal about the broken window.
15. Dad locked his keys in the car again.
16. A group toured the new library at the university.
17. I bought some film for my camera.
18. My older brother took Mom to dinner for her birthday.

C. Write each sentence. Draw one line under the main verb. Draw two lines under the helping verb.

19. The plumber has repaired the leaky faucet at last.
20. Your sister is talking on the telephone again.
21. The bus will arrive on schedule.
22. Some kinds of whales are becoming rare.
23. The President was holding a press conference.
24. Floods have destroyed several buildings near the river.
25. Derek had eaten the last slice of ham.

Tenses of Verbs

tense ● The **tense** of a verb shows the time of the action. *page 96*

Present: The students <u>prepare</u> reports.
Past: Each person <u>selected</u> a topic.
Future: They <u>will</u> <u>present</u> the reports next week.

present tense ● A verb in the present tense must agree with the subject of the sentence. *page 98*

A lion roar<u>s</u>. Cats like milk.
Juan like<u>s</u> music. Lou and Vi wash dishes.
She fix<u>es</u> cars. They fix the radio.

spelling of verbs ● The spelling of some verbs changes when *-es* or *-ed* is added. *page 100*

I reply. You shop.
He repl<u>ies</u>. We shop<u>ped</u>.
We repl<u>ied</u>.

MORE PRACTICE 1 Tenses of Verbs

Write the verb in each sentence. Then write *present, past,* or *future* to show what tense it is in.

1. The parade will begin at noon in front of City Hall.
2. The commercial compares two brands of breakfast cereal.
3. Officers Peter Nemeth and John Gray worked at the police station in our neighborhood.
4. We hang coats and umbrellas on a wooden rack at the back of the room.
5. The fire engines responded to a false alarm.
6. Your paycheck will arrive in tomorrow's mail.
7. Sometimes the early bird catches the worm.
8. The helicopter reports traffic news for drivers during morning and evening rush hours.
9. The janitor replaced two light bulbs in the auditorium.
10. The cafeteria served tacos twice last week.

MORE PRACTICE 2 Tenses of Verbs

A. Each underlined verb below is in the present tense. Write each sentence. Change the verb to the tense shown in parentheses ( ).

1. Alice and I count the profits from the car wash. (past)
2. The gardeners water the seedlings every other morning. (future)
3. The dog buries bones all over the backyard. (past)
4. Frightening creatures appear at the door on Halloween. (past)
5. These new mysteries fascinate every reader. (future)
6. Grandma whistles cheerful melodies to her canaries. (past)
7. We paint safety posters for a contest at school. (future)
8. The travelers carry two large suitcases. (future)
9. The tiny kitten shivers by the open window. (past)
10. The coaches explain the strategy for today's game. (future)

B. Write each sentence. Use the correct form of the verb in parentheses ( ).

11. The setting sun (look, looks) like a red ball of fire.
12. Grace (throw, throws) a baseball with her left hand.
13. The voters (elect, elects) new senators every four years.
14. The band members (wear, wears) green and white uniforms.
15. The school nurse (teach, teaches) a first-aid class.
16. The weeds (multiply, multiplies) very quickly in our garden.
17. Her parents (work, works) for a large airline.
18. Mr. Douglas (organize, organizes) a craft fair every winter.
19. That parrot (tell, tells) corny jokes.
20. Many commuters (travel, travels) to work on subways.
21. The contestants (pay, pays) a small entry fee for the race.

C. Write each verb. Then write its past-tense form.

22. occupy
23. flip
24. grip
25. satisfy
26. slam
27. worry
28. copy
29. apply
30. plan

MORE PRACTICE 3   Tenses of Verbs

A. Write the verb in each sentence. Then write *present, past,* or *future* to show what tense it is in.

1. We saved a dollar by purchasing two tickets at once.
2. The cast presents a performance twice daily.
3. A famous author will autograph books at the shopping mall.
4. This machine prepares coffee automatically at a certain time.
5. The witness responded nervously to the lawyer's questions.
6. The store manager will train three new sales clerks.
7. We heard the news of the hurricane in Florida last night.
8. Many varieties of wild flowers bloom at Morris Park.
9. The newspaper will print my letter in tomorrow's edition.
10. The bride tossed the bouquet from the top step.
11. This vegetable casserole contains too much salt.
12. The hungry wren spied an unsuspecting worm.

B. Write each verb. Then write its *-es* present-tense form.

13. hurry   16. copy   19. marry
14. terrify   17. supply   20. qualify
15. rely   18. testify   21. bury

C. Write each sentence. Use the correct present-tense form of the verb in parentheses ( ).

22. The best chefs _____ as little salt as possible. (use)
23. Hot pepper always _____ me sneeze. (make)
24. Those circus acrobats _____ some amazing stunts. (perform)
25. A cactus _____ very little moisture to survive. (need)
26. Astronauts _____ weightlessness during space flights. (experience)
27. Flash floods _____ sometimes in the desert. (occur)
28. Our Irish setter _____ us every morning at seven. (wake)
29. She always _____ a life jacket on the sailboat. (wear)
30. That movie about vampires _____ me. (terrify)

MORE PRACTICE 4 Tenses of Verbs

A. Write each sentence. Use the past tense of the verb in parentheses ( ).

1. Nicholas (unwrap) the gifts before dinner.
2. The little girl (grip) the balloon's string tightly.
3. Susan's sister (apply) to medical school in Calfifornia.
4. In the cartoon an ostrich (bury) its head in the sand.
5. The teacher (pin) the schedule of events on the bulletin board.
6. I (slam) the car door shut with my right hand.
7. My first cousin (marry) an opera singer.
8. Our family (plan) a surprise for my grandparents' wedding anniversary.

B. Write each sentence. Use the correct present-tense form of the verb in parentheses ( ).

9. The construction workers _____ for lunch at noon. (break)
10. Your tag _____ you as a hospital visitor. (identify)
11. The drill-team members _____ at least four hours a week. (practice)
12. The recipe _____ a full cup of milk and two eggs. (require)
13. A glass of orange juice _____ my sweet tooth. (satisfy)
14. James _____ the movie projector when it breaks down. (fix)
15. My grandfather _____ a class in art history. (attend)
16. The city library _____ for overdue books. (charge)

C. Each underlined verb below is in the present tense. Write each sentence. Change the verb to the tense shown in parentheses ( ).

17. Class elections take place in November. (future)
18. Mr. O'Brien exchanges the sweater for a larger size. (past)
19. I qualify for the advanced swim class. (past)
20. These companies replace defective equipment for free. (future)
21. The tomato plants freeze if the temperature drops. (future)
22. The planetarium opens at eleven during the summer. (past)
23. I capture my friends' attention with a funny joke. (future)
24. Our class presents a puppet show for the younger children. (past)
25. The spider traps a fly in its silvery web. (past)

Irregular Verbs

irregular verbs ● **Irregular verbs** do not form the past and past participle by adding *-ed.*   *page 102*

Present	Past	Past Participle
come	came	(has, have, had) come
do	did	(has, have, had) done
eat	ate	(has, have, had) eaten
fall	fell	(has, have, had) fallen
fly	flew	(has, have, had) flown
give	gave	(has, have, had) given
go	went	(has, have, had) gone
grow	grew	(has, have, had) grown
ride	rode	(has, have, had) ridden
run	ran	(has, have, had) run
see	saw	(has, have, had) seen
take	took	(has, have, had) taken
wear	wore	(has, have, had) worn
write	wrote	(has, have, had) written

MORE PRACTICE 1   Irregular Verbs

Write each sentence. Use the past tense of the verb in parentheses (   ).

1. Gail and Theresa (go) to the movies yesterday.
2. Elliot (give) me part of his egg salad sandwich.
3. Alicia (run) in a mini-marathon last July.
4. Calvin (know) the combination to my locker.
5. We (eat) at that burger stand often before it closed.
6. I (fall) at least twelve times the first time I went skating.
7. Jeff (ride) by Melissa on a unicycle.
8. The shopping mall (do) a holiday window display.
9. Nobody (see) the dog sneak away with the lamb chop.
10. The warm weather (come) early this year.

MORE PRACTICE 2 Irregular Verbs

A. Write each sentence. Use the past tense of the verb in parentheses (   ).

1. The cat (take) a nap in the warm sunlight.
2. The African violets (grow) nicely near the front window.
3. Everyone (see) the drill team perform at the rodeo.
4. The driver (take) the wrong exit off the freeway.
5. Pablo (write) a letter to the newspaper about pollution control.
6. The team mascot (wear) a gorilla suit at all the home games.
7. Steve and Jackie (do) a report about magnetism for extra credit.
8. The school chorus (give) a concert for senior citizens at the park.
9. Dr. Jensen (go) to the hospital twice on Saturday.
10. Once Elizabeth (ride) on a camel.
11. Two witnesses (see) the driver run the red light.
12. Mrs. Lopez (do) three batches of cookies for our bake sale.
13. We (give) a surprise birthday party for my great-grandmother.
14. Tommy (take) the last slice of pizza off the plate.
15. The clown (wear) one blue shoe and one red shoe.

B. Write each sentence. Use the past participle of the verb in parentheses (   ).

16. My aunt has (fly) over the International Date Line twice.
17. Cassie had (take) my coat by mistake yesterday.
18. Lester has (write) the correct date on the chalkboard.
19. The officers have (give) a talk about traffic safety.
20. Joey had (go) to return the library books.
21. Nothing had (fall) off the shelves during the mild earthquake.
22. Some pilots have (fly) around the world solo.
23. I had never (eat) kiwi fruit before.
24. Jane has (ride) with Sally on a bicycle built for two.
25. We had (do) three loads of wash by ten o'clock.
26. You have (grow) at least a foot since I last saw you!
27. This envelope for dad has (come) by express mail.
28. They have (go) to watch the boat races at the lake.
29. The cafeteria had (run) out of mayonnaise again.
30. The officer had (give) an order to the soldiers.

GRAMMAR HANDBOOK

Irregular Verbs

irregular verbs ● Some irregular verbs follow a pattern in the way they are formed. *page 104*

Present	Past	Past Participle
bring	brought	(has, have, had) brought
catch	caught	(has, have, had) caught
find	found	(has, have, had) found
say	said	(has, have, had) said
think	thought	(has, have, had) thought
break	broke	(has, have, had) broken
choose	chose	(has, have, had) chosen
freeze	froze	(has, have, had) frozen
speak	spoke	(has, have, had) spoken
drink	drank	(has, have, had) drunk
ring	rang	(has, have, had) rung
sing	sang	(has, have, had) sung
swim	swam	(has, have, had) swum

MORE PRACTICE 1   Irregular Verbs

Write each sentence. Use the past tense or the past participle of the verb in parentheses (   ).

1. Tamara had (catch) a bad cold during the last storm.
2. Sandy (find) a wallet full of money at the bus stop.
3. My brother has (swim) in a number of races this year.
4. Everyone had (bring) a different dish to the pot-luck dinner.
5. The vase (break) into hundreds of pieces when I dropped it.
6. Cynthia had (think) the party was starting at eight o'clock.
7. On hot afternoons we have (drink) glass after glass of cold lemonade.
8. The lake (freeze) over during the last weekend of January.
9. My grandfather (say) he would make some raspberry jam.
10. The coach has (chose) the players for tomorrow's game.

MORE PRACTICE 2 Irregular Verbs

Write each sentence. Use the past tense or the past participle of the verb in parentheses ( ).

1. The officer (speak) in a kind voice.
2. Barbara has (sing) on local television.
3. The telephone had (ring) at midnight.
4. The contestant (choose) the first category.
5. I (drink) the steaming cocoa slowly.
6. My friends (bring) flowers to the hospital when I was sick.
7. People have (say) she looks just like her mother.
8. The playful kitten (break) my mug.
9. Luis (speak) clearly and slowly.
10. The dinner bell has (ring) already.
11. Mollie (catch) a sea bass from the pier.
12. Every winter the Polar Bear Club has (swim) in the icy bay.
13. We each (choose) our favorite flavor.
14. Lynn and I (sing) along with the radio.
15. George has (find) his lost dog.
16. The tomatoes have (freeze) on the plants in the garden.
17. I have (speak) by telephone with my cousins in France several times.
18. She has (bring) the latest records to the party.
19. Mr. Carbone (say) the elevator is still out of order.
20. The outfielder has (catch) the final ball of the game.
21. The bank's computers have (break) down.
22. Someone has (drink) my apple juice.
23. Ping Lee (break) a school record.
24. The mechanic (think) the car needed a new carburetor.
25. Our science teacher has (say) the reports are due on Friday.
26. The telephone (ring) for a long time.
27. The judges have (choose) Rita's drawing for first prize.
28. We all (think) the movie was boring.
29. The performer (sing) my favorite song in English and in Spanish.
30. I (find) a mystery magazine on the desk.

GRAMMAR HANDBOOK

Troublesome Verb Pairs

**the verbs
<u>can</u> and <u>may</u>**
- Use the verb *can* to mean "to be able to do something." Use the verb *may* when you ask for or give permission. *page 106*

<u>Can</u> you play the accordion? <u>May</u> I listen?

**the verbs
<u>sit</u> and <u>set</u>**
- Use the verb *sit* to mean "to rest." Use the verb *set* to mean "to put or place something." *page 106*

Rosa <u>set</u> the cup on the table.
I <u>sit</u> beside Tommy in math class.

MORE PRACTICE 1 Troublesome Verb Pairs

Write each sentence. Use the correct verb in parentheses ( ).

1. I always (sit, set) and rest a while after exercising.
2. Mrs. Graham (sit, set) the big rubber-tree plant near the window in the living room.
3. The detective in this book (can, may) solve any mystery.
4. The gardener (sit, set) the rake down carefully so that no one would trip over it.
5. (Can, May) you skate backwards?
6. It is not comfortable to (sit, set) for long periods of time on the wooden bleachers at the stadium.
7. My brother (can, may) turn cartwheels using just one hand!
8. At the Japanese restaurant we (sit, set) our shoes outside the sliding door.
9. Do you prefer to (sit, set) in the front or the back of the bus?
10. You (can, may) help yourself to some cheese and crackers if you are hungry.
11. Cynthia (can, may) say quite a few words in German.
12. Where did that messenger (sit, set) the note from the principal?
13. The baby (can, may) drink from a cup already.
14. We (can, may) watch television when we have finished all our homework.
15. Uncle Fritz likes to (sit, set) in a big wooden rocking chair.

MORE PRACTICE 2 Troublesome Verb Pairs

A. Write each sentence. Use the correct verb in parentheses (   ).

1. You (can, may) borrow my tape recorder if you are careful.
2. Who (can, may) reach the box of crayons on the top shelf of the supply closet?
3. If you (sit, set) that glass near the table edge, it will probably fall off.
4. Mother cannot remember where she (sit, set) her key ring down.
5. Our science teacher said we (can, may) leave our books open for this test.
6. It is fun to (sit, set) around a campfire at night and tell ghost stories.
7. The guest of honor did not (sit, set) down for a minute all evening.
8. Some plants in the yard (can, may) be poisonous to pets.
9. The dentist (sit, set) out some instruments.
10. (Can, May) I have another glass of milk?

B. Write each sentence. Use *can, may, sit,* or *set* to complete each sentence.

11. The front seat of Dad's car is big enough for three people to _____ comfortably.
12. Frank _____ always beat me in a game of dominoes.
13. This calculator _____ fit inside my shirt pocket!
14. On warm evenings during the summer we _____ in a big swing on the front porch.
15. Dorothy _____ her sunglasses on top of her head.
16. _____ I join you, or is this chair taken already?
17. You _____ change the station on the radio if you would like to listen to something else.
18. The officer _____ a sign that said "Road closed" in the middle of Grant Avenue.
19. _____ you do thirty push-ups without stopping?
20. My kitten likes to _____ on my lap.

Pronouns

pronoun • A **pronoun** takes the place of a noun or nouns.   *page 130*

The <u>players</u> threw the <u>ball</u>. <u>They</u> threw <u>it</u>.

subject pronoun • The **subject pronouns** are *I, you, she, he, it, we,* and *they*.   *page 132*

<u>Maureen</u> is absent today. <u>She</u> is absent today.

object pronoun • The **object pronouns** are *me, you, her, him, it, us,* and *them*.   *page 134*

Suzanne called <u>Michael</u>. Suzanne called <u>him</u>.

possessive pronoun • A **possessive pronoun** shows ownership.   *page 136*

<u>Pablo's</u> bicycle is green. <u>His</u> bicycle is green.
<u>Lucy's</u> bicycle is blue. The blue bicycle is <u>hers</u>.

MORE PRACTICE 1   Pronouns

Write each sentence. Underline the pronoun in it.

1. Max drew a pyramid on his paper.
2. We searched everywhere for the lost watch.
3. Henry led them right to the spot where the treasure was buried.
4. I cannot wait another minute for dinner!
5. The magic slipper fit her perfectly.
6. Is this sleeping bag mine?
7. Joyce found it in an old brown paper bag at the bus top.
8. Would you prefer to have hamburgers or hot dogs for lunch?
9. They saved two dollars by buying the tickets in advance.
10. The teacher's announcement about the schedule change surprised us.
11. Marnie Pierce practices her cello early every morning.
12. My brother trimmed all the hedges and bushes along the driveway.
13. Their favorite show is being shown one hour later tonight.
14. The Smiths gave me a ride to school last week.
15. Which movie is your sister going to see this afternoon?

MORE PRACTICE 2   Pronouns

A. Write both sentences in each pair. Underline the pronoun in sentence **b.** Underline the noun or nouns in sentence **a** that the pronoun replaces.

1. **a.** Dina's hair is curly.
   b. Her hair is curly.
2. **a.** Randy and Sue are twins.
   b. They are twins.
3. **a.** Oscar won the raffle.
   b. He won the raffle.
4. **a.** Jane invited Lois and Paul.
   b. Jane invited them.
5. **a.** The cat played with yarn.
   b. It played with yarn.

6. **a.** Betsy sneezed and coughed.
   b. She sneezed and coughed.
7. **a.** Ms. Lee asked Dad a question.
   b. Ms. Lee asked him a question.
8. **a.** The Scouts carried flags.
   b. The Scouts carried them.
9. **a.** The students gave reports.
   b. They gave reports.
10. **a.** This guitar is Lauren's.
    b. This guitar is hers.

B. Write each sentence. Underline the subject pronoun.

11. On Saturdays you can go to the movies for half price.
12. He forgot to buy film and batteries for the camera.
13. In Switzerland they speak German, French, and Italian.
14. After dinner we will visit a sick friend in the hospital.
15. She told a funny story about sleeping bears.
16. It fell off the table and shattered into a thousand pieces.
17. You should see Jack's photographs of Hawaii.
18. I couldn't possibly eat another bite after that huge meal!

C. Write the object pronoun in each sentence.

19. The ringing of the alarm clock startled me.
20. At the circus the audience watched him on the high wire.
21. Leah will tell you about the plans for the trip after school.
22. Ramon carried it slowly and carefully across the kitchen.
23. The police officer warned them about jaywalking.
24. The van will pick you up at seven o'clock sharp.
25. The mayor praised her for helping at the Special Olympics.

GRAMMAR HANDBOOK

MORE PRACTICE 3   Pronouns

A. Write each sentence. Use a subject pronoun in place of the underlined word or words.

1. Dr. Roslyn Winters won an award for scientific research.
2. Naomi, Jay, and Toni collected seashells at the beach.
3. Mount Vesuvius is still an active volcano in Italy.
4. Jocelyn and I wore the same costume to the Halloween party.
5. This calendar is out of date.
6. The jury members reached a verdict of "not guilty."
7. At school Ronald is the chairperson of the fire-safety committee.
8. Debra's mother is a vice president at the city's largest bank.

B. Write each sentence. Use an object pronoun in place of the underlined words.

9. The bus took the players, band members, and cheerleaders to the game.
10. Sally asked Gordon and me to decorate a float for the parade.
11. The newspaper editor invited Aunt Edna to a luncheon for writers.
12. I prefer pickle relish to mustard on cheeseburgers.
13. His music teacher urged Dan Ramos to enter the songwriting contest.
14. Nathan described the country of Norway as having beautiful waterfalls.

C. Write the sentences. Complete each sentence with the singular (S) or plural (P) subject or object pronoun you use to talk about yourself.

15. The movie scared (P).
16. (S) lost my gloves.
17. (P) laughed for hours.
18. Tim called (S) yesterday.

D. Write the possessive pronoun in each sentence.

19. I thought yours was the most clever limerick in the class.
20. Has Rhoda seen her cousin lately?
21. That last can of apple juice in the refrigerator is mine.
22. Somebody borrowed his Spanish dictionary without permission.
23. This jacket is missing a button from its left sleeve.
24. Saturday is our grandparents' fortieth wedding anniversary.
25. Their house has a roof that leaks during heavy rainstorms.

MORE PRACTICE 4 Pronouns

A. Write each sentence. Use the correct pronoun in parentheses (   ).

1. Joanna loaned (her, hers) stopwatch to Pete.
2. (My, Mine) backpack has a broken zipper.
3. Colleen said this box of crayons is (your, yours).
4. (Their, Theirs) house is on the corner of Spruce and Hayes.
5. We need to plan (our, ours) strategy carefully.
6. We think the nicest drawings in the museum are (her, hers).
7. Mr. Kawakami agrees with (your, yours) suggestions.
8. I wish this beautiful golden retriever puppy were (my, mine).
9. Which sets of skis are (their, theirs)?
10. The cat with one blue eye and one brown eye is (our, ours).

B. Write each sentence. Use a possessive pronoun in place of the underlined word or words.

11. Lisa read George's poem at the assembly on Friday.
12. This kind of cereal is Ronnie's and Valerie's favorite.
13. A delivery truck backed over the curb and dented Juan's and my bicycles.
14. I lost the piece of paper on which I had written the locker's combination.
15. The hat with the propeller on top of it is Jason's.
16. The desk nearest the front door of the classroom is Cora's.
17. The A-frame tent set up in the yard is Walter's and Freddie's.
18. Danny braided the pony's mane with red ribbons.
19. Marie Curie's husband was a scientist also.
20. When the puppy is six weeks old, it will be my sister's and mine.

C. Write the pronoun in each sentence below.

21. Your lunch is ready.
22. I forgot to wind the clock.
23. Jo saw him at the market.
24. They already played that song.
25. The dog hurt its foot.
26. Bring my book tomorrow.
27. Kim told them the truth.
28. Wesley taught her the words.
29. Jim gave us the extra sandwich.
30. We have a new school.

Using Pronouns

subject pronoun ● Use a subject pronoun as the subject of a sentence. *page 138*

<u>We</u> went to the movies. <u>I</u> saw Marsha there.

object pronoun ● Use an object pronoun after an action verb. *page 138*

Joe called <u>her</u> on Friday. Chris visited <u>us</u> today.

MORE PRACTICE 1 Using Pronouns

A. Write the pronoun in parentheses ( ) that correctly completes each sentence.

1. (I, Me) left my jacket at the library last week.
2. Mickey's parents drove (we, us) to the lake for a picnic.
3. (They, Them) are rehearsing a play in the auditorium after school every day this week.
4. Alexandra and (I, me) sold more tickets than anyone else for the children's hospital raffle.
5. Size 5 shoes fit (I, me) perfectly.
6. Marco and (we, us) get off the bus at the same corner every day.
7. (He, Him) sang a funny song about monkeys at the talent show.
8. (She, Her) and the other students are taking a first-aid class.
9. The fire chief showed Richard and (I, me) around the station.
10. You and (she, her) read the train schedule incorrectly.

B. Write each sentence. Use the correct pronoun in parentheses.

11. Mrs. Reynolds sent (they, them) to the grocery store on the corner for more milk and eggs.
12. Dad needs Esther and (her, she) to move their bicycles out of the driveway immediately.
13. My sisters and (I, me) trade our clothes back and forth often.
14. You may see him and (we, us) at the Fourth of July picnic on Monday.
15. We did not see (he, him) when Uncle Teddy appeared on that local television show.

MORE PRACTICE 2 Using Pronouns

A. Write each sentence. Use the word or words in parentheses that correctly complete the sentence.

1. (Loretta and I, I and Loretta) really enjoyed listening to your report about home computers.
2. (He, Him) and Dad have been friends for over twenty years.
3. (They, Them) spent hours arguing about the best fast-food restaurant.
4. The sales clerk told (Andy and me, me and Andy) about binoculars.
5. Our cousins and (we, us) call each other on holidays.
6. Calvin and (she, her) tied for first prize in the short story contest.
7. I contacted you and (she, her) for more information about the craft fair.
8. Our neighbors invited the O'Malleys and (we, us) to a barbecue.
9. (They, Them) and Sharon plan to participate in the track meet.
10. (My family and I, I and my family) went to the delicatessen for lunch on Sunday.

B. Write each sentence. Use the pronoun in parentheses ( ) that correctly completes the sentence. Then write whether the pronoun you used is a subject pronoun or an object pronoun.

11. Danielle thanked Sammy, Gloria, and (I, me) for the birthday gifts.
12. (They, Them) and I are in the same gymnastics class.
13. Fran and (she, her) were surprised at the results of the election.
14. Dr. Kincaid showed my parents and (I, me) the X rays of my foot.
15. The sad news upset (her, she) and her brother for days.
16. Simon and (they, them) are building a birdhouse.
17. You and (me, I) should hurry!
18. Erin reminded Doug and (us, we) about the special meeting.
19. I escorted Mrs. Henning, Mr. Davis, and (he, him) to the nurse's office.
20. When the kittens were hungry, I fed (they, them).

GRAMMAR HANDBOOK

Adjectives

adjective • An **adjective** describes a noun or a pronoun. *page 170*
Adjectives answer the question *how many* or *what kind.*
The articles *a, an,* and *the* are a special kind of adjective.

<u>Beautiful</u> chimes in <u>the</u> tower played for <u>five</u> minutes.

predicate adjective • An adjective that follows a linking verb describes the subject of a sentence. *page 172*

The bacon was <u>crisp</u>. Breakfast tasted <u>delicious</u>.

comparison of adjectives • Use the *-er* form of an adjective to compare two persons, places, or things. *page 174*

• Use the *-est* form of an adjective to compare three or more persons, places, or things. *page 174*

The Amazon is a <u>longer</u> river than the Mississippi.
The Nile is the <u>longest</u> river in the world.

• The words *more* and *most* are often used with adjectives of two or more syllables to make comparisons. *page 176*

Silver is <u>more valuable</u> than copper.
Gold is the <u>most valuable</u> of the three metals.

MORE PRACTICE 1   Adjectives

Write the adjectives in each sentence. Include articles.

1. He lost three dimes in the broken telephone.
2. Aileen lives on a busy street near some stores.
3. I bit into an apple and chipped a front tooth.
4. Lonnie read forty pages of a new mystery.
5. We visited an aquatic park to see the clever dolphins.
6. Wild geese flew over the frozen lake.
7. Three letters arrived for the special guest.
8. Christopher delivers a weekly newspaper printed by a small publisher.
9. Mix equal portions of milk and flour.
10. The antique store displayed a large collection of old-fashioned toys.

MORE PRACTICE 2 Adjectives

A. Write each sentence. Underline the adjectives that tell *what kind* once. Underline the adjectives that tell *how many* twice. Do not include articles.

1. The weary skier drank several mugs of hot cocoa.
2. She threw the rubber ball to the eager puppy.
3. Some countries sent many representatives to the important conference.
4. Six wooden puppets danced on hidden strings.
5. The timid deer darted across the misty meadow.
6. Curious Goldilocks spent a few hours in an unfamiliar neighborhood.
7. I ate one sour pickle.
8. Vera picked twelve fresh roses.
9. Four people walked out of the boring movie.

B. Write each sentence. Use *a* or *an* to complete it.

10. We heard _____ ambulance.
11. _____ hammer hit my thumb.
12. She ordered _____ omelet.
13. I brought _____ umbrella along.
14. He has _____ pair of glasses.
15. _____ operator placed the call.

C. Write each sentence. Underline the predicate adjective once. Underline twice the noun or pronoun it describes.

EXAMPLE: The ripe watermelon was sweet.
ANSWER: The ripe watermelon was sweet.

16. Evelyn seemed sorry about the misunderstanding.
17. We were breathless after climbing the hill.
18. After a visit to the barber, my hair was short again.
19. The new store was ready for its first customers.
20. Mirror Lake is popular with swimmers and boaters.
21. The woman felt calm after the accident.
22. Ronald's parents were happy with his report card.
23. The house was vacant for many months.
24. Dr. Lopez was patient with the terrified kitten.
25. Green apples taste delicious with mild cheese.

A. Write sentences for each of the following pairs of adjectives and nouns. Use a linking verb and use the adjective as a predicate adjective.

EXAMPLE: long tunnel
ANSWER: The tunnel was long.

1. famous author
2. juicy peaches
3. careless pedestrian
4. exciting conclusion
5. friendly Nancy Evans
6. clever limerick
7. talented musician
8. enthusiastic cheerleaders
9. hungry Patty Ann
10. annoying flies

B. Write the word in parentheses ( ) that correctly completes each sentence.

11. Wool is a (warmer, warmest) fabric than cotton.
12. The (faster, fastest) runner on the track team is Heather.
13. Grant Alley is the (narrower, narrowest) street in our city.
14. Western Oregon is (greener, greenest) than Eastern Oregon.
15. The Grand Canyon is (deeper, deepest) than Bryce Canyon.
16. Is this skyscraper the (higher, highest) building you've ever seen?
17. California redwoods are the world's (taller, tallest) trees.
18. My brother is (shorter, shortest) than I am.
19. The star named Sirius is the (brighter, brightest) star in the sky.
20. Uncle Edward chose a (smaller, smallest) puppy than we did.

C. Write each sentence. Use the form of the adjective shown in parentheses ( ).

21. That song about monkeys has the (silly + -est) words I've heard.
22. Winter was the (rainy + -est) season.
23. Cedar Road is (hilly + -er) than El Rancho Avenue.
24. The (busy + -est) intersection in town is Fourth and Heatherton.
25. I thought Sunday was the (nice + -est) day in months.
26. The Great Salt Lake is (large + -er) than Lake Placid.
27. She is a (funny + -er) storyteller than her partner.
28. The players on that team are (big + -er) than our team members.
29. Some plants grow better in a (wet + -er) climate.
30. That program had the (strange + -est) ending you could imagine!

GRAMMAR HANDBOOK

MORE PRACTICE 4 Adjectives

A. Write each adjective below. Then write the two forms used to compare persons, places, or things.

1. expensive
2. good
3. quick
4. hilarious
5. fascinating
6. comfortable
7. terrible
8. small
9. fine
10. bad
11. elegant
12. strange

B. Write each sentence. Use the correct form of the adjective in parentheses ( ).

13. February is the (short) month of the year.
14. During the first half of the game the fans were (enthusiastic) than during the second half.
15. Jacqueline was the (impatient) person waiting in the line.
16. Today's orchestra rehearsal was (good) than yesterday's.
17. I think Buttons the Clown is (comical) than Ruffles.
18. That is the (ridiculous) excuse for being late that anyone could possibly think of!
19. A gentle breeze is (pleasant) than a strong wind on a boating trip.
20. This is the (bad) sore throat I have ever had.
21. Is Superhero really (powerful) than a speeding space shuttle?
22. Loma Linda Cafe serves the (good) cheesecake in the country.
23. I find reading a book (enjoyable) than watching television.
24. Is overwatering (harmful) to plants than underwatering?
25. Bert thinks that drying the dishes is a (bad) job than washing them.
26. That geography class seemed like the (long) hour in the history of the world!
27. That roller coaster ride is the (exciting) attraction in the park.
28. My cousin Yolanda is (friendly) with Robin than with Mark.
29. Your class seems to be (cooperative) with a substitute teacher than mine.
30. The alarm clock in the kitchen has a (soft) ring than the one in the bedroom.

GRAMMAR HANDBOOK

Adverbs

adverb

- An **adverb** may describe a verb, an adjective, or another adverb. *pages 202, 206*

  An <u>incredibly</u> large dog waited <u>patiently</u> by the gate. We arrived <u>too</u> late to see it.

adverbs that compare

- Adverbs have forms that are used to compare actions. *page 204*

  Jack left <u>early</u> for school. Bobby left <u>earlier</u> than Jack. Earl left the <u>earliest</u> of all.
  Amanda ate <u>quickly</u>. Pablo ate <u>more quickly</u> than Amanda. Judy ate the <u>most quickly</u> of the group.

using adverbs and adjectives

- Use adjectives to describe nouns and pronouns. *page 208*
- Use adverbs to describe verbs, adjectives, and other adverbs. *page 208*

Adjectives	Adverbs
Rachel has a <u>soft</u> voice.	She speaks <u>softly</u>.
Healthy folks feel <u>well</u>.	They dance <u>well</u> together.
I felt <u>bad</u> yesterday.	Did the team play <u>badly</u>?

negative words

- **Negative words** mean "no." Avoid using two negative words in the same sentence. *page 210*

  Our bus <u>never</u> arrives on time. Our bus does <u>not</u> ever arrive on time. Our bus <u>doesn't</u> ever arrive on time.

MORE PRACTICE 1 Adverbs

In the sentences below, the verbs are underlined. Find the adverb in each sentence and write it.

1. She always <u>wears</u> a red flower.
2. Yesterday I <u>went</u> to the store.
3. The butterfly <u>landed</u> gently.
4. We <u>climbed</u> the fence carefully.
5. The children <u>played</u> outside.
6. Sometimes I <u>forget</u> my own name!

MORE PRACTICE 2 Adverbs

A. Write each sentence and underline the adverb. Then write *how, when,* or *where* to show what the adverb tells about the verb.

EXAMPLE: My little brother gripped my hand tightly.
ANSWER: My little brother gripped my hand tightly. (how)

1. Tamara mows the lawn often.
2. The baby giggled happily at the dancing bear.
3. The pedestrian stepped carelessly into the street.
4. We are fortunate to have a new library nearby.
5. The team captain accepted the trophy proudly.
6. My school is getting a new principal soon.
7. Jay spelled every word perfectly on this week's test.
8. A special-delivery letter arrived yesterday.
9. The bus will leave here at four o'clock on Friday.
10. Once I tried to waterski at Canyon Lake.

B. Write each sentence. Then write the adverb that describes the underlined adjective or adverb.

11. Summer temperatures are extremely high in the desert.
12. Everyone thought the test was incredibly difficult.
13. Don't you think this soup is rather salty?
14. My sister and I visit our grandparents fairly often.
15. The trail up the mountain seems awfully steep for a beginning hiker.
16. Edward arrived too late to buy a ticket for the show.
17. My tenth birthday is almost here!
18. The twins' personalities are certainly different.
19. The cream and butter make this dessert quite rich.
20. I am afraid my favorite shoes have become too small.

C. For each adverb below, write the form that is used to compare two actions. Then write the form that is used to compare three or more actions.

21. loudly   22. well   23. neatly   24. early   25. badly

MORE PRACTICE 3 Adverbs

A. Write each sentence. Use the adverbs below to complete the sentences.

so   extremely   very   too   rather

1. Summer vacation seemed to pass ____ quickly this year.
2. Don't you think Randy appears ____ pale today?
3. The high altitude made us ____ dizzy.
4. Please be ____ careful when you light a match.
5. Marta and Willie eat their lunches ____ slowly.

B. Write the sentences. For each adverb in parentheses ( ), add *more* or use the *-er* form.

6. Steve climbed the rope (easily) than I did.
7. The car rides (smoothly) since its tune-up.
8. Sometimes we sleep (late) on Saturdays than during the week.
9. I write (neatly) this year than I did last year.
10. Can a kangaroo jump (high) than a person can?

C. Write the sentences. For each adverb in parentheses ( ), add *most* or use the *-est* form.

11. The drums played the (loud) of all the instruments.
12. Of all the speakers, Desmond spoke (clearly) into the microphone.
13. Greg's box kite flew the (high) of all the kites in the sky.
14. Leslie ran the (fast) in the hundred-yard dash at the meet.
15. Darla waited (patiently) of anyone in line.

D. Write the sentences. Underline the negative words.

16. Nobody on our block has seen our lost pet.
17. I can't eat another bite!
18. Nancy has never been to my house before.
19. Nothing tastes as good as a cold, crisp apple.
20. None of the batters today got to first base.

MORE PRACTICE 4 Adverbs

A. Write the word in parentheses ( ) that correctly completes each sentence.

1. That wool blanket is very (warm, warmly).
2. You seem (unusual, unusually) quiet today.
3. All the lights went out quite (sudden, suddenly).
4. The teenagers played the radio (loud, loudly) on the beach.
5. Mother cut the watermelon with a (sharp, sharply) knife.
6. The clerk was (rude, rudely) to the customers.
7. She fastened her seat belt (tight, tightly).
8. Their story is (strange, strangely) but true.
9. Martin has a (bad, badly) case of measles.
10. I could see many fish in the (clear, clearly) water.

B. Choose the word in parentheses ( ) that correctly completes each sentence. Write the sentence. Then write whether *good, well, bad,* or *badly* is an adjective or an adverb in the sentence.

EXAMPLE: The team played (bad, badly) in the tournament.
ANSWER: The team played badly in the tournament. (adverb)

11. Eating healthful foods helps people stay (good, well).
12. The band played the marching song (good, well).
13. The movie at the Strand Theater is really (good, well).
14. Donald has a (bad, badly) bruise on his leg.
15. He bruised his leg (bad, badly).

C. Write the word in parentheses ( ) that correctly completes each sentence. Avoid double negatives.

16. Nobody (ever, never) beats Joel at checkers.
17. Hasn't (anyone, no one) unlocked the front door yet?
18. There aren't (any, no) more staples in this stapler.
19. None of my friends (never, ever) heard that joke before.
20. We have not heard (anything, nothing) from them in months.

GRAMMAR HANDBOOK

Prepositions

preposition
- A **preposition** relates a noun or pronoun to another word in the sentence. *page 244*

object of the preposition
- The noun or pronoun that follows the preposition is called the **object of the preposition.** *page 244*

  Jacob entered <u>through</u> the <u>door</u>. He talked <u>to me</u>.

prepositional phrase
- A **prepositional phrase** includes the preposition, the object, and all the words that come between them. *page 246*

  Little Ms. Muffet sat <u>on a tuffet</u>.

prepositions and adverbs
- Some words can be either prepositions or adverbs. *page 248*

  We peered <u>inside</u> the cave. Nancy walked <u>inside</u>.

using prepositional phrases
- Use object pronouns in prepositional phrases. *page 250*

  Chuck explained the plans <u>to us</u>.

using <u>between</u> and <u>among</u>
- Use the prepositions *between* and *among* correctly. *page 250*

  I could not decide <u>between</u> chocolate and strawberry.
  The prize money was divided <u>among</u> the five winners.

MORE PRACTICE 1 Prepositions

Write each sentence. Underline the preposition.

1. The sun always sets in the west.
2. The first lunar landing took place during the late sixties.
3. Harold took photographs with his new instant camera.
4. Flowering trees are blossoming along Market Street.
5. We waited a long time at the busy intersection.
6. The breeze blew the papers off Julia's desk.
7. I found my library book under the bed.
8. Some bicycle riders rode across the United States last summer.

MORE PRACTICE 2   Prepositions

A. Write each sentence. Underline the preposition once. Underline the object of the preposition twice.

1. The vase fell off the shelf.
2. After school Karen takes an aerobic dancing class.
3. I was pleased with my report.
4. She told the fable of the greedy fox.
5. Walter and I bought a birthday present for him.
6. The spaghetti should boil for ten minutes.
7. A tremendous jet could be seen above the clouds.
8. The batter hit the baseball over the fence.
9. We jogged around the lake's edge.
10. Have you heard the joke about the forgetful elephant?

B. Write each sentence. Underline the prepositional phrase.

11. Please bring me some tea without sugar.
12. My cousins and I often go to the movies.
13. The reporter wrote a story about home computers.
14. Lois left her tennis racket at the park.
15. I climbed carefully down the shaky ladder.
16. My cousins will visit us during their summer vacation.
17. The tiny kitten darted out the open door.
18. Terry took a very nice picture of you.
19. I would like my hamburger with everything!
20. The parade passed before the city hall.

C. Write each sentence. Then write whether the underlined word is a preposition or an adverb.

21. The baby woke and looked <u>around</u>.
22. The sailboat passed <u>under</u> the Golden Gate Bridge.
23. We ate a picnic lunch <u>near</u> the Colorado River.
24. Everyone in the room stood <u>up</u>.
25. The new shopping center is quite <u>near</u>.

GRAMMAR HANDBOOK

MORE PRACTICE 3 Prepositions

A. Write the prepositional phrase in each sentence. Underline the preposition once. Underline the object of the preposition twice.

EXAMPLE: I need some batteries for my radio.

ANSWER: for my radio

1. That thin glass might shatter in the dishwasher.
2. I watched the game with Cindy's binoculars.
3. Under the old newspapers you might find today's edition.
4. Put the leftovers inside this plastic container.
5. The young colt galloped beside its mother.
6. I can't find anything on this messy desk!
7. Did a letter come for Mom today?
8. The money disappeared without a trace.

B. Write each sentence. If the underlined part is an adverb, change it to a prepositional phrase. If it is a prepositional phrase, change it to an adverb.

EXAMPLE: Josh dropped the letter in the mailbox.

ANSWER: Josh dropped the letter in.

9. I parked my bicycle below.
10. Everyone looked inside the room.
11. Francesca walked over.
12. The police officer drove around the parking lot.
13. The museum is near.
14. Kevin went out the emergency exit.

C. Write the word that correctly completes each sentence.

15. I laughed when Marla told the story to (I, me).
16. Lori sits (between, among) Rita and Daniel in social studies class.
17. The judges must choose (between, among) ten talented contestants.
18. We looked for (them, they) at the meeting.
19. I marched (between, among) two other Scouts in the parade.
20. Seth spotted a swan (between, among) the turkeys, geese, and ducks.

MORE PRACTICE 4 Prepositions

A. Write the prepositional phrase in each sentence. Underline the preposition once. Underline the object of the preposition twice.

1. Last night I had a dream about a purple cow.
2. Does walking under a ladder bring bad luck?
3. Eileen never leaves the house without her keys.
4. We drove by the new restaurant.
5. They took the elevator to the fortieth floor.
6. Darlene always talks during our last class.
7. Somebody has painted a bright green line across the playground.
8. Do not open this package before your birthday!
9. Everyone told scary stories around the campfire.
10. What will you do over the long holiday weekend?
11. The athlete threw a towel over his shoulders.
12. Have you seen the latest exhibit at the art museum?
13. My muscles were very stiff after the long hike.
14. The squirrel ran quickly up the tree trunk.
15. From the airplane window you could see the entire city.

B. Choose the pronoun in parentheses ( ) that correctly completes each sentence. Write the sentence.

16. Dad asked me to save a piece of cherry cheesecake for (he, him).
17. Grandma sent a post card to (they, them) from England.
18. I ate lunch with Howard and (he, him) on Tuesday.
19. I brought enough fruit for Julie and (we, us).
20. Sandy borrowed a pen from (she, her) and has not returned it yet.
21. The clowns skipped around (us, we) at the fair.
22. Jackie would love to have dinner with you and (she, her).
23. I could listen to (them, they) play music all day long.
24. Mrs. Levin rode by (we, us) on her bicycle.
25. Roy owes two dollars to (I, me) for the show ticket.

Compound Subjects and Predicates

compound subject

- A **compound subject** is two or more simple subjects that have the same predicate. *page 278*

<u>Gabriela</u> and my <u>sister</u> are best friends.

compound predicate

- A **compound predicate** is two or more verbs that have the same subject. *page 282*

Ms. Weinstock <u>cleaned</u> and <u>waxed</u> her car.

MORE PRACTICE 1 Compound Subjects and Predicates

A. Write the complete subject in each sentence. If the subject is compound, write *compound* after it.

1. Hail and rain fell during the terrible storm.
2. The costumes are kept backstage at the theater.
3. Dennis Shepard and Cheryl Eneboe were finalists in the contest.
4. Sailboats and small yachts are docked at the marina.
5. Mumps, measles, and chicken pox are usually considered childhood diseases.
6. Regina and I played a piano duet at the school talent show.
7. Crispy bacon is my favorite breakfast food.
8. Salt and pepper are spices found in most kitchens.

B. Write the complete predicate in each sentence. If the predicate is compound, write *compound.*

9. The cast members dance and sing during every performance.
10. I dusted and vacuumed the entire living room on Saturday.
11. Marty Brewer draws pictures of ships and boats.
12. Lenny washed and dried all the dinner dishes last night.
13. The audience clapped and cheered for the acrobats.
14. The track team jogs several miles every afternoon.
15. My grandparents water and weed their garden every day during the summer.

MORE PRACTICE 2 Compound Subjects and Predicates

A. Write each sentence. Underline the compound subject.

EXAMPLE: Celery and spinach appeared on the salad counter.
ANSWER: <u>Celery</u> and <u>spinach</u> appeared on the salad counter.

1. The table and chairs were made of oak.
2. Tulips and daffodils bloom in the spring.
3. Balloons and streamers decorated the room.
4. Salad and cole slaw come with each sandwich.
5. Books, magazines, and records are available at the public library.
6. Children and adults like circuses.
7. Juice, milk, and water are all excellent thirst-quenchers.
8. Wool and cotton are natural fibers.
9. A newspaper and two letters arrived in today's mail delivery.
10. Roberto, Jake, and Ellen work together on the safety patrol.
11. Televisions and radios help people to know the news.
12. Raisins and peanuts are healthy, tasty snacks.

B. Write each sentence. Underline the verbs in the compound predicate.

EXAMPLE: Betty slipped and fell on the staircase.
ANSWER: Betty <u>slipped</u> and <u>fell</u> on the staircase.

13. Terry bathed and dressed the baby.
14. My best friend lost and found ten dollars on the same day.
15. We baked and decorated a cake for the surprise party.
16. The kindergarten children laughed and giggled at the puppet show.
17. I peeled and chopped an onion.
18. The police officer followed, stopped, and warned the driver.
19. Many people collect and trade postage stamps from foreign countries.
20. Bonnie combed and brushed her hair.
21. The kitten purred, yawned, and fell asleep.
22. We cut and pasted magazine pictures.
23. At the flea market people buy and sell used merchandise.
24. The sun rises and sets once every 24 hours.
25. Many jets arrive and depart each day.

GRAMMAR HANDBOOK

Subject-Verb Agreement

subject-verb agreement

- Compound subjects joined by *and* use the form of a verb that is used with a plural noun.   *page 280*

Elizabeth and Wally <u>ride</u> horses.
The students and the teacher <u>enjoy</u> math class.

MORE PRACTICE 1   Subject-Verb Agreement

A. Write the verb in parentheses that correctly completes each sentence.

1. A hammer and some nails (was, were) in the carpenter's tool box.
2. An alarm clock and a rooster (do, does) a good job of waking up everyone on the farm each morning.
3. Colds and sore throats (occur, occurs) in all kinds of weather.
4. Envelopes, post cards, aerograms, and stamps (is, are) available at the post office.
5. Some doctors and a lawyer (has, have) offices on the twelfth floor of the First City Bank Building downtown.

B. Write each sentence. Use the correct form of the verb in parentheses (   ).

6. Bright balloons and colorful streamers (make, makes) any room look like a party.
7. Beans and peas (grows, grow) on vines.
8. Our dog and your cat (plays, play) nicely together.
9. Mushrooms and eggs (make, makes) a wonderful omelet.
10. Chocolate and coffee (is, are) the two flavors that make mocha.
11. Bicycle riders and skaters (spends, spend) lots of time at Madison Park on weekends.
12. Manuel and Patsy (play, plays) checkers almost every day.
13. A woodpecker and a squirrel (live, lives) in that big tree.
14. Valentine's Day and Groundhog Day both (comes, come) in the shortest month of the year.
15. Grapefruit, oranges, and lemons (grow, grows) in Arizona.

MORE PRACTICE 2 Subject-Verb Agreement

A. Write the verb in parentheses (   ) that correctly completes each sentence.

1. Lemonade, ice tea, and orange juice (is, are) very refreshing on a hot summer's day.
2. Parrots and mynah birds (imitate, imitates) human voices.
3. Candles and oil lamps (help, helps) in power failures.
4. Cars, trucks, and jets all (uses, use) some form of oil products for fuel.
5. My black shoes and brown boots (need, needs) polish.
6. Carnations and roses (makes, make) beautiful bouquets.
7. Engineers, secretaries, and mechanics (study, studies) many different subjects at night school.
8. Roslyn and Jorge (is, are) learning about computers in a special computer class.
9. Model sports cars and jeeps (was, were) shown at the county fair.
10. The judge and the jury (try, tries) to make a fair decision in a legal case.

B. Write each sentence. Use the correct form of the verb in parentheses (   ).

11. Singers and musicians (deliver, delivers) funny messages for a new business called Tune-a-gram.
12. Sometimes heavy winds and rain (cause, causes) traffic accidents.
13. Skeletons and several ghosts usually (appears, appear) at our door on Halloween.
14. The earth and the other planets (revolve, revolves) around the sun.
15. Hot dogs and hamburgers (is, are) often served on rolls or buns.
16. Many singers and some dancers (takes, take) classes at the music conservatory.
17. Joseph and his grandfather (likes, like) to play tennis together.
18. My cousin and my best friend (live, lives) near each other.
19. Zucchini and pumpkins (is, are) both members of the squash family.
20. Chickens, ducks, and turkeys (eats, eat) the seeds that the farmer scatters around the barnyard.

Compound Sentences

subject-verb agreement

- A **compound sentence** contains two or more simple sentences joined by a conjunction. *page 284*

  I have finished.   You have just started.
  I have finished, but you have just started.

compound sentence

- A comma is used before the conjunction *and, or,* or *but* in a compound sentence. *page 286*

  Dr. Becker is very busy today, but she can see you at two o'clock tomorrow.

run-on sentence

- A **run-on sentence** is two or more sentences not separated by correct punctuation or connecting words. *page 286*

  The team runs onto the field people cheer wildly.

MORE PRACTICE 1   Compound Sentences

A. Write *simple, compound,* or *run-on* for each sentence.

1. My brother and I brush our teeth at least two times a day.
2. Leila Kimura wrote a poem, and Lee Glickstein read it at the assembly on Martin Luther King Day.
3. Fido scratched at the door Stevie let the puppy in.
4. We wanted to play baseball, but the rain changed our plans.
5. Dad wrapped and mailed a package to Aunt Elise.
6. Many people entered the contest only one lucky winner was selected.
7. You can wait for me near the front entrance, or I can meet you on the second floor of the library.

B. Write each compound sentence. Underline the two simple sentences in it.

8. A sudden rain shower fell, and a beautiful double rainbow appeared.
9. The telephone rang thirty times, but no one was home to answer it.
10. Jill may bring fruit salad, or she might decide to make coleslaw for the pot-luck dinner.

MORE PRACTICE 2 Compound Sentences

A. Write each sentence. Add a comma before the conjunction.

1. Everyone is very hungry but lunch will not be ready for another hour.
2. You can ride your bicycle to the library or you can walk along Hyde Street to get there.
3. The audience clapped and cheered for ten minutes and the singer came back on stage to sing another song.
4. The pelican dived towards the water but the fish got away.
5. Many of my friends like science fiction but I prefer to read mystery stories.
6. Janice went to Holly's apartment but her friend had gone to the dentist for a filling.
7. Willie told Jason about the book and the other boy decided to find it at the library.
8. Some people have curly hair and some people have hair that is completely straight.
9. You may finish your homework now or you may do the assignment after dinner.
10. I would love to taste the cheesecake but I am too full to eat dessert right now.

B. Correct these run-on sentences. Write each as a compound sentence by adding a comma and a conjunction.

11. Eleanor works after school at the grocery story she is saving her money for a bicycle.
12. I ran up the stairs to answer the telephone I was too late.
13. Enrico ordered a roast beef sandwich on rye bread the food server brought him ham and cheese on whole wheat toast.
14. Mary Jane went shopping she bought bright green socks and a new belt.
15. Elizabeth Stone and I want to go to the movies today the show begins in twenty minutes.

Paragraphs

paragraph
- A **paragraph** is a group of sentences that tells about one main idea. *page 30*

topic sentence
- The **topic sentence** states the main idea of a paragraph. *page 32*

supporting sentences
- **Supporting sentences** develop the main idea. *page 32*

- The first word of a paragraph is indented.

Indent → Topic sentence

Supporting sentences

Mercury is a strange liquid metal. It is a liquid that is dry. You can touch it with your finger, and your finger will not get wet. Mercury is always a liquid, even when it's cool. No other metal acts this way. Most liquids trickle in a stream when they run downhill. Mercury stays in a little puddle. The whole puddle slides downhill! If you give a puddle of mercury a little push, it breaks into hundreds of tiny round globs. If these globs are pushed together, they form a puddle again.

PRACTICE

A. Write a topic sentence for each of these topics.

1. a favorite pet
2. what to do on a rainy day
3. why I like (name of sport or game)
4. what I want to be when I grow up
5. my opinion about (a TV show, a movie, a book, or something that happened recently)

B. Choose one of the topic sentences you wrote for **Practice A** above. Then write a paragraph, using that topic sentence as your first sentence. Make sure that the other sentences in your paragraph are supporting sentences. They should tell more about the idea stated in your topic sentence. Don't forget to indent the first sentence of your paragraph.

Writing Forms: Friendly Letters

- A **friendly letter** has five parts: the heading, greeting, body, closing, and signature. *page 152*

- The **heading** shows the address of the writer and the date. Proper nouns are capitalized. A comma is used between the city and the state and between the date and the year.

- The first word of the **greeting** is capitalized as well as the proper noun. The greeting is followed by a comma.

- The **closing** is followed by a comma. Only the first word in the closing is capitalized.

Heading

121 South Main Street
Carthage, MO 64836
July 17, 1986

Greeting

Dear Greg,

Body

I'm so glad you're coming to visit us next Monday! Just let me know what train you're taking, and I'll be at the station to meet you.
Don't forget your bathing suit!

Closing

Your cousin,

Signature

Jim

PRACTICE

Using the form shown above, write a friendly letter to a friend or relative. Give that person some news about yourself. Tell what you have been doing lately. Use the form shown on page 374 of this Young Writer's Handbook to address the envelope correctly.

Writing Forms: Business Letters

business letter
- A **business letter** has six parts: the heading, inside address, greeting, body, closing, and signature. *page 154*

- When you write a business letter, make your message clear and brief. *page 154*

heading
- The **heading** gives the writer's address and the date.

inside address
- The **inside address** gives the name and address of the person or company to whom the letter is sent. Notice where commas and capital letters are used in the sample below.

greeting
- In a business letter, the **greeting** is followed by a colon.

closing
- Only the first word in the **closing** is capitalized. Acceptable closings include: *Respectfully, Yours truly, Sincerely.*

signature
- If the letter is typed, the writer's name is typed four lines below the closing, under the writer's **signature.**

Heading

```
                          3105 W. Penn Street
                          Corry, PA 16407
                          August 2, 1986
```

Inside address

```
Ms. Diane O'Brien, Manager
Outdoor Gear, Inc.
232 First Avenue
Caribou, ME 04736
```

Greeting

```
Dear Ms. O'Brien:
```

Body

```
     Please send your new fall catalog to me at
the above address.
```

Closing
Signature

```
                          Sincerely,
                          Sally Moyer
                          Sally Moyer
```

PRACTICE

Write a business letter to a real or made-up company or organization. You may wish to ask for information or write a suggestion or complaint. Use the form on page 374 to address the envelope correctly.

Writing Forms: Thank-You Notes and Invitations

- A **thank-you note** is a short letter of thanks for a gift or favor. It follows the form of a friendly letter.

thank-you note

23 King Street
Largo, FL 33540
June 4, 1986

Dear Aunt Agatha,
I really enjoyed the book you sent me for my birthday, *The Case of the Curious Computer.* It was fascinating, and it taught me a lot about computers, too!

Love,
Kristy

- An **invitation** is a note or letter that invites someone to an event. It should name the event, tell where and when it is being held, and tell who sent the invitation.

invitation

You are invited to *my Halloween party*
Place: *122 Coover Avenue*
Date and Time: *Oct. 31, 2:00–4:00 P.M.*
Held by: *Jeff Conti*
Wear a costume!

PRACTICE

A. Write a thank-you note to a real person or someone you make up.

B. Write an invitation to a party or other special event.

Writing Forms: Outlines

outline
- An **outline** organizes information into main ideas and supporting ideas. *page 230*

- Each main idea is listed as a main topic in an outline, and each supporting idea is listed as a subtopic.

main topic
- A **main topic** is numbered with a Roman numeral, followed by a period. The first word begins with a capital letter.

subtopic
- A **subtopic** is listed under its main topic and is indented. Each subtopic is labeled with a capital letter, followed by a period. The first word begins with a capital letter.

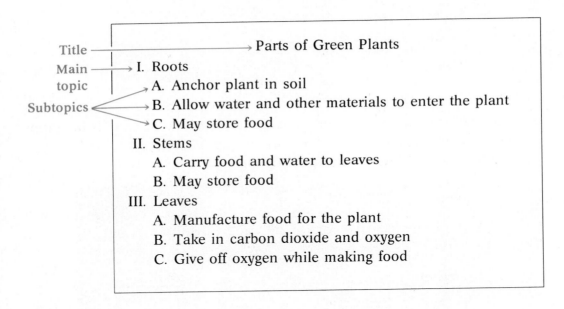

Title → Parts of Green Plants

Main topic → I. Roots

Subtopics →
A. Anchor plant in soil
B. Allow water and other materials to enter the plant
C. May store food

II. Stems
A. Carry food and water to leaves
B. May store food

III. Leaves
A. Manufacture food for the plant
B. Take in carbon dioxide and oxygen
C. Give off oxygen while making food

PRACTICE

Making an outline is an excellent way to review and remember material you have read. It is a good way to prepare for a test. Outline a lesson from this book, or outline part of a chapter from a social studies or science book. Use the headings and subheadings in the book to help you decide on your main topics and subtopics. Use your own words in your outline. You do not need to write complete sentences.

Writing Forms: Book Reports

- A **book report** tells what a book is about and gives an opinion of the book.   *page 74*

- A **book title** is underlined.

Study this book report form. It shows what kind of information to include in a book report.

Title *The Saturdays*

Author *Elizabeth Enright*

Setting *New York City*

The four Melendy children, their father, and the housekeeper. They don't have a mother anymore.

What the book is about *The Saturdays tells how the Melendy family spends each Saturday to make it the most interesting day of the week. Each week they put their spending money together and take turns deciding what to do on Saturday. They have lots of adventures as they visit famous places, such as the Statue of Liberty.*

Your opinion *I especially enjoyed this book because it made me feel that I was in New York, too!*

PRACTICE

Copy the book report form above. Use it to write a report about a book you read recently and would like to recommend to your classmates.

Addressing Letters: Envelopes

- When you address an envelope, you write the return address and the receiver's address.

return address
- Write your name and address in the upper left-hand corner. This is the **return address.** It shows where to return the letter if it cannot be delivered.

receiver's address
- In the center of the envelope, write the **receiver's address.** This is the name and address of the person who will receive the letter. For business letters, the receiver's address is an exact copy of the inside address.

state abbreviations
- You may use an abbreviation for the name of a state. Use the two-letter abbreviation approved by the Postal Service. See the list of state abbreviations on the next page.

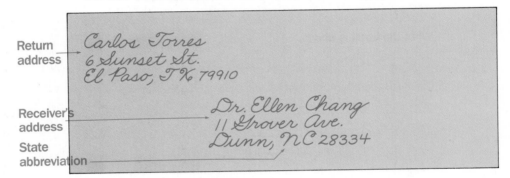

Return address — Carlos Torres / 6 Sunset St. / El Paso, TX 79910

Receiver's address — Dr. Ellen Chang / 11 Grover Ave. / Dunn, NC 28334

State abbreviation

PRACTICE

Using a ruler, draw three envelopes like the sample above. Then address each one, using the information given below.

1. *Return address:* Robert Gula   418 Monroe St.   Oxford, CT 06483
   Receiver's address: Ms. Theresa Kwon   4 Lake Rd.   Aztec, NM 87410

2. *Return address:* Jesse A. Stanton   31 Wayne Ave.   Lodi, NJ 07644
   Receiver's address: Mrs. Ann Tully   28 Reed Rd.   Cody, WY 82414

3. *Return address:* Vincent Ricci   8 Budd Ave.   Barre, VT 05641
   Receiver's address: Mr. Scott Macey   27 Cedar Dr.   Bristol, TN 37620

Addressing Letters: State Abbreviations

- Use these abbreviations of state names when you write addresses. Notice that periods are not used in the abbreviations.

Alabama	AL	Maine	ME	Oregon	OR
Alaska	AK	Maryland	MD	Pennsylvania	PA
Arizona	AZ	Massachusetts	MA	Rhode Island	RI
Arkansas	AR	Michigan	MI	South Carolina	SC
California	CA	Minnesota	MN	South Dakota	SD
Colorado	CO	Mississippi	MS	Tennessee	TN
Connecticut	CT	Missouri	MO	Texas	TX
Delaware	DE	Montana	MT	Utah	UT
Florida	FL	Nebraska	NE	Vermont	VT
Georgia	GA	Nevada	NV	Virginia	VA
Hawaii	HI	New Hampshire	NH	Washington	WA
Idaho	ID	New Jersey	NJ	West Virginia	WV
Illinois	IL	New Mexico	NM	Wisconsin	WI
Indiana	IN	New York	NY	Wyoming	WY
Iowa	IA	North Carolina	NC	* * *	
Kansas	KS	North Dakota	ND	District of	
Kentucky	KY	Ohio	OH	Columbia	DC
Louisiana	LA	Oklahoma	OK		

PRACTICE

A. Write the abbreviation for each of these state names.

1. Arizona
2. Colorado
3. Maine
4. Michigan
5. Tennessee
6. Arkansas
7. Georgia
8. Texas
9. Utah
10. Iowa

B. See how many words you can form by combining state abbreviations. Write them in a list. For example, ME + ND form the word *mend*. GA + IL form the name *Gail*. Then trade papers and see if your partner can name the states whose abbreviations form each word.

YOUNG WRITER'S HANDBOOK

REVIEW AND PRACTICE HANDBOOKS   375

Editing Marks

- Use editing marks to make changes when you revise and proofread your writing.

Mark	Meaning	Example
——	cross out	It is a ~~most~~ perfect day for a picnic.
		It is a perfect day for a picnic.
∧	add	*mystery* Have you read this ∧ story?
		Have you read this mystery story?
↰ (circle with arrow)	move	Take ∧ to school today (your lunch).
		Take your lunch to school today.
≡	capital letter	Have you visited the g̲r̲and c̲anyon?
		Have you visited the Grand Canyon?
/	small letter	I'll meet you at the D̸rugstore.
		I'll meet you at the drugstore.
¶	indent	¶The largest railroad station in the world is Grand Central Terminal in New York City. It covers 48 acres.
		The largest railroad station in the world is Grand Central Terminal in New York City. It covers 48 acres.
◯ (circle)	check spelling	*received* I never (recieved) the letter.
		I never received the letter.

Proofreading Checklist

When you write something for others to read, be considerate of your audience. Proofread your paper for errors. If you find a mistake, correct it neatly, using the editing marks. The proofreading checklist below will help you find errors. Notice that the writer has checked *No* for questions 3 and 5. The checks help the writer notice what kind of errors he or she is making. Copy the checklist form if you wish.

It is generally a good idea to check for just one thing at a time. For example, first check for spelling errors. It is easier to spot these if you start at the end of your composition and move to the beginning. Check each word separately, looking only for spelling errors. Next check for sentence sense, and so on.

Questions	YES	NO
1. Did I indent the first word of each paragraph?	✔	
2. Did I begin each sentence with a capital letter and end it with the correct punctuation mark?	✔	
3. Did I use capital letters correctly?		✔
4. Did I spell each word correctly?	✔	
5. Did I use my best handwriting?		✔

Capitalization

- A **proper noun** begins with a capital letter. *page 54*

people and pets
- Capitalize the names of people and pets. *page 54*

Gregory   Jamie Lynn Murray
the Jacksons   Rex

titles and initials
- Capitalize titles, such as *Miss* or *Mr.*, and initials.

Miss Doreen Gray   Mr. H. L. Jones
Ms. Constance Cook   Dr. Jeanne A. Ramos
President John F. Kennedy   Judge A. L. Green

place names
- Capitalize every important word in the names of particular places and things. *page 54*

Clover Hill Road   San Francisco
South Dakota   Lake Michigan
New Zealand   Mount Everest
Golden Gate Bridge   Avenue of the Americas

special groups
- Capitalize the names of nationalities and languages.

Irish   Latin   Japanese
Canadian   Spanish   Mexican

- Capitalize the names of clubs, organizations, and business firms.

Westfield Garden Club   Boy Scouts of America
Ace Manufacturing Company   Computers Unlimited, Inc.

calendar words
- Capitalize every important word in the names of months, days, holidays, and special days. *page 54*

October   Wednesday   February
Thanksgiving   Labor Day   Armed Forces Day
Halloween   Fourth of July   Groundhog Day

- The pronoun *I* is always capitalized. *page 130*   **pronoun I**

  When I go to Florida, I'll visit Uncle Harry.

- Capitalize the first word, the last word, and all important words in the title of a book. *page 74*   **book title**

  The Lion, the Witch, and the Wardrobe
  The Fellowship of the Ring

- Capitalize the first word, the last word, and all important words in the title of a story, poem, or report.   **title of story, poem, or report**

  "The Case of the Black Hat" (story)
  "A Sea-Song from the Shore" (poem)
  "The World's Highest Mountain" (report)

PRACTICE 1   Capitalization

A. Write each name correctly.

1. mr george m. brown
2. president franklin d. roosevelt
3. dr. kimberly ann nickell
4. mrs. e. l. cunningham
5. ms. roxanne richards
6. black beauty
7. miss ana r. perez
8. queen elizabeth II
9. rover
10. w. a. richards

B. Write each sentence. Use capital letters correctly.

11. Did raymond name his dog lassie or ginger?
12. The report james wrote was about president dwight d. eisenhower.
13. Both mr. tom a. perry and miss diane jackson applied for the job.
14. Is barbara's music teacher mrs. stein or dr. warfield?
15. The letter joanne wrote is addressed to ms. arlene d. chiang.
16. When will matt introduce ray to elizabeth?
17. The horse is named liberty belle.
18. Was carrie permitted to interview mayor alma g. hansen?

PRACTICE 2 Capitalization

A. Write each address. Use capital letters correctly.

1. miss jennifer lee griffin
   18 valley view road
   mint hill, north carolina 28212

2. mr. michael s. eagan
   28 long hill drive
   forest park, georgia 30050

3. dr. j. l. vega
   46 north essex street
   yazoo city, mississippi 39194

4. ms. diane n. verzi
   93 birch run avenue
   blair, nebraska 68008

5. mrs. helen t. keyes
   82 rising sun boulevard
   benton, arkansas 72015

B. Write each sentence. Use capital letters correctly.

6. Joanne can speak english, french, and spanish.
7. Shall we go to an italian, a chinese, or a mexican restaurant for our birthday celebration?
8. The union county coin collectors' club meets every tuesday.
9. This camera was made by the apex camera corporation.
10. When was the girl scouts of america founded?
11. On wednesday the latin teacher was absent.
12. Mrs. Harrington wrote letters to the alpine furniture company and the casper carpet company.
13. The adirondack mountain club has many members.
14. James has formed a toy company called toy town, inc.
15. This german novel has been translated into english, dutch, danish, and swedish.

PRACTICE 3 Capitalization

A. Write these days and dates. Use capital letters correctly.

1. saturday, june 22
2. new year's day
3. friday, august 23
4. mother's day
5. wednesday, november 4
6. thursday, april 29
7. washington's birthday
8. columbus day
9. tuesday, july 15
10. armistice day

B. Write each sentence. Use capital letters correctly.

11. Since monday was labor day, i had a three-day weekend.
12. Every halloween i make my own costume.
13. Of course, i love the pumpkin pie we have on thanksgiving!
14. Even though i am not irish, i celebrate st. patrick's day.
15. Dad will like the present i'm making for him for father's day.

C. Write each sentence. Use capital letters correctly.

16. May i borrow the book the cricket in times square?
17. No, i haven't read king of the wind.
18. A book i'd recommend is island of the blue dolphins.
19. After i read sea star, i looked for other books by the same author.
20. The book i will report on is secret of the tiger's eye.

D. Write each sentence. Use capital letters correctly.

21. My report is called "the climate of mars."
22. The poem "the purple cow" is by Gelett Burgess.
23. Have you read the story "three strong women"?
24. The story "when the stones were soft" is a folktale from Africa.
25. Our class recited the poem "where the sidewalk ends."
26. The title of Jake's report is "the loch ness monster."
27. The poem "a modern dragon" describes a train.
28. I read "the three little pigs" to my young cousin.
29. Lisa's report, "first aid for burns," gives useful information.
30. The poem "some fishy nonsense" has a catchy rhythm.

Punctuation

comma

- Use a **comma** after *yes, no,* or *well* at the beginning of a sentence. *page 252*

  Yes, that is the glove I lost.

- Use a **comma** to set off the name of a person spoken to. *page 252*

  James, the phone call is for you.
  Tell me, Susan, why you were late this morning.

- Use a **comma** to separate the last name and first name of a person when the last name is written first. *page 252*

  Washington, George

- Use a **comma** to separate words in a series. *page 178*

  Maria, Frank, Bob, and Jenny are on our team.

- Use a **comma** to separate the name of a city and a state and to separate the date and the year.

  Philadelphia, Pennsylvania   July 4, 1776

- If a two-word place name or a date is within a sentence, use a **comma** both before and after the name of the state (or country) and before and after the year.

  Eugene was born on February 16, 1889, in Annapolis, Maryland, a town near the nation's capital.

- In a quotation, use a **comma** to separate the quotation from the speaker. The comma comes before the quotation marks. *page 118.*

  Carlos said, "The Eagles are ahead by one touchdown."

apostrophe

- In a contraction, use an **apostrophe** to show where a letter or letters have been left out.

  does + not=doesn't   they + will = they're

- Use **quotation marks** to show the exact words of a speaker. *page 118*

page 118

> Stacey said, "Today is my brother's birthday."
> "Last week," she added, "was my mother's birthday."

- Use **quotation marks** before and after the title of a story, poem, article, or report when you write about it.

> The poem "Eletelephony" is amusing.
> That magazine has an interesting article, "Tidal Waves."

- **Underline** the title of a book, magazine, newspaper, or movie.

<u>Soup and Me</u> (book)   <u>National Geographic</u> (magazine)
<u>Dallas News</u> (newspaper)   <u>Star Wars</u> (movie)

- Most abbreviations end with a **period.**

Below are some common abbreviations. Notice that each begins with a capital letter and ends with a period.

Mr. = Mister (a man)	St. = Street
Ms. = a woman	Ave. = Avenue
Mrs. = a married woman	Rd. = Road
Dr. = Doctor	Blvd. = Boulevard

A.M. = before noon	P.M. = after noon

Mon.	Tues.	Wed.	Thurs.	Fri.	Sat.	Sun.

Jan. = January	Sept. = September
Feb. = February	Oct. = October
Mar. = March	Nov. = November
Apr. = April	Dec. = December
Aug. = August	

quotation marks

underlining

period with abbreviations

YOUNG WRITER'S HANDBOOK

PRACTICE 1 Punctuation

A. Write each sentence. Use commas correctly.

1. No I didn't order this magazine.
2. Well today turned out to be a good day after all.
3. Yes school will be closed for Memorial Day.
4. No there isn't any more pizza.
5. Well let's not go to the movies today.

B. Write each sentence. Use commas correctly.

6. Jessica will you please answer the phone?
7. If you look on the shelf Mike you'll find your glasses.
8. Mr. Greentree you are the lucky winner of our contest!
9. Thank you so much Aunt Grace for the lovely gift!
10. Camille are you listening to me?

C. Write each sentence. Use commas correctly.

11. She filled out the form and signed her last name first: Jones Rita.
12. The recipe calls for carrots oil honey flour and baking powder.
13. The author card gave the author's last name first: Somers Ann.
14. Sparrows robins cardinals and chickadees ate the seeds we put out.
15. I invited Joe Annie Charlene Steve and Doug to my party.

D. Write these place names and dates. Use commas correctly.

16. Chicago Illinois
17. December 2 1849
18. Rome Italy
19. May 15 1985
20. Charlottesville Virginia
21. February 2 1774

E. Write each sentence. Use commas correctly.

22. The actor was born in Benson Vermont on September 2 1938.
23. Harvard College was founded on October 28 1636.
24. George Washington was born in Wakefield Virginia.
25. On November 4 1841 the first wagon train reached California.

PRACTICE 2   Punctuation

A. Write the contraction for each pair of words.

  1. it is   **2.** they are   **3.** we have   **4.** do not   **5.** he will

B. Write these sentences. Use quotation marks and commas correctly.

  6. Ramon said You'll never guess what happened to me.
  7. Jane replied No, that is not my hat.
  8. I was never said Dan more surprised in my life!
  9. Mark asked Do we have a science test tomorrow?
  10. The soccer game will not be called off said Jim if it rains.

C. Write these titles. Use quotation marks and underlining correctly.

  11. The Wright Brothers (book)
  12. Three Golden Oranges (story)
  13. Wall Street Journal (newspaper)
  14. Saturday Evening Review (magazine)
  15. Millions of Strawberries (poem)

D. Write the abbreviation for each of the following.

  16. November   **21.** February
  17. a married woman **22.** Wednesday
  18. Boulevard   **23.** Mister
  19. after noon   **24.** Friday
  20. Doctor   **25.** April

E. Write the sentences. Replace the underlined words with abbreviations.

  26. Your appointment with Doctor Green is for 2:00 after noon.
  27. Mister Harris moved to 23 Oak Street on Monday, March 4.
  28. Field Day will be held on Tuesday at 10:00 before noon.
  29. The accident happened at the corner of Central Avenue and Harrison Street last Thursday.
  30. On Saturday, October 14, we are going to the circus.

The 10 Most Useful Spelling Rules

1. If a word ends in *e*, drop the *e* when you add a suffix that begins with a vowel.

   drive + ing = driving   late + er = later

   Keep the *e* when you add a suffix that begins with a consonant.

   sure + ly = surely   peace + ful = peaceful

2. If a word ends in a vowel and *y*, keep the *y* when you add a suffix.

   turkey + s = turkeys   stay + ed = stayed

3. If a word ends in a consonant and *y*, keep the *y* when you add a suffix that begins with *i*.

   cry + ing = crying   baby + ish = babyish

   Change the *y* to *i* when you add a suffix that does not begin with *i*.

   happy + ness = happiness   cry + es = cries

4. If a one-syllable word ends in one vowel and one consonant, double the final consonant when you add a suffix that begins with a vowel.

   drop + ing = dropping   sad + er = sadder

5. When you choose between *ie* and *ei*, usually choose *ie*.

   field   shriek   friend

   Choose *ei* after *c* or for the long *a* sound.

   receive   deceit   ceiling
   neighbor   weigh   vein

   (Exceptions: *leisure, seize, neither, weird*.)

6. The suffix -*s* can be added to most nouns and verbs. If the word ends in *s, ss, sh, ch, x,* or *zz,* add -*es.*

gas	gases	hiss	hisses
push	pushes	match	matches
fox	foxes	buzz	buzzes

7. If a word ends in a single *f* or *fe,* usually change the *f* to *v* when you add -*s* or -*es.*

calf	calves	elf	elves
knife	knives	wife	wives

8. The letter *q* is always followed by the letter *u* in English words.

question   quarrel   equal

The letter *v* is always followed by another letter; it is never the last letter in a word.

love   have   give

9. Add an apostrophe and *s* ('s) to a singular noun to show possession, but do not add them to a pronoun. Special pronouns show possession.

doctor's	spider's	Mary's
his	hers	its
ours	yours	theirs

10. Use an apostrophe (') in a contraction to show where a letter or letters have been left out.

is	+ not	= isn't	I	+ am	= I'm
we	+ are	= we're	it	+ is	= it's
you	+ will	= you'll	they	+ have	= they've
could	+ not	= couldn't	she	+ is	= she's

100 Words Often Misspelled

1. ache
2. again
3. aisle
4. all right
5. always
6. among
7. answer
8. anything
9. assignment
10. been
11. beginning
12. believe
13. break
14. business
15. busy
16. calendar
17. children
18. color
19. coming
20. committee
21. cough
22. could
23. country
24. different
25. doctor
26. done
27. early
28. easy
29. especially
30. every
31. exaggerate
32. experience
33. February
34. foreign
35. forty
36. friend
37. governor
38. grammar
39. guess
40. handkerchief
41. hear
42. heard
43. height
44. here
45. imagine
46. interested
47. it's
48. knew
49. know
50. knowledge
51. laid
52. library
53. loose
54. lose
55. many
56. meant
57. minute
58. much
59. necessary
60. neighbor

61. often
62. once
63. opposite
64. piece
65. pretty
66. raise
67. receive
68. said
69. separate
70. shoes
71. since
72. some
73. sometime
74. stationary
75. sugar
76. sure
77. surprise
78. their
79. there
80. therefore

81. they
82. though
83. threw
84. through
85. tired
86. together
87. too
88. truly
89. Tuesday
90. two
91. unusual
92. very
93. Wednesday
94. where
95. whether
96. woman
97. women
98. would
99. writing
100. you're

PRACTICE

Read the pairs of words below. One or both of the words in the pairs are often misspelled. Write a sentence for each word to illustrate the meaning of the word. You may use a dictionary if you wish.

1. hear, here
2. loose, lose
3. stationary, stationery
4. it's, its

5. their, they're
6. threw, through
7. too, two
8. whether, weather

Handwriting Models

a b c d e f g h i
j k l m n o p q r
s t u v w x y z

Circle letters

a b d o p q

Curved letters

c e f h m n r u

Double-curved letter

s

Straight-line letters

b d h i k l t

Slant-line letters

k v w x y z

Below-the-line letters

g j p q y

A B C D E F G H I
J K L M N O P Q R
S T U V W X Y Z

Handwriting Models

a b c d e f g h i
j k l m n o p q r
s t u v w x y z

Upward-loop letters

b e f
h k l

Rounded letters

m n v
x y z

Oval letters

a c d
g o q

Pointed letters

i j p r
s t u w

A B C D E F G H I
J K L M N O P Q R
S T U V W X Y Z

Used with permission from Zaner-Bloser *Handwriting: Basic Skills and Application.*
Copyright © 1984, Zaner-Bloser, Inc., Columbus, Ohio.

7 Tips for Taking Tests

1. Be prepared. Have several sharp pencils and an eraser.

2. Read or listen to the directions carefully. Be sure you know what you are to do and where and how you are to mark your answers.

   > Match the synonyms in columns A and B.
   > Circle the correct answer.
   > Cross out the wrong answer.
   > Fill in the circle next to the correct answer.

3. Answer the easy questions first. Quickly read all the questions on the page. Then go back to the beginning and answer the questions you are sure you know. Put a light check mark next to those you are not sure of or don't know.

4. Next try to answer the questions you are not sure you know. You may have a choice of answers. If so, narrow your choice. First eliminate all the answers you know are wrong. Try to narrow your selection to two answers. Then mark the answer you think is right.

5. Answer the hardest questions last. If you can't answer a question at all, don't waste time worrying about it. Skip the question and go on to the next. (Sometimes a percentage of wrong answers is subtracted from the number of correct answers.)

6. Plan your time. Don't spend too much time on just one question. Check your watch or a clock from time to time as you take the test. If you spend too much time on one part of the test, you won't have time to finish the rest. You will also need to save some time to check your answers.

7. Check your answers when you have finished. Make sure you have marked your answers correctly. Unless you're sure you made a mistake, you probably should not change an answer.

5 Guides for Helping Others Improve Their Writing

When you work with a partner to respond to each other's writing, you help that person by making specific comments. You have a chance to tell your classmate what you like about the writing and why you like it. Learning how to make helpful suggestions is a valuable skill. The guidelines below show you how to get started.

1. Ask your partner to read his or her composition out loud twice. The first time, listen to the whole composition. During the second reading, listen and also take notes.

2. Be positive. Discuss the best parts of the composition first. Give specific examples of what you like, and make comments such as this:

   - I like the beginning because it tells what this composition is about.
   - I like the beginning because you created suspense.
   - I like the way you used action verbs.
   - I like the way you included specific details.
   - I like the way you told about what you saw and heard.

3. Show sincere interest. Make comments such as this:

   - I would like to know more about …
   - After hearing your writing, I feel as if …
   - I agree (or disagree) when you say …

4. To give positive suggestions in a helpful way, make comments such as this:

   - Could you change the beginning? Try a sentence like this …
   - Could you make this ending stronger by moving this sentence to the end?

5. Remember, the purpose of working on writing with a partner is to support the writer and help the writer communicate.

Thesaurus

What Is a Thesaurus?

In a thesaurus, entry words are listed in alphabetical order. Under each entry word, synonyms and antonyms are shown. Below is part of a thesaurus entry from this book.

Entry word→ **clear** (adj)— **1** not hazy or cloudy. The <u>clear</u> night sky was flooded with stars. **2** easy to see through, to hear, or to understand. Her directions were quite <u>clear</u>.

Synonym → *transparent*— transmitting light so that bodies lying beyond are distinctly visible. Automobile windshield glass is <u>transparent</u>.

Antonym → ANTONYM: indistinct

An entry word appears in dark type: **clear**
The synonyms appear in italic type: *transparent*
The antonyms appear in blue type: indistinct

How to Use the Thesaurus Index

To find a word, use the Thesaurus Index. An entry word is shown this way:

clear (adj) 401

A synonym is followed by its entry word. The example below means "To find *transparent* look under the entry for **clear**, which begins on page 401."

transparent **clear** (adj) 401

An antonym is followed by its entry word. The example below means "To find indistinct, look under the entry for **clear**, which begins on page 401."

indistinct **clear** (adj) 401

A cross-reference (marked "See also") lists an entry that gives additional synonyms, related words, and antonyms.

clear (adj) 401
See also **definite** (adj) 402

To learn more about a thesaurus, turn to the lesson "Using a Thesaurus" on page 28.

THESAURUS INDEX

A list of all the words in this thesaurus

THESAURUS

great **large** (adj) 405
great (adj) **little** (adj) 406
grief **joy** (n) 405
grit **spirit** (n) 410

H

habitat **place** (n) 408
handsome **beautiful** (adj) 401
happiness **joy** (n) 405
harsh **rough** (adj) 409
hastily **fast** (adv) 404
have (v) 405
have **want** (v) 413
hazy **clear** (adj) 401
heart **courage** (n) 402
heavy (adj) **light** (adj) 406
heroism **courage** (n) 402
hilarity **joy** (n) 405
history **story** (n) 411
honest **good** (adj) 405
hover **fly** (v) 404
huge **large** (adj) 405
huge **little** (adj) 406
humble **famous** (adj) 403
hunger **want** (v) 413

I

identical **same** (adj) 409
ignore **see** (v) 410
illustrious **famous** (adj) 403
imagine **think** (v) 411
immature **young** (adj) 414
immense **large** (adj) 405
immense **little** (adj) 406
imperfectly **well** (adv) 414
important **little** (adj) 406
inconsistent **same** (adj) 409
incorrect **wrong** (adj) 414
indefinite **definite** (adj) 402
indistinct **clear** (adj) 401
indistinguishable **same** (adj) 409
inertia **energy** (n) 403
inflammatory **exciting** (adj) 403
inform **tell** (v) 411
infrequent **many** (adj) 407

infrequent **rare** (adj) 409
inherit **get** (v) 404
initial (adj) **last** (adj) 405
inquire **ask** (v) 401
insecurely **fast** (adv) 404
insert **put** (v) 408
inside **outside** (adj) 408
insignificant **little** (adj) 406
install **put** (v) 408
instruct **tell** (v) 411
intensity **vigor** (n) 412
interior (n) **outside** (n) 408
interrogate **ask** (v) 401
in the face of **before** (prep) 401
in the presence of **before** (prep) 401
introductory **last** (adj) 405
irregular **rough** (adj) 409

J

jagged **rough** (adj) 409
jet **fly** (v) 404
joy (n) 405
judge **think** (v) 411
junior **young** (v) 414
just **good** (adj) 405

K

kind **warm** (adj) 413

L

lack (v) **have** (v) 405
lack **want** (v) 413
large (adj) 405
large **little** (adj) 406
lasso **trap** (v) 411
last (adj) 405
leave (v) **come** (v) 402
leave (v) **wait** (v) 413
legend **story** (n) 411
lethargy **vigor** (n) 412
level (adj) **rough** (adj) 409
lifelessness **spirit** (n) 410
light (adj) 406
linger **wait** (v) 413

listen **tell** (v) 411
little (adj) 406
little **large** (adj) 405
liveliness **energy** (n) 403
liveliness **spirit** (n) 410
locale **place** (n) 408
locate **find** (v) 404
loosely **fast** (adv) 404
lose **find** (v) 404
lose **get** (v) 404
lovely **beautiful** (adj) 401
loyal **true** (adj) 411
lucid **clear** (adj) 401
lure **trap** (v) 411

M

make (v) 406
　See also **do** (v) 403
manufacture **do** (v) 403
many (adj) 407
massive **large** (adj) 405
mature (adj) **young** (adj) 414
mention **say** (v) 410
messy **neat** (adj) 407
microscopic **little** (adj) 406
mild **warm** (adj) 413
minor **little** (adj) 406
minute (adj) **large** (adj) 405
minute **little** (adj) 406
misadventure **accident** (n) 401
miserable **nice** (adj) 408
misery **joy** (n) 405
misfortune **accident** (n) 401
mishap **accident** (n) 401
mislay **find** (v) 404
misplace **find** (v) 404
miss (v) **find** (v) 404
monotonous **exciting** (adj) 403
monotonous **same** (adj) 409
much **many** (adj) 407
must **need** (n) 407
myth **story** (n) 411

N

narrate **tell** (v) 411
narrative **story** (n) 411
near **come** (v) 402

THESAURUS

A

accident (n)—An unfortunate event that happens by chance and that results in loss, injury, or death. There is an automobile accident almost every month at that dangerous intersection.

calamity—an extremely grave event or misfortune marked by great loss and lasting distress; a disaster. The fire was a calamity to the family whose home was destroyed.

catastrophe—a sudden or widespread tragic event or disaster; a great calamity. The earthquake that devastated most of the city is a catastrophe that will not be easily forgotten.

disaster—a sudden event that causes much damage, suffering, or loss. The train wreck was a disaster that fortunately took no lives.

misadventure—an unfortunate accident; a piece of bad luck. I knew that our vacation trip was a misadventure when it began to rain on the very first day.

misfortune—bad luck; adverse fortune. By misfortune I arrived on the island just ahead of the typhoon.

mishap—an unfortunate accident. Falling from her bicycle was a mishap that left Kim badly bruised.

ask (v)—**1** to question; to call on to answer. I asked my brother questions about geography. **2** to make a request for something. I asked the waiter for more water.

inquire—to ask about someone or something. Have you inquired about the time that the game will be played?

interrogate—to question systematically. The police officer interrogated the woman who saw the accident.

question—to ask for the purpose of finding out. Mark questioned me about my science project.

quiz—to question carefully. Our teacher quizzed us on yesterday's homework assignment.

request—to ask for. I requested extra help in math after school.

ANTONYMS: answer (v), reply (v), respond

B

beautiful (adj)—very pleasing to see or hear; delighting the mind or the senses. That is a beautiful painting.

attractive—pleasing; winning attention and liking. You are wearing an attractive sweater.

dazzling—brilliantly shining; splendid. Dazzling gems sparkled in the jewelry store display cases.

glorious—having great beauty; splendid; magnificent. This crisp and clear autumn day is truly glorious.

handsome—pleasing or impressive in appearance. That limousine is certainly a handsome automobile.

lovely—beautiful in mind, appearance, or character; delightful. Having dinner at that new restaurant sounds like a lovely idea.

pretty—pleasing by delicacy or grace. Look at this pretty bouquet of daisies.

ANTONYMS: ugly, unattractive

before (prep)—**1** preceding in time; earlier than. Does Memorial Day come before Flag Day? **2** in the sight or presence of. Bill was standing before the principal. **3** in front of. There is a curtain before the window.

ahead of—in front of. I saw Jean ahead of me in line.

in advance of—prior to. The thunderstorms along the cold front should arrive in advance of the cooler air.

in the face of—in the presence of; confronting. In the face of danger, Susan remained calm and did not panic.

in the presence of—in front of; before. Was she ever in the presence of royalty?

prior to—earlier than. We had breakfast prior to our departure.

ANTONYMS: after (prep), behind (prep)

C

clear (adj)—**1** not hazy or cloudy. The clear night sky was flooded with stars. **2** easy to see through, to hear, or to understand. Her directions were quite clear.

audible—loud enough to be heard. The volume control is turned down so low that the sound is barely audible.

cloudless—free from clouds; clear. The full moon shone brilliantly in the cloudless winter sky.

distinct—easily heard, seen, or understood; plain. Sharon drew the distinct outline of a jet airplane.

clear *(continued)*

THESAURUS

explicit—clearly expressed or distinctly stated. The auto manual had explicit instructions.

lucid—easy to understand or follow. He gave a lucid explanation of his whereabouts.

transparent—transmitting light so that bodies lying beyond are distinctly visible. Automobile windshield glass is transparent.

See also *definite* (adj).

ANTONYMS: cloudy, hazy, indistinct, obscure, unclear, vague

come (v)—**1** to move toward or approach. Come here as soon as you can. **2** to arrive at a certain place, end, or conclusion. We came to this town five years ago.

advance—to move forward. The long freight train is steadily advancing toward the tunnel.

approach—to come nearer to. Brad approached the busy intersection with caution.

arrive—to reach the end or destination of a journey; to come to a place. The plane will arrive in Dallas at four o'clock.

attain—to arrive at or reach by living or by developing. That department store has attained a reputation for quality.

near—to come close to; to approach. When you begin to see skyscrapers in the distance, you will be nearing New York City.

reach—to arrive at; to get to. The mountain climbers reached the summit of Mt. Rainier on Wednesday.

ANTONYMS: depart, go, leave (v), retreat (v), withdraw

courage (n)—the strength of mind or will to face danger. Fire fighters showed courage in battling the blaze.

boldness—show of scorn for danger; daring. The boldness of the plan surprised us.

bravery—fearlessness in the face of danger or difficulty; courage. The bravery of the hostages was astounding.

heart—enthusiastic courage. It takes heart to persist.

heroism—willingness to take risks to help others; valor. Davy Crockett's heroism is admired.

valor—willingness to take risks to help others; heroism. Knights of old showed valor in battle.

See also *spirit* (n).

ANTONYMS: cowardice, fear (n), timidity

cut (v)—**1** to separate, divide, or remove with a knife or any tool that has a sharp edge. Cut the paper in two pieces with scissors. **2** to make by or as if by cutting. The sculptor will cut a human figure from that block of wood.

carve—**1** to cut into pieces or slices. When will you carve the Thanksgiving Day turkey? **2** to make by cutting. Which Presidents are carved on Mt. Rushmore?

cleave—to cut, split open, or divide. The construction crew will cleave those giant rocks by using jackhammers.

engrave—to form by cutting; to carve in an artistic manner. The jeweler will engrave your initials on the back of the ring.

prune—to cut undesirable twigs or branches from a bush, a tree, or a vine. I must prune some of the older branches from the forsythia bushes.

score—to cut, scratch, or line. Before baking the ham, score it by cutting shallow grooves into it with a knife.

slice—to cut into flat, broad pieces. Slice the roast beef very thin, please.

D

definite (adj)—**1** exact or clear; precise; not vague. The dark clouds and strong winds are definite signs that a thunderstorm is approaching. **2** having certain limits; restricted. There are definite procedures to follow in case of an emergency.

certain—without any doubt; sure. I am certain that the concert is at seven o'clock.

defined—having settled limits or boundaries. This fence forms a clearly defined property boundary between the two lots.

explicit—clearly expressed or distinctly stated. Carol's explicit remarks about the basketball game could hardly be misinterpreted.

specific—definite; particular; precise. Every pair of shoes has a specific size.

unequivocal—having no doubt or ambiguity; straightforward; blunt and plain. Martin's unequivocal refusal to attend the meeting was a surprise to everyone.

unmistakable—not capable of being misunderstood or mistaken; clear. A 747 aircraft has an unmistakable shape.

See also *clear* (adj).

ANTONYMS: ambiguous, equivocal, imprecise, indefinite, undefined, vague

do (v)—**1** to carry through to the end any action or piece of work; to perform; to complete. Juan did a report on conservation. **2** to produce or make. He does beautiful landscapes in watercolors.

construct—to make by combining parts; to put together; to build. The workers have already constructed a new bridge over the river.

execute—to carry out fully; to do. A plan of action is useless unless it is properly executed.

manufacture—to make by hand or by machinery; to make something that is useful. That corporation manufactures paper towels.

perform—to do or to carry out; to go through and finish; to accomplish. Since you must perform that difficult task, be sure to ask questions about what you do not understand.

practice—**1** to do something again and again to learn to do it well. Great violinists practice several hours a day. **2** to work at a profession or occupation. He has practiced law for over ten years.

produce—to bring into existence by labor; to create; to make from various materials; to manufacture. How many automobiles does that company produce in one year?

See also *make* (v).

E

energy (n)—the ability for forceful action; the capacity for doing work. Toby had enough energy to run five miles.

liveliness—high spirits; the quality of being full of life and spirit. The liveliness of the kittens was evident in their spirited play.

power—force or strength; might; the ability to act or do. Does that railroad locomotive have enough power to pull one hundred freight cars?

stamina—power to resist that which weakens; endurance; staying power. Derrick has the stamina to run long distances.

strength—the condition or quality of being strong; force; power; vigor. I do not have the strength to move that heavy table.

vigor—strength or force; flourishing physical condition; intensity of action. Pam does push-ups and sit-ups with vigor.

vitality—vital force; the power to live and develop. My little sister is a happy and healthy young girl who is filled with vitality.

See also *vigor* (n).

ANTONYMS: fatigue, inertia, powerlessness, sluggishness, tiredness, weakness

exciting (adj)—producing excitement or a feeling of agitation; arousing; stirring. Traveling by airplane is always an exciting and enjoyable experience for me.

breathtaking—thrilling; exciting. The view from the scenic overlook just off the interstate highway is breathtaking.

inflammatory—tending to arouse or excite; tending to excite anger or disorder. The manager of the baseball team made several inflammatory remarks regarding the umpires.

stimulating—rousing to action; inspiring; stirring. Cold, stimulating mornings in winter wake me up in a hurry.

stirring—exciting; rousing; inspiring. The mayor's stirring speech left everyone applauding and cheering.

suspenseful—characterized by or full of suspense; causing the condition of being mentally uncertain, especially such a condition induced by craft in order to hold the attention of an audience or reader. Alfred Hitchcock directed some of the most suspenseful and terrifying movies ever made.

thrilling—characterized by excitement, or causing a sudden sharp feeling of excitement. Riding a roller coaster is a thrilling experience for most people.

ANTONYMS: dull, monotonous, tedious, uneventful, unexciting

F

famous (adj)—well-known; much talked about or written about; celebrated; noted. The famous singer gladly signed autographs after the concert.

celebrated—well-known; much talked about. The celebrated ballet dancer will perform tomorrow evening.

eminent—above most or all others; outstanding; famous. The eminent scientist made a profound discovery that left most of her peers in awe.

illustrious—brilliantly outstanding because of

THESAURUS

THESAURUS

achievements or actions. His illustrious motion-picture career included several award-winning performances.

notable—remarkable; worth noticing; striking; important. Winning a gold medal in the Olympic Games is certainly a notable achievement.

notorious—generally known and talked about because of something bad; having a bad reputation. The notorious gang robbed many banks a long time ago.

popular—liked by most people; liked by associates or acquaintances. That toy is so popular that most stores do not have any left to sell.

ANTONYMS: humble, inconspicuous, obscure, undistinguished, unknown

fast (adv)—**1** in a rapid manner; quickly; swiftly. I walked fast in order to get to the bus stop in time. **2** in a fixed or firm manner; tightly. The window frame is stuck fast.

firmly—solidly or securely. Make sure that the handle on that pan is firmly attached.

hastily—in a hurried manner; in a rash or careless manner. It was obvious by the numerous errors in spelling and punctuation that the letter was written hastily.

quickly—with haste; rapidly; very soon. Go quickly to your room.

rapidly—in a manner marked by a high rate of motion, succession, or occurrence. The seasons seem to be rapidly flying by.

securely—firmly or solidly. The steel railing is bolted securely to the bridge.

swiftly—in a fast or speedy manner. A deer ran swiftly across the road.

ANTONYMS: insecurely, loosely, slow (adv), slowly

find (v)—to come upon by chance; to discover by searching. We could not find the glove that Lori had misplaced.

catch—to hold or capture, especially after a chase. After several days of detective work, the police finally caught the thief.

detect—to discover the presence, existence, or fact of. I detect the odor of gas near the kitchen stove.

discover—to see or learn of for the first time; to find out. Astronomers continually discover new stars in the universe.

encounter—to meet or come upon unexpectedly.

Tourists driving on narrow mountain roads often encounter dangerous hairpin turns.

locate—to seek out the exact position of. The forest rangers located the hungry deer and gave them food.

trace—to follow by means of tracks, signs, or other evidence. Scientists easily traced the source of the town's air pollution.

ANTONYMS: lose, mislay, misplace, miss (v)

fly (v)—to move through the air with wings; to travel in an airplane or a spacecraft; to wave or float in the air. We will fly to Chicago next week.

flutter—to wave back and forth lightly and quickly. The flag in front of our school fluttered in the breeze.

glide—to move along effortlessly, smoothly, and evenly. The bird calmly glided in a circular pattern high above the treetops.

hover—to remain in or near one place in the air; to hang suspended or fluttering in the air. The helicopter hovered above the traffic jam.

jet—to fly by jet airplane. You can jet across the country in a relatively short time.

soar—to fly in the air, often at a great height; to fly upward. The rocket soared into the sky and soon disappeared from view.

G

get (v)—to come to have; to gain possession of; to obtain. Allen will get a new pair of glasses tomorrow.

acquire—to get by one's own efforts; to come to have. Through years of work he acquired a large fortune.

contract—to get, usually without choice. Ellen contracted the flu last week.

earn—to get in return for service or work. I earned extra money by delivering newspapers.

inherit—to receive after someone dies. The Benson family inherited their beautiful house many years ago.

obtain—to get through effort or diligence; to come to have. Sharon obtained two tickets to the basketball game.

receive—to take into one's hands; to be given. I received a wonderful birthday present from my parents.

ANTONYMS: give, lose, relinquish

good (adj)—**1** having high quality; superior. A good rocking chair lasts a long time. **2** as it ought to be; right; proper; agreeable. Doing what is good sometimes takes courage. **3** clever; skillful. He always tells a good joke.

beneficial—producing good; helpful. Proper exercise is beneficial to good health.

excellent—very good; better than others. The food in this restaurant is excellent.

honest—not lying, stealing, or cheating; truthful. An honest person does not cheat others.

just—fair; right; impartial. The judge made a just decision.

pleasant—giving pleasure; agreeable. A person with a pleasant disposition usually has a warm smile.

proficient—well advanced in an art, science, or subject; skilled. A proficient carpenter can do excellent work quickly.

ANTONYMS: awful, bad, disagreeable, dishonest, incompetent, worthless

H

have (v)—**1** to hold in one's possession or in one's keeping. Do you have a pencil I could borrow? **2** to experience. Henry has a terrible toothache.

command—to have power over; to be in authority over; to control by position. The fortress commands the harbor entrance.

endure—to put up with; to tolerate; to experience. I endured a terrible sore throat for about three days.

experience—to feel; to live through. That famous actress experienced many thrilling moments.

own—to have or hold as property; to possess. They own two automobiles.

possess—to have as a knowledge, an attribute, or a skill; to have as property. Ron possesses exceptional artistic ability.

undergo—to go through; to experience. The library will undergo a major renovation during the next couple of years.

ANTONYMS: lack (v), need (v)

J

joy (n)—a glad feeling; a strong feeling of pleasure; happiness. On a morning this beautiful, I feel joy at being alive.

bliss—great happiness or joy. Walking in the park on a warm morning in spring is sheer bliss.

delight—great pleasure or joy. The little boy ate his ice-cream cone with delight.

ecstasy—a feeling of very great joy; strong feeling that thrills or delights. The older man was filled with ecstasy when he saw his brother for the first time in many years.

glee—great delight or lively joy; merriment. We laughed with glee as we watched the monkeys at the zoo.

happiness—a state of contentment and well-being; joy; gladness. Sometimes happiness cán be found in the simplest things.

hilarity—great mirth or enjoyment; boisterous or noisy merriment. My friends and I talked and laughed with hilarity at the party.

ANTONYMS: despair (n), grief, misery, sadness, sorrow (n), unhappiness

L

large (adj)—of more than the usual amount, size, or number; big. The large tray was filled with delicious sandwiches.

considerable—in large quantity; much. A considerable number of people will take part in the Fourth of July parade.

enormous—extremely large; huge. That enormous tree must be over one hundred years old.

great—large in amount, extent, number, or size; big. Many great boulders line the shoulder of the road.

huge—very large; unusually large in bulk, dimensions, or size. A huge stalled tractor blocked the entrance to the freeway.

immense—very big; vast; huge. The state of Alaska covers an immense area.

massive—large and solid; big and heavy; huge. The massive wall was over four feet thick.

ANTONYMS: little, minute (adj), slight (adj), small, tiny

last (adj)—coming after all others; being at the end; final; conclusive. I know someone who likes to read the last page of a novel before reading the rest of it.

closing—being the final portion or last stage of an item. The closing chapter of the book was by far the most exciting.

last *(continued)*

THESAURUS

conclusive—convincing; decisive; final. Those X rays gave conclusive proof that the tennis player had fractured her wrist.

farewell—parting; last; final. The farewell address of our retiring principal was truly inspiring.

farthest—most distant in time or space. Are satellites now exploring the farthest reaches of outer space?

final—being the last; at the end. The final game of the season takes place tomorrow afternoon at two o'clock.

ultimate—most remote in time or space; farthest; last in a series of steps; extreme. Her ultimate goal is to win a gold medal in the Olympics.

ANTONYMS: beginning (adj), first (adj), inconclusive, initial (adj), introductory, opening (adj)

light (adj)—**1** not heavy; having little weight. Those suitcases are surprisingly light when empty. **2** easy to do or bear. Ted has to do some light chores. **3** of little importance. Sheila enjoys light reading just before bedtime.

effortless—showing or requiring little use of energy; easy. The gymnast performed with seemingly effortless skill and grace.

feathery—light and delicate; almost weightless. With a feathery touch the pianist produced delicate tones that could hardly be heard.

simple—easy to do, understand, or solve. Assembling that model airplane was simple.

superficial—of or on the surface; lying on or affecting only the surface. Although she tripped on the step, she received only a superficial scratch on her knee.

trivial—not important; insignificant. We talked about trivial things like the weather.

weightless—having little or no weight. Astronauts experience weightless conditions when they travel in space.

ANTONYMS: burdensome, cumbersome, difficult, heavy (adj), profound, strenuous

little (adj)—**1** not big or great; small. The diamond stylus on a stereo phonograph is little. **2** small in amount, number, or importance. There is little time remaining before the end of this class.

insignificant—having little influence or importance; too small to be important. An insignificant amount of snow fell last night, so we were able to get to school easily.

microscopic—unable to be seen without using a microscope; extremely small; minute; tiny. Those microscopic dots on the leaves of the plant are actually tiny insects.

minor—inferior in importance, size, or degree; smaller. Get the job done without worrying about minor details.

minute—very small. That restaurant served minute portions of food.

slight—lacking in strength or importance; having a slim build. The movie has a slight plot, but, after all, it is a comedy.

small—not large; little in size; not large in comparison with other things of the same kind. Be sure to buy only a small loaf of bread and a quart of milk.

ANTONYMS: big (adj), great (adj), huge, immense, important, large (adj)

M

make (v)—**1** to bring into being; to build, form, put together, or shape. I can make a bowl from this modeling clay. **2** to cause to; to force to. Will you make us run three laps around the entire track?

assemble—to put or fit together. Brian assembled that model airplane in less than five days.

build—to make by putting materials together; to construct. Did you build the shelves in this closet?

compel—to urge or drive with force; to force. The high-wind warnings compelled us to keep the boat close to the shore.

create—to make something which has not been made before; to bring into being. The florist created a beautiful floral centerpiece for the dinner party.

force—to make someone act against his or her will. My sister forced me to wash all the dishes.

form—to make in a certain shape; to give shape to. Take the three strips of cardboard and form a triangle.

See also *do* (v).

ANTONYMS: destroy, wreck (v)

many (adj)—consisting of a large number; numerous. There are many new office buildings in this part of town.

abundant—more than enough; amply supplied. There was an abundant harvest of wheat this year.

frequent—happening often or every little while. We have frequent bus service to and from the city.

much—in great degree or amount. Try not to eat too much food at the picnic.

numerous—very many; consisting of great numbers of individuals or units. I have swum in that lake on numerous occasions.

plentiful—more than enough; ample. We are fortunate to live where food is plentiful.

several—more than two, but fewer than many. Michele was late for school several times last month.

ANTONYMS: few (adj), infrequent, rare, scant (adj), sole (adj).

N

neat (adj)—clean and in order; marked by tasteful simplicity. Joe keeps his room neat.

orderly—in order; with regular system, arrangement, or method. When the alarm sounds for the fire drill, proceed to the exits in an orderly fashion.

organized—arranged in some order or pattern; put into working order. He has the most organized loose-leaf binder in our class.

tidy—neat and in order; trim; orderly. He keeps the inside of his car as tidy as his home.

trim—in good order or condition; tidy; neat. Their trim apartment is obviously well taken care of.

uncluttered—not littered; in order; neat. This uncluttered living room appears very spacious.

well-groomed—well dressed and very neat; neat and trim. Even on extremely hot days, Alex always wears a tie and maintains a well-groomed appearance.

ANTONYMS: cluttered (adj), disorderly, disorganized (adj), messy, sloppy, untidy

need (n)—**1** the lack of a desired or useful thing; a want. There is a desperate need for more room in the overcrowded hospital. **2** something that has to be; a requirement; a necessity. The reason for the need for quiet when working in a library is obvious.

absence—the state of being without; a lack. The absence of rainfall has greatly diminished the water supply in the reservoir.

deficiency—an absence or lack of something needed; incompleteness. Because of a deficiency of funds, a new municipal building could not be built.

must—something that is necessary; an obligation. Seeing that exciting new movie is a must.

necessity—that which cannot be done without; a needed thing. Good lighting is a necessity when you are reading.

requirement—something needed; a necessity. One requirement for that job is the completion of a special training course to handle medical emergencies.

shortage—too small an amount; a deficiency; a lack. During the water shortage the watering of lawns was prohibited.

ANTONYMS: abundance, adequacy, excess (n)

next (adj)—**1** nearest. The next town is Pleasantville. **2** immediately following. The next train will arrive at this station in about fifteen minutes.

adjacent—lying close or near, or touching; adjoining or neighboring. Do adjacent apartments usually have soundproof walls between them?

adjoining—being next to or in contact; adjacent; bordering. Those two adjoining buildings are connected to each other by a glass-enclosed pedestrian mall.

following—that immediately follows; next after. On the following day huge waves pounded the already-battered rocky shore as the storm grew even more fierce.

nearest—closest; least distant. The nearest service station must be at least ten or twelve miles from here.

neighboring—being or living near; adjacent; bordering. The neighboring county is almost entirely made up of rolling acres of rich productive farmland.

succeeding—following in time, place, or order. The mystery story will be continued in the next three succeeding issues of the magazine.

THESAURUS

THESAURUS

nice (adj)—pleasing or satisfying. It will be a nice afternoon if the sun comes out.

agreeable—suiting one's pleasure. We will do everything possible to be sure our guests have an agreeable stay.

blissful—full of great happiness or joy. The child spent a blissful afternoon playing with the new toy.

delightful—enjoyable and very pleasing. Most of the movie was delightful, but the ending made me cry.

fine—excellent; very good. The new community center has fine facilities, including an indoor ice-skating rink.

refreshing—pleasantly different or unusual. After you spend all day in the house, a long walk can be a refreshing activity.

splendid—grand; wonderful. Everyone is still talking about this year's splendid school carnival.

ANTONYMS: awful (adj), disagreeable, dreadful, miserable, terrible, unpleasant

O

outside (n)—the outer part of something. I would like to try on the jacket that has pockets on the outside.

coating—the layer that covers a surface. The table and chairs come in different colors of plastic coatings.

covering—the outer part of something, which protects or hides what is inside. It is difficult to tell what is in that package with the plain, paper covering.

exterior—the outside. They live in the new apartment building with the brick exterior.

face—the front, top, or outer side of something. The face of her watch has many dials that glow in the dark.

shell—a hard outer covering. I cannot crack the shell of this walnut with my fingers.

surface—the outer part of something solid; the top level of a liquid. I would use the paper with the shiny surface for the bulletin-board display.

ANTONYMS: center (n), core (n), inside (n), interior (n)

P

piece (n)—a part of a whole. Be careful not to step on a piece of glass from the broken window.

allotment—a person's share of the whole. Each band member was given an allotment of tickets to sell.

chunk—a short, thick piece. Would you like a chunk of cheese with your lunch?

fragment—a piece broken off something. They found a fragment from an antique pot near the ruins.

portion—a part that is divided or separated from the whole. Each person may take a small portion of mashed potatoes.

share—the part belonging to one person. Carolyn did more than her share of work on the project.

shred—a small strip that is torn or cut off. Maybe there is a shred of paper caught in the copying machine.

ANTONYMS: all (n), entirety, whole (n)

place (n)—the space occupied by or intended for a person or thing. The cross-country skiers looked for a place to stop and rest.

area—an open space used for a special purpose. There is a large area for parking behind the shopping center.

dwelling—a place where someone lives. This museum was originally a family dwelling.

habitat—the place where an animal or plant grows or lives. The photographer traveled to India to observe the animals in their natural habitat.

locale—the scene of an event or some action. Several reporters dashed to the locale of the blazing fire.

site—a particular place where something is, was, or will be located. The site chosen for the monument is near the river.

territory—a section of land. The settlers claimed the undeveloped territory for farmland.

put (v)—to lay or cause to be in some place or position. At the end of the day, the librarian always puts the books back on the shelves.

arrange—to put in a proper or desirable order. Marcus arranged the name cards in alphabetical order.

deposit—to set down. We deposited items for the garage sale on a long table.

insert—to put into something. I'll try, but I don't think I can insert this bent key into the lock.

install—to put in position and fix for use. Someone from the store will <u>install</u> our new washing machine tomorrow.

position—to put in a particular place. Sandy carefully <u>positioned</u> the clock on the mantel.

rest—to place something to prevent it from falling. Michelle <u>rested</u> her bicycle against a tree while she waited for her friend.

ANTONYMS: displace, remove, withdraw

R

rare (adj)—**1** uncommonly found or happening. A snowstorm in April is <u>rare</u> here. **2** unusual in quality, often valuable. The <u>rare</u> gem is priceless.

exceptional—not like it usually is; not like others. The choir director was impressed by Christopher's <u>exceptional</u> voice.

infrequent—not occurring often. Our trips to the beach have been <u>infrequent</u> because of the poor weather.

uncustomary—not the usual way of acting or doing something. It is <u>uncustomary</u> for her to go to bed this early.

unique—being the only one of its kind. Katie's aunt made her a <u>unique</u> wooden jewelry box.

unusual—out of the ordinary; different. We tasted many <u>unusual</u> foods at the international bazaar.

See also *unusual* (adj).

ANTONYMS: common (adj), everyday (adj), ordinary (adj), regular (adj), routine (adj), usual (adj)

report (n)—a written or spoken account of something. Before Steve wrote his <u>report</u>, he researched his topic carefully.

address—a formal speech. In his <u>address</u>, the senator said he would support the housing bill.

announcement—a report that is given to bring something to the public's attention. The principal sent out a newsletter to make several <u>announcements</u> about the new school year.

bulletin—a brief report of the latest news. The television program was interrupted to present an important news <u>bulletin</u>.

chronicle—a record of events in time sequence. The speaker showed slides to go with the <u>chronicle</u> she had written about her worldwide journey.

critique—a review of something in which personal judgment is expressed. The judges gave a <u>critique</u> of each drawing entered in the contest.

rumor—a story or report that is told to others, but has not been proven to be true. Did you hear the <u>rumor</u> that Joshua is moving to another state?

rough (adj)—not smooth, even, or level; bumpy. This floor is too <u>rough</u> to roller-skate on.

bristly—having a texture like that of short, stiff, coarse hairs. You will need strong soap and a <u>bristly</u> sponge to scrub those mud-caked tires.

coarse—rough in appearance or texture. The tent is made of a <u>coarse</u> material.

harsh—rough or unpleasant to the touch or other senses. The stiff towel felt <u>harsh</u> against my face.

irregular—uneven. The ceiling is <u>irregular</u> because some of the tiles have come loose.

jagged—having sharp points sticking out. Adam cut his foot on a piece of <u>jagged</u> glass.

rugged—having an irregular, broken surface. The northern part of the state has a cold climate and a <u>rugged</u> terrain.

ANTONYMS: even (adj), flat (adj), level (adj), silky, smooth (adj), soft

S

same (adj)—being alike or unchanged; not different. My brother and I listen to the <u>same</u> kind of music.

consistent—without changing one's way of thinking or acting. She believes in <u>consistent</u> exercise and good eating habits.

identical—exactly alike in every way. Pat and Kim laughed when they realized they were wearing <u>identical</u> coats.

indistinguishable—not able to be recognized by differences. The street signs are <u>indistinguishable</u> in this thick fog.

monotonous—not varying or changing; boring. Do we have to play that <u>monotonous</u> game again?

stable—not likely to change or move; steady. Barbara would like to have a <u>stable</u> job after she completes the training program.

uniform—like all others; all the same. The gardener planted the bushes so they would be a <u>uniform</u> height.

same (*continued*)

THESAURUS

THESAURUS

ANTONYMS: contrasting (adj), different, dissimilar, distinct, inconsistent, variable (adj)

save (v)—**1** to keep or make free from harm or danger. Lona saved the baby bird from falling out of its nest. **2** to lay aside; to have or hold on to. Should we save the empty cartons or throw them away?

conserve—to keep from being used up. You can conserve electricity by turning off the light when you leave a room.

economize—to keep from waste. The office workers are economizing their supplies so they do not run out before the end of the year.

preserve—to keep from change; to keep safe from harm. Matina preserves her favorite photographs in a picture album.

reserve—to hold back, usually for a brief period of time. The librarian said he would reserve the book for me until tomorrow.

salvage—to save from being ruined or wrecked. The citrus growers salvaged a part of the orange crop from the severe frost.

store—to put away for later use. We store old clothes and toys in the attic.

ANTONYMS: consume, discard (v), endanger, risk (v), spend, waste (v)

say (v)—to speak; to put into words. Carlotta did not say where she was going.

comment—to make a brief statement, giving a personal judgment about something. Many people commented on the colorful decorations we made for the party.

declare—to make known by publicly announcing. In the broadcast, the city official declared her acceptance of the job.

exclaim—to speak with force, usually when surprised or angry. "I can't believe that I really won!" exclaimed the tennis champion.

expound—to explain in detail in order to make something clear or understood. The famous doctor expounded the results of his latest research study.

mention—to speak about or refer to briefly. Did anyone mention what time the next train will be arriving?

reveal—to say what was not known before. At the next meeting, the club president will reveal her plans for a charity event.

See also *tell* (v).

see (v)—**1** to perceive by use of the eyes; to look at. Can you see that beautiful little bird in the dogwood tree? **2** to form a picture in the mind. I can still see the castle we visited two years ago.

glimpse—to catch a quick or brief view of. We glimpsed the express train as it sped through the station.

observe—to see and note; to notice; to carefully examine; to watch; to study. Peter observed the cooking demonstration with great interest.

picture—to form an image of in the mind. I pictured the hotel to be much larger than it actually is.

view—to look at; to see. As her mother drove the car, Teena viewed the majestic countryside of Montana.

visualize—to form a mental picture of. Try to visualize the store as it was the last time you were there.

witness—to observe; to see for oneself. Jonathan witnessed a landing of the space shuttle.

ANTONYMS: disregard (v), ignore

spirit (n)—liveliness; courage; vigor; enthusiasm. Her cheery smile shows that she has spirit.

enthusiasm—eager interest; zeal; strong excitement of feeling. The fans cheering loudly at the game were filled with enthusiasm.

fervor—intense enthusiasm, emotion, or earnestness. After she received some encouragement and helpful advice from her teacher, Patty continued working on her science project with renewed fervor.

grit—courage; endurance; pluck. Showing true grit, she finished running the marathon even though she was on the verge of total collapse.

liveliness—the quality or condition of being full of life and spirit; vigor. The liveliness of kittens at play is a joy to behold.

vitality—life force; the power to live. The bustling city has a vitality of its own.

zest—keen enjoyment; an exciting or pleasant quality. With a zest for the beauty of nature, he watched the sun slowly disappear beneath the motionless pines.

See also *courage* (n).

ANTONYMS: dullness, lifelessness, spiritlessness, timidity

story (n)—an account of a happening or group of happenings. Do you enjoy reading adventure stories as much as I do?

biography—a written story of a person's life. Jeff has just read a biography of Abraham Lincoln.

history—a record or story of important events, usually including an explanation of their causes. Every day I learn more of the history of the United States.

legend—a story coming down from the past, especially one that many people have thought of as true. The stories about King Arthur are legends.

myth—a story or legend, usually one that tries to explain something in nature. Is there a myth that explains the causes of thunder and lightning?

narrative—an account or story; a tale. Who was the author of the funny narrative that our teacher read to us?

tale—a story of an incident or event, especially a fictional story. I just read an exciting tale about pirates.

T

tell (v)—to express in words; to say; to give an account of; to relate. Tell me what you think of it.

advise—to give advice to; to counsel; to offer an opinion to. Would you advise me about what to get my mother for a birthday present?

communicate—to give news or information by speaking or writing; to telephone; to write. Have you communicated recently with your sister in New Mexico?

inform—to supply with facts, knowledge, or news; to tell. I was not informed of the change in plans until today.

instruct—to teach; to train; to give knowledge to; to give orders or directions to. I was instructed to hand out the drawing materials.

narrate—to tell the story of; to relate. He will narrate the well-known story, which has been set to music.

report—to tell of something seen, done, heard, or read; to state or announce. Allison reported the results of her science experiment to us.

See also *say* (v).

ANTONYM: listen

think (v)—**1** to exercise the powers of the mind; to have an idea or thought in the mind. I think about many different things all of the time. **2** to have an opinion. I think the librarian is a very nice person.

believe—to think something is real or true. I believe that the rocky cliffs along the coastline are being slowly worn away by the pounding surf.

conclude—to reach certain decisions or opinions by reasoning; to infer. The jury concluded that the defendant was not guilty of the crime for which he was being tried.

dream—to think, see, hear, or feel while sleeping. Did you ever dream that you were trying to run but could not move?

imagine—to form a picture of something in the mind. Juan imagined that he was an astronaut floating in space.

judge—to make up one's mind about; to conclude; to think. Can you judge the distance from this side of the lake to the other?

suppose—to consider as possible; to assume; to consider as probably true. Do you suppose we could all fit in that little car?

trap (v)—to catch; to entrap. The police trapped the crafty criminal.

capture—to take captive; to take by force, skill, or trickery. The troops captured the enemy headquarters.

catch—to take and hold; to capture; to seize. The shortstop caught the hard-hit ground ball.

entrap—to catch in a trap; to bring into danger. The small boat was entrapped by the huge ice floes in the river.

lasso—to catch with a long rope that has a running noose at one end. The rancher lassoed the stray steer.

lure—to attract or tempt, as with a bait. When fishing, people often lure fish by using worms.

net—to catch in a net. Many fish were netted by the trawlers that day.

ANTONYMS: discharge (v), extricate, free (v), release (v), remove

true (adj)—**1** agreeing with fact; not false. The story about the adventures of the explorer was true. **2** genuine, real. The miners found true gold. **3** loyal, faithful. He was true to his word and returned as he had promised.

authentic—coming from the stated source; not

true *(continued)*

THESAURUS

THESAURUS

copied; real; genuine. The signature on the document is <u>authentic</u>.

factual—concerned with something known to be true. The <u>factual</u> account of the admiral's visit to the South Pole was fascinating.

genuine—actually being what it seems or is claimed to be; true. How can you tell if that gemstone is a <u>genuine</u> diamond?

loyal—faithful and true to duty, promise, love, or other obligations. A <u>loyal</u> fan roots for the same team whether it wins or loses.

real—existing as a fact; not made up or imagined; true; actual; not artificial; genuine. The mountain scene depicted on the stage was so well made that the mountains looked <u>real</u>.

steadfast—loyal; firm of purpose; not changing; unwavering. Kathy remained <u>steadfast</u> in her desire to finish the fifty-mile hike.

ANTONYMS: artificial, counterfeit (adj), false, fictitious, untrue, untrustworthy

turn (v)—**1** to move around as a wheel does; to revolve; to move partway around in this manner. Please <u>turn</u> the handle counterclockwise. **2** to take the opposite direction or a new direction. After about two miles the road <u>turns</u> westward.

bend—to curve out of a straight position. The branches of white birch trees usually <u>bend</u> under the weight of heavy snow or ice.

circle—to move in or as if in a circle; to form a circle. The seagull <u>circled</u> above the fishing boat.

curve—to bend in a line that has no straight part; to move in the course of such a line. The rising tiers of seats <u>curve</u> gracefully around the center of the arena.

revolve—to move in a curve around a point; to move in a circle. The planets of the solar system <u>revolve</u> around the sun.

spin—to revolve or turn around rapidly. The pinwheel <u>spins</u> whenever a strong breeze blows.

twist—to turn around; to have a winding course or shape; to curve or wind. The steep trail <u>twisted</u> through the rugged terrain.

U

unusual (adj)—out of the ordinary; different; not commonly seen, used, or happening; uncommon. That <u>unusual</u> plant grows in the tropical areas of the world.

rare—uncommonly found or happening; unusual. Some species of birds are <u>rare</u>.

singular—unusual; extraordinary; strange. With <u>singular</u> devotion to duty, the soldier carried out the difficult assignment.

uncommon—unusual or rare; exceptional or remarkable. He had many <u>uncommon</u> minerals in his rock collection.

unexpected—not expected; not anticipated; unforeseen. The <u>unexpected</u> major snowfall caught everyone by surprise.

unfamiliar—not well-known; strange; unusual. While traveling in Europe, we sampled many <u>unfamiliar</u> foods.

unique—being the only one of its kind. This <u>unique</u> painting was done nearly a century ago.

See also *rare* (adj).

ANTONYMS: common (adj), commonplace (adj), customary, familiar, routine (adj), usual (adj)

use (v)—**1** to put into action or service; to utilize; to practice or employ actively; to exercise. Whenever I <u>use</u> tools, I keep safety in mind. **2** to consume or take regularly. That old automobile <u>uses</u> too much gasoline.

consume—to use up; to spend; to destroy. The forest fire <u>consumed</u> hundreds of acres of trees.

employ—to use; to use the services of. Chris <u>employed</u> a pair of tweezers to remove that tiny wire from the model.

exercise—to actively use to cause improvement or to give practice and training. If you <u>exercise</u> every day, you may actually begin to feel healthier.

exhaust—to empty completely; to drain. The campers <u>exhausted</u> their food supply within a week.

operate—to keep at work; to run or drive. May I <u>operate</u> the model train set?

utilize—to make use of; to put to a practical use. A good student <u>utilizes</u> his or her time wisely when studying.

ANTONYMS: conserve (v), preserve (v), save (v)

V

vigor (n)—strength or force; flourishing physical condition; intensity of action. He begins each day with surprising <u>vigor</u>.

drive—initiative, energy, vigor. Being a person with drive, she pushed herself beyond the normal limits of endurance.

energy—the ability for forceful action; the capacity for doing work. Mowing the lawn takes a great deal of energy.

fervor—great warmth of feeling; intense earnestness, enthusiasm, or emotion. With fervor in his eyes, the artist gazed at his masterpiece.

intensity—vigorous activity or strong feeling; great strength. My parents said they never saw anyone play tennis with more intensity than Jimmy Connors.

vim—energy, force, vigor. The joggers began their daily run with vim.

vitality—vital force; the power to live and develop. I never saw anyone with as much vitality as that actress.

See also *energy* (n).

ANTONYMS: **apathy, feebleness, lethargy, slowness, sluggishness, weakness**

W

wait (v)—to stop doing something or to stay until something happens or someone comes. Please wait here until I return.

dawdle—to waste time; to be idle; to dally. If you dawdle over your homework, you will never finish it.

delay—to put off until a later time. Severe thunderstorms delayed the departure of our plane for over an hour.

linger—to be slow in quitting something or in parting, as if unwilling to leave. Some of the guests lingered for quite some time after the wedding reception had ended.

remain—to continue in a place; to stay. We remained indoors through much of the sub-freezing weather.

stay—to continue in a place or condition; to remain. We will stay here until it is time to board the train.

tarry—to delay leaving; to stay, to remain. If you tarry any longer, you will not get to school on time.

ANTONYMS: **depart, go, leave (v)**

want (v)—**1** to feel that one needs or would like to have; to wish for; to desire. I want to visit Hawaii someday. **2** to fail to possess, especially in the required or customary amount; to be without. The ballet dancer's performance was good, but at times it wanted gracefulness.

crave—to desire very much; to long for. The new student craved friendship.

desire—to long or to hope for; to wish earnestly for. Above all else he desired happiness.

hunger—to feel uncomfortable because of not having eaten; to be hungry. At about the same time every evening, Gene hungers for a snack.

lack—to be without; to not have enough; to need. Although she plays basketball well, she lacks the desire to become an outstanding player.

need—to be in want of; to be unable to do without; to require. This houseplant needs water right now.

wish—to have a desire for; to want. I wish I could go swimming today.

See also *wish* (v).

ANTONYMS: **decline (v), have, own (v), possess, refuse (v), reject (v)**

warm (adj)—**1** more hot than cold; having or giving off heat to a moderate or adequate degree; having some heat. Is it warm outside today? **2** marked by or showing affection, gratitude, or sympathy. Being a warm person, he is always considerate of other people's feelings.

affectionate—having or showing fondness or tenderness. The new mother gave her baby an affectionate kiss.

compassionate—wishing to help those that suffer; sympathetic; pitying. The compassionate doctor comforted the seriously ill patient.

kind—doing good rather than harm; sympathetic; friendly; gentle. The kind woman gave her sweater to the shivering child.

mild—calm; warm; moderate; not severe or harsh. We had a mild winter with less snow than usual.

temperate—neither very hot nor very cold; moderate. Places with a temperate climate generally have summers that are not too hot and winters that are not too cold.

tepid—slightly or moderately warm; lukewarm. My hot tea had become tepid before I had a chance to drink it.

ANTONYMS: **coldhearted, cool (adj), cruel, uncaring, unfriendly, unsympathetic**

THESAURUS

well (adv)—in a satisfactory, good, or proper manner; all right. She did her work well.

capably—in a competent manner; with ability; ably. During the captain's illness, the next officer in rank capably commanded the ship.

efficiently—ably producing the effect wanted without waste of energy or time. Working efficiently, I was able to finish my homework in much less time than it usually takes me.

excellently—in a manner better than others; very well; superiorly. Kim's teacher said that her composition was excellently done.

expertly—in a skillful or knowledgeable manner; adroitly. That diagram was expertly drawn.

ingeniously—in an inventive, resourceful, original, or clever manner. She solved that difficult puzzle ingeniously.

skillfully—with expert ability; expertly. The technician skillfully adjusted the equipment.

ANTONYMS: badly, imperfectly, improperly, poorly, unsatisfactorily

wish (v)—**1** to have a desire for; to express or feel a desire for; to desire something for someone. I wish we were going to the zoo today. **2** to command or request a person to do something. Mark wishes you to attend his birthday party.

ask—to make a request for something. He asked the movers to be careful with the large couch.

crave—to desire very much; to long for. The lonely child craved affection.

demand—to ask or call for, either as a right or with authority. My parents demand my respect.

desire—to long or hope for; to wish earnestly for. Francis desired to play on the team.

request—to ask for. Terry requested a map of the city.

want—to feel that one would like to have; to wish for; to desire. Tom wants a new bicycle for his birthday.

See also *want* (v).

wrong (adj)—**1** not right; unjust, bad. Cheating on a test is wrong. **2** not correct; not according to truth or facts; inaccurate. You gave a wrong answer to the question. **3** not proper or right according to a code or standard. A sweat suit is the wrong thing to wear to a wedding.

improper—not in accordance with accepted standards; not suitable; wrong. It is improper for spectators to shout when a tennis player is about to serve.

inappropriate—not right for an occasion; not suitable; not fitting. A tuxedo is inappropriate clothing for a camping trip.

incorrect—not correct; containing mistakes or errors; faulty; wrong. That clock keeps incorrect time.

unjust—characterized by the absence of justice; not fair. It is unjust to force one person to do the work of many.

unlawful—against the law; contrary to law; prohibited by law; illegal. It is unlawful to drive faster than the speed limit.

untrue—not true to the facts; incorrect; false. That story you heard about me is untrue.

ANTONYMS: correct (adj), fair (adj), proper, right (adj), suitable, true

Y

young (adj)—in the early part of life, growth, or development; not old; of, belonging to, or having to do with youth; having the vigor, freshness, looks, or other qualities of youth. That young woman graduated from college last year.

budding—being in an early stage of development; in the process of emergence. The budding astronomer made her first visit to the planetarium.

fresh—newly arrived, gathered, or made; recent; looking young or healthy. I enjoy eating peaches that are fresh and not yet mushy.

immature—not full-grown; not completely developed; not ripe. These immature seedlings must be protected from extreme cold.

junior—**1** the younger (used chiefly to distinguish a son with the same given name as his father). William Dobbs, Junior, is on the phone. **2** of or for younger people; youthful. Do you sing in the junior chorus?

new—never having been before; now first made, heard of, or discovered; not old. Charlene is moving into a new house.

youthful—young; suitable for young people; having the qualities or looks of youth; vigorous; fresh. My grandfather, who jogs every morning, is a youthful person.

ANTONYMS: adult (adj), ancient (adj), mature (adj), old (adj), ripe, senior (adj)

THESAURUS

Index

420

5 6 7 8 9 10—KP—90 89 88 87 86